THE HISTORY OF

THE
WORLD SERIES

Also by Glenn Dickey:

The History of American League Baseball
The History of National League Baseball
Champs and Chumps
The Great No-Hitters
The Jock Empire
The History of Professional Basketball

THE HISTORY OF

THE WORLD SERIES

SINCE 1903

GLENN DICKEY

𝔰𝔡

STEIN AND DAY/*Publishers*/New York

First Published in 1984
Copyright © 1984 by Glenn Dickey
All rights reserved, Stein and Day, Incorporated
Designed by Louis Ditizio
Printed in the United States of America
Stein and Day/*Publishers*
Scarborough House
Briarcliff Manor, N.Y. 10510

Library of Congress Cataloging in Publication Data

Dickey, Glenn.
  The history of the World Series since 1903.

  Bibliography: p.
  Includes index.
  1. World series (Baseball)—History.   I. Title.
GV863.A1D52   1984   796.357′782   83-40365
ISBN 0-8128-2951-4

To my wife, Nancy, and son, Scott,
who are my constant inspiration

Contents

Introduction

by REGGIE JACKSON

The World Series is like nothing else I've ever been involved with. Everything is magnified, bigger than life-size.

During the season, there are maybe 40 million people who come out to watch major league baseball games. For the World Series, there are 100 million people watching on TV. That means there are 60 million people watching who don't see baseball during the year, and they judge you by what you do in the World Series.

Everything is critiqued and analyzed—overcritiqued and overanalyzed. You can be a hero or a goat based on what you do in just seven games. In the regular season, seven games is nothing; in the World Series, it's everything.

I know my own reputation is based on what I did in the World Series, especially the 1977 Series. People remember that more than the fact that I was MVP in 1974 with the A's. I'm known as "Mr. October." Well, you don't hit as many home runs as I've hit or drive in as many runs as I've driven in by hitting just in October. But people remember what I've done in the Series.

How do you handle that pressure? In my case, I always concentrated on making sure I got my sleep and read the scouting reports thoroughly, so I'd be well prepared. That's all you can do, really.

In a way, I was fortunate that I didn't play in the first World Series my team was in—the 1972 Series—because that gave me a chance to see what the World Series really meant. Because I was injured, I had to watch as my Oakland A's teammates beat the Cincinnati Reds.

That just made me more determined that I was going to play in a World Series. I told my teammates the next year, "Hey, I'm going to be in the World Series this year. You guys want to come along?" That sounds like bragging, but I meant it in a lighthearted way, and they knew it.

Those three straight World Series championships with the A's were exciting, but the most memorable one for me had to be 1977, when I hit three straight home runs in the last game. In a sense, that made up for everything that had happened that year.

It had been a tough year for me. There had been disputes with (manager) Billy Martin, a flareup with Thurman Munson. Guys had been down on me, but this was a vindication for me. It's like I was saying, "Hey, I'm not such a bad guy. I can win for you."

I'll never forget that game. I really felt good before the game. I'd hit home runs in the last couple of games, and I pumped about 15 into the seats in batting practice. I got a standing ovation for that! I knew I was swinging the bat as well as I could swing it.

The first time up, I walked on four straight pitches and I was really frustrated. Feeling the way I was feeling, I wanted to swing the bat. So, the next time up, when the first pitch was in there, I hit it. I knew it was out when I hit it.

The next time, I hit the ball so hard, I wasn't sure it would go out. I thought it might just stay on a line and hit the fence. But then, it started rising and went out.

Then they brought in a knuckleballer and I thought, "This is really my day," because I had always hit knuckleballers. I could hardly wait to get up to the plate the last time. I thought, "I want to get up there before I lose this feeling." And I hit that home run probably even harder than the others.

There have been other times in my career when I've had that same kind of feeling in a game, that I could hit a home run any time I got my pitch. But in the regular season, you don't have the same kind of public attention you get in the World Series, and you don't have that dramatic buildup, so it doesn't mean as much. That World Series stands alone for me.

On the other side, I've had my disappointments. The California Angels team I played on in 1982 won a divisional title and set an American League attendance record. We were known as the "Hammerin' Halos" because I hit 39 home runs, Doug DeCinces hit 30, Brian Downing hit 28, Don Baylor hit 24, and Freddie Lynn hit 21.

But nobody remembers any of that today because we didn't get into the World Series. The Milwaukee Brewers did.

I've been fortunate, though, because I've had my chance to play in the World Series. For a professional, that's the ultimate. Your career is incomplete if you haven't made it to the Series.

There's nothing like playing in the World Series, but reading this book is the next best thing. It captures the excitement of the World Series and makes you feel you're there. It's a book every sports fan should have.

Preface

There are many way to approach a subject as dramatic and diverse as the World Series. Mine has been to take the most memorable Series and use them as examples of what this great sports event means.

Memorable can mean many things. A Series can be memorable for an individual performance, such as Reggie Jackson hitting homers on three consecutive pitches in 1977. It can be memorable because it is the first, or because it heralds the start of an era or even a switch of power from one league to the other. It can be memorable simply because it features such crackling good play; who can ever forget the 1975 Cincinnati–Boston Series?

The selection of most memorable, of course, is one man's opinion. You may have a favorite that was left out—but arguing about baseball is really the National Pastime, isn't it?

In the back of the book, there are statistics on every World Series, to settle some arguments and probably start others.

Finally, a personal note: The most difficult part of this book was winnowing out the Series to write about, because the level of excellence has been so high, remarkably so for any form of entertainment. Broadway should be so lucky.

THE HISTORY OF
THE
WORLD SERIES

1. In the Beginning

The World Series is a truly unique event. Unlike other American sports championships, it matches teams that have not met during the regular season, which heightens the suspense and increases the arguments between supporters of the teams.

Because baseball has no inter-league play, the World Series is seen—rightfully or not—as the true measure of the relative strength of the two leagues. Few people really care whether an American or a National Conference team wins the Super Bowl, because those are artificial divisions, but baseball fans will root for a team in the World Series simply because it is a representative of the league with which they identify.

Unlike the Super Bowl, its only competition for the designation of America's premier sports event, the World Series is held in the parks of the competitors, and the partisan fans become an important part of the scene.

The parks themselves are important; baseball in Fenway Park is quite different from baseball in Dodger Stadium. With the advent of artificial turf, another element has been added. Games within an individual Series will vary greatly when play shifts back and forth from grass to artificial turf.

The Series itself changes the game. During the regular season, baseball is a leisurely game. Because the season is a long one, fans take the games more casually than they would a football game; they know their team will have many chances to recover from a loss, or even a string of losses. There is no need to hang on every pitch. Games are a time to talk with friends, to discuss strategy, to compare teams and players of previous years as well as the current season.

But in the Series, the tension level is always high. One pitch, one play can make a big difference in a game, and one game can make a big difference in a short Series. The classic pitcher-batter duel becomes a suspenseful one, and fans explode with excitement at every hit and every strikeout.

The tension in a World Series can do strange things to players. Some of the best players—Ted Williams, Ty Cobb—have had embarrassingly bad Series. Conversely, some ordinary players—Billy Martin, Gene Tenace—have played like All-Stars in the World Series. Don Larsen was literally perfect in one World Series game, but before and after that, he was known more for what he did off the field than on.

Because the games are so important and the tension is so high, there have been many memorable games and individual efforts, and the level of play and excitement in the World Series has been consistently high—again, much more than in the Super Bowl, which is often more spectacle than game.

The idea of a championship series matching the winners in two leagues was such a natural that it was tried as early as 1882, between the National League champion (Chicago) and the American Association champion (Cincinnati).

Even the name, World Series, dates back to that era; it was apparently the idea of sportswriter Alfred Spink, who was later to found *The Sporting News,* the famed "Baseball Bible." It was a peculiarly American idea, that a championship could be so designated when the baseball "world" did not even extend to the south and west of the United States!

When the American Association folded in 1890, that competition ended. In 1894, the National League started a competition called the Temple Cup; lasting for four years, it matched the first- and second-place teams in the league.

But those competitions, both the early "World Series" and the Temple Cup, were mainly experiments, only a rough precursor of what was to come. There was relatively little interest in the competitions, particularly in the Temple Cup.

There was no set format for the competitions. There were as many as 15 games and as few as two, the first one ending at the latter number after each team had won a game and bickering ended the Series before any more games could be played.

The 15-game Series was played in 1887, St. Louis of the American Association winning ten of the games against National League champion Detroit. It was more of a carnival than a competition, with games being played in ten cities. In addition to the home cities, games were played in Pittsburgh, Brooklyn, New York, Philadelphia, Boston, Washington, Baltimore, and Chicago.

Even that Series, though, was less of a travesty than the 1885 competition, which matched the St. Louis Browns of the American Association and the Chicago White Stockings of the National League.

The Series ended in a tie, each team winning three games with one a tie, and it was so poorly played as to make the designation of championship a mockery. Between them, the teams made 103 errors in the seven games, an incredible 27 coming in the final game.

In the middle of the Series, play was suspended while the Browns played the St.

Louis Maroons of the National League for the championship of St. Louis. The wonder is that they resumed the Series after the Browns disposed of the Maroons.

Because of the variety of formats and the erratic play, these early competitions are only a footnote in the history of the World Series. Baseball historians generally consider the World Series to have started in 1903, when the champions of two stable leagues, the National and American, met for the first time. For the purpose of this book, I will make the same distinction.

The great rivalry between the two baseball leagues actually began in 1901, when Ban Johnson declared his American League to be a major league.

Johnson, one of the great baseball pioneers, had been working to that point since, in 1893. Leaving his job as a Cincinnati sportswriter then, he had become president of the Western League, a minor league centered in the midwest.

Under Johnson's direction, the league thrived. He brought solid financial support to the league, gave umpires an authority that was uncommon at the time, and encouraged owners to improve and police their parks, so women would be encouraged to come to the games.

It was always Johnson's dream to make the Western League into a major league, but he probably would not have been able to make it without some unwitting help from the National League owners.

The first helpful move came when the National League cut back to eight teams from 12 after the 1899 season, dropping teams in Washington, Baltimore, Cleveland, and Louisville. Johnson persuaded the owners of the Grand Rapids franchise to move into Cleveland, and Charles Comiskey moved his St. Paul franchise to Chicago. With that, Johnson renamed his league the American League, trying to give it more of a national identity.

But the league, by any name, was still a minor league, because it didn't have the quality players the National League had. And the National Agreement, a document of the time that set operating rules for all of baseball, designated the National League as the only major league.

After the 1900 season, Johnson made his next move. He announced that his league was withdrawing from the National Agreement and that it would not honor the reserve clause of National League player contracts. He put franchises into Boston, Philadelphia, Baltimore, and Washington, making his league as national in scope as the National League itself, and declared that the American League would operate as a major league.

There was still the question of players. It's easy enough to call a league a major league, but if the players aren't good enough, nobody is fooled. Once again, the National League owners came to the rescue. With their seeming monopoly on the game, they had established a salary limit of $2,400, so National League stars were quite willing to listen to offers from American League owners.

In the 1901 season, 111 of the 182 American League players were those who had jumped from the National League, and many of them were stars. Nap Lajoie, a second baseman who moved from the Philadelphia Phillies to the Philadelphia Athletics, won the American League triple crown by hitting .422 with 14 home runs and 125 RBIs. Cy Young, the winningest pitcher of all time, jumped to the new league, as did his fellow star pitchers, Eddie Plank and Joe McGinnity. John McGraw, who later jumped back to become a great manager in the National League, Jimmy Collins, Roger Bresnahan, and Wilbert Robinson all played in the American League in 1901, and all of these players eventually were elected to the Hall of Fame.

The American League, through these player raids, built itself up so quickly and successfully that a truce between the leagues was reached in 1903, to prevent any more player raids. Johnson was dealing from strength in these negotiations, and he knew it. He successfully resisted the full merger that National League owners wanted; the leagues remained separate. The American League teams were allowed to keep all the players they had lured from the National League and, despite the protests of the Giants, kept a team in New York, the Highlanders, later to become the Yankees.

Thus, the stage was set once again for inter-league competition, and it was quick to come. Although it might have seemed more natural for the newer league to make the first move, it was actually the National League that first proposed the World Series.

By August of that year, it was clear who was going to win in both leagues. Pittsburgh, which had been in first place since June 19, eventually won the National League pennant by 6½ games and the Boston Pilgrims, who were to become the Red Sox, coasted home in the American League by 14½ games.

Pittsburgh owner Barney Dreyfus was confident his team could beat the Pilgrims. The Pirates had won three straight National League pennants and hadn't been hurt by the American League raiding, probably because Dreyfus ignored the salary limit and was generous by the standards of the times.

Dreyfus approached Henry Killilea, the Boston owner, with the idea that the teams play a postseason championship. Killilea asked the advice of Johnson. "If you think you can beat them, play them," said Johnson.

The two owners worked out a format for a nine-game Series, the first three and last two games at Boston, the middle four in Pittsburgh.

Dreyfus had reason to be confident when he made the arrangements. He had a great team—it had won a then-record 102 games the previous season—and the best player in the game, shortstop Honus Wagner, who excelled as a fielder, hitter, and base runner.

But by the time the Series approached, the Pirates were not the team they had been earlier. Wagner had injured his right leg and, though he played, was limping badly. Pittsburgh's leading pitcher, 25-game winning Sam Leever, had injured his shoulder in a trapshooting tournament and pitched only briefly and ineffectively in the Series (10 innings, two losses). The 16-game winning Ed Doheny succumbed to mental illness and was hospitalized before the Series.

The Boston fans were also a factor in this Series. "The fans were part of the game in those days," the Pittsburgh third baseman Honus Wagner told Lawrence Ritter in *The Glory of Their Times* years after the fact. "They'd pour right out onto the field and argue with the players and the umpires. Was sort of hard to keep the game going sometimes, to say the least."

The Pilgrims had a group called the Royal Rooters, whose leader was a man named Mike McGreevey, known as "Nuf Sed" because that was his way of ending any and all baseball arguments.

The Boston fans got under the skin of the Pirates players in an unusual way—by singing a song, or at least, their version of the song.

Taking the tune of a popular song of the day called "Tessie," the Royal Roosters sang things to the Red Sox players like, "Jimmy (Collins), you know I love you madly."

When the slumping Wagner came to bat, they sang:

> Honus, why do you hit so badly,
> Take a back seat and sit down.
> Honus, at bat you look so sadly,
> Hey, why don't you get out of town.

Compared to what was usually said to players of that era, this was pretty mild stuff, but the Pirates didn't like it. Maybe they were music critics at heart.

What bothered the Pirates even more, though, was their lack of pitching. With Doheny out and Leever ineffective, the Pirates only had Deacon Phillippe, a 24-game winner during the regular season, left from their regular starting rotation. Phillippe alone couldn't do it for the Pirates, although he gave it a game try.

It might have been an omen for the Pirates when owner Dreyfus had to pay to get into the Boston park. "Imagine paying to see my own team play!" he said.

It was worth it that day, though, as the Pirates jumped on the 28-game-winning Young for four runs in the first inning and went on to a 7–3 win behind Phillippe.

Bill Dineen got the Pilgrims back into a tie when he pitched a 3–0 shutout in the second game. Pittsburgh's playing manager, Fred Clarke, started Leever, but the sore-armed pitcher gave up two runs before conceding in the first inning.

Clarke went back to Phillippe in the third game, on only one day of rest, and Phillippe came through again with a 4–2 complete game victory, disappointing the noisy Boston fans. The crowd of 18,801 overflowed the stands into the outfield, resulting in seven ground-rule doubles during the game.

The next day, a Sunday, was a travel day, and rain postponed the Monday game, so Clarke sent Phillippe out once again. And, once again, Phillippe responded with a win, 5–4 over Dineen, despite a three-run Boston rally in the ninth.

With a 3–1 lead and the prospect of playing the next three games in Pittsburgh, the Pirates seemed to have this first-ever Series under control. But their injuries were starting to take effect and Clarke couldn't pitch Phillippe in every game, though he certainly tried.

Boston broke out of its hitting slump in the fifth game, scoring six times in the sixth inning and another four times in the seventh, en route to an 11–2 win.

The next day, Dineen notched his second win, this one by 6–3, and the clubs were even. The momentum of events had obviously turned.

The next day was cold, and Dreyfus decided it was too cold to play, postponing the seventh game of the Series. Perhaps, but there were other factors that probably weighed more heavily than the cold in his decision: (1) the fact that he could get a larger crowd for the game on Saturday, when it was played, than on Friday, when it was scheduled; and (2) the postponed game gave Phillippe an extra day of rest.

But this time, Phillippe—whose right arm must have been just short of falling off—wasn't up to the challenge. Young beat him, 7–3. It gives some idea of how desperate Pittsburgh's pitching situation was that, though Boston had a 4–1 lead after four innings and a 6–2 lead after six, Clarke left Phillippe in to pitch another complete game.

Heading back to Boston with a one-game lead and his two aces, Young and Dineen, both available if the Series went its full nine games, Boston manager Collins could afford to be optimistic. After all, Phillippe couldn't pitch both games, could he?

We'll never know, because the Pilgrims wrapped it up in the eighth game. The travel day and another rain delay gave Phillippe the relative luxury of two days rest but he'd have had to pitch a shutout to stay even that day as Dineen won his third game, again by a 3–0 score. As good as Dineen was in the Series, the outstanding player in the Series had to be Phillippe, who had won all three of the Pirates' victories and pitched five complete games.

The Series had been a resounding success from the standpoint of fan interest. More than 100,000 fans had watched the eight games, in parks that seated well under 20,000. In each city, there had been a game where the crowd was larger than capacity.

The Pirates were disappointed as a team, and no individual was unhappier than the great Wagner, who was virtually playing on one leg. He went hitless in the last three games and batted only .222 for the Series, and he made six errors, two of them during Boston's six-run flurry in the sixty inning of the fifth game.

But the Pirate players did better than the winning Pilgrims financially. Dreyfus donated his share to the players, who thus made $1,316 each. Boston's Killilea, meanwhile, wasn't giving away anything; in addition to Dreyfus, the Pittsburgh sportswriters had also had to pay their way into the Boston park. The Boston players got only $1,182, but Killilea took $6,699 for his share—and then sold the team to John I. Taylor, son of the owner of the *Boston Globe.*

The outcome of the Series didn't surprise Boston manager Collins, who had said before the Series, "The Pittsburghs do not look so strong to me. They show up strong because they are in a poorer league than the American. Why, the American League is fifty percent stronger than the National. I think we can show them some baseball when the time comes."

After the Series, Collins had another comment, for *Sporting Life*: "I should not be surprised to see postseason games each fall as long as there are two big leagues. There is no reason, when the games are played out on their merits, as they were in this case, why they should not be successful. They give the public a high article of baseball and enable the championship teams to pick up a bit of prize money for the cold winter."

In 1904 the Pilgrims won again in the American League, but only by a game and a half over the New York Highlanders, and they were deprived of the chance to defend their World Championship when the New York Giants, National League champions, refused to play them.

"There is nothing in the constitution or playing rules of the National League which requires its victorious club to submit its championship honors to a contest with a victorious club in a minor league," said New York Giants owner John Brush, somewhat illogically in view of the American League's victory in the first World Series.

"If the Giants do not want to play the champions of the American League," retorted Chicago White Sox owner Charles Comiskey, "the followers of the game can draw their own conclusions."

At this date, with the principals all long since in their graves, the reasons for the Giants' refusal to play in the World Series can only be the subject of speculation. But there are some obvious factors.

One is that both Brush and Giants manager John McGraw disliked American League president Ban Johnson. As a sportswriter in Cincinnati before he got into baseball, Johnson had been quite critical of Brush, then the Cincinnati owner.

Johnson and McGraw had had several run-ins when McGraw was playing manager of the Baltimore franchise in the American League, primarily because of McGraw's umpire-baiting. Those problems had caused McGraw to jump to the National League.

Apart from those personal animosities, however, McGraw and Brush probably suspected that Collins's opinion was the correct one: The American League was superior, though not by the margin Collins claimed, because it had raided the National League of so many star players.

A standout third baseman in his playing days, John McGraw later managed the New York Giants—and held them out of a proposed World Series in 1904. *(George Brace)*

The Giants, who were preeminent in New York because they had been there longer, didn't want to take a chance that the Highlanders might win the American League pennant and then supplant them in the eyes of the fans by winning the World Series. (As the Yankees, the Highlanders eventually did just that, of course, but not until the arrival of Babe Ruth.)

The feeling at the time was that it had been McGraw who had not wanted to play and then Brush who agreed. Some thought McGraw had changed his mind by late-season, but by that time, Brush's prestige was on the line. He would have seemed a fool if he had changed his mind at the last moment.

Lending credence to that theory is the fact that it was Brush who proposed after that season that the World Series be made mandatory—though he had said in a September statement that winning the National League pennant was "the greatest honor that can be obtained in baseball."

Since that time, the World Series has been played every year without fail. Neither scandal (the Black Sox Series), nor hard time, nor even world wars stopped it.

2. The Hitters Lay a Goose Egg

By 1905, John McGraw was ready for the American League. His Giants had led the National League from April 23 and had won the pennant by nine games, while the Philadelphia Athletics had struggled to win by two games in the American League.

For the Series, McGraw had a psychological weapon: new uniforms. The Giants took the field that fall in black uniforms with white trim and "Giants" spelled out in white across the front. Black uniforms were quite appropriate for the Giants; as long as McGraw managed them, they were hated everywhere outside of New York.

"I will never forget the impression created in Philadelphia and the thrill I got personally when the Giants suddenly trotted out from their dugout," McGraw later wrote in his autobiography, *My Thirty Years in Baseball.*

"I have heard army men say that the snappiest-looking outfit is usually made up of the best fighters," he added. "I can well understand that. The psychological effect of being togged out in snappy uniforms was immediately noticeable upon the players. The Athletics in their regular-season uniforms appeared dull. . . ."

Uniforms, no matter how snappy, are no help if you don't have the players, but McGraw had put together a very strong team.

The Giants had been a last place team when he had come to New York in 1902, but he had brought some good players with him: catcher Roger Bresnahan, one of the best of all time; pitcher Joe McGinnity, nicknamed "Iron Man" because he sometimes pitched both games of a doubleheader; and first baseman Dan McGann and second baseman Billy Gilbert, both solid if unspectacular players.

McGraw had traded well. He had gotten shortstop Bill Dahlen from Brooklyn and his entire outfield from other clubs—right fielder George Brown (Phillies), center fielder Mike Donlin (Cincinnati), and left fielder Sandow Mertes (Cubs). The only rookie on the 1905 team was third baseman Art Devlin.

But, most of all, McGraw had Christy Mathewson, who is still the winningest pitcher in National League history.

Mathewson towered above his competitors and colleagues, literally and figuratively. At 6-1½, he was literally a giant in that era, when players—and everybody else—were considerably shorter than they are today.

Sportswriters of that time tended to exaggeration and hyperbole, and Mathewson was accordingly portrayed as a saint, which was not quite true. Although he was thought not to drink or smoke, Mathewson—according to Fred Lieb who knew him as a player—would take an occasional drink and did smoke cigarettes.

In his book, *Baseball As I Have Known It,* Lieb noted that Mathewson loved to gamble. "He was good at card games of any sort and usually won—he was smarter, had a quicker mind and knew cards and percentages better than most of them. He studied opposing card players much as he studied batsmen when he was pitching, and this gave him a decided advantage."

Lieb remembered a dice game when Mathewson bet $1,000 on a roll, an enormous amount in those days. When McGraw learned about the game, he fined the other players $10 and Mathewson $100 ". . . because you should have set a better example for these men who don't have your intelligence."

But those chinks in Mathewson's armor were small ones indeed. Compared to other players of the day, Mathewson *was* a saint, so it's no surprise that he was portrayed that way in the literature of the day.

In an era when most players were uneducated, ill-mannered ruffians, Mathewson was a college graduate (Bucknell) and a model of decorum, on and off the field. He never questioned an umpire's decision nor criticized a teammate during a game. His modesty was such that when he wrote a book, *Pitching in a Pinch* in 1912 (reissued in 1977), he discussed the 1911 Series in which he had problems but not the 1905 Series in which he starred.

He was basically a reticent man. Lieb recalled times when the Giants' train pulled into small cities and Christy pulled down the shade on the window next to him so he couldn't be seen by people on the platform. But, despite his reticence, he talked frequently to groups of youngsters about the evils of drinking and smoking and the virtue of education.

He refused to pitch on Sunday because of a promise to his mother. As Lieb points out, that wasn't a difficult promise to keep at a time when Sunday ball was allowed only in three National League cities, Chicago, St. Louis, and Cincinnati. Still, it was consistent with Mathewson's beliefs as he was a regular churchgoer (Episcopalian).

Mathewson was the most admired player of his time. Parents felt comfortable in holding him up as an idol to their children, and when fathers took their sons to their first baseball game it was, whenever possible, to watch Mathewson pitch.

They were seldom disappointed. Mathewson was a marvelous pitcher, as much in control of the game as any pitcher who has ever lived. Although he five times led the National League in strikeouts, including what was then a league-record 267 in 1903, he seldom tried for a strikeout, preferring to get hitters out on fewer pitches.

His fast ball, Lieb thought, ranked somewhat below that of Rube Waddell, Walter Johnson, Lefty Grove, Bob Feller, and Nolan Ryan, but his motion was so smooth that it was often in on hitters before they realized it. He had a good curve and a pitch that was called a "fadeaway" then and known as a screwball today, breaking away from left-handed hitters.

Mostly, though, Mathewson had great control. In one year, 1913, he went 68 consecutive innings without yielding a walk; for the year, he walked a mere 21 batters in 306 innings, an average of only slightly more than one every 15 innings.

Although he approached the game scientifically, studying hitters' weaknesses and moving the ball around so they could not discover a pattern, Mathewson's basic philosophy was simple: Let the batter hit the ball. With his great control, he could usually make the batter hit a pitch on the corner of the plate and, in that dead ball era, he seldom had to worry about a home run.

Lieb remembered a game against Cincinnati when Mathewson allowed 14 hits and still pitched a shutout! In each of the first seven innings, he gave up two singles; in the eighth and ninth, he retired the Reds 1–2–3. He did not allow a walk in the game, of course.

Mathewson had 13 seasons in which he won at least 20 games and four in which he won 30 or more, en route to his career total of 373. His best season was probably 1908 when he led the league in nine separate categories, including wins (37), earned run average (1.43), strikeouts (259), and shutouts (12).

But 1905 wasn't bad, either. He was 31–8 (his third straight season with at least 30 wins), with an ERA of 1.27, nine shutouts, and 206 strikeouts—all league-leading marks.

That kind of success gave Mathewson great confidence, of course. Strangely, that confidence wasn't shared by his teammates; except for Mathewson and Bresnahan, the Giant players voted to share their Series earnings equally with the Athletics, win or lose. That decision enraged McGraw, whose passion for winning was unequalled in baseball.

"I was disgusted . . . at their unwillingness to take a chance," he wrote in his autobiography.

That decision seemed even stranger because the Athletics were coming into the Series at less than full strength. Rube Waddell, their great left-handed pitcher who had won 26 games during the regular season and struck out 287 batters, could not pitch because of an injured shoulder.

Waddell had injured the shoulder tripping over a suitcase on a train, while trying to take a straw hat off the head of fellow pitcher Andy Coakley during a victory celebration in September.

Philadelphia fans, at least some of them, thought Waddell had been bribed by gamblers to pretend that he was injured. After the Series, there were newspaper stories making the same claim, talking of a betting coup by those gamblers who had put their money on the Giants.

Throwing games was not an uncommon practice at that time, when both interest and players' salaries were considerably lower than they are today. But, there was never any substantiation of those claims—which were repeated off and on for 30 years after the fact—and Waddell did not appear to be the kind of player who would throw a game. Money held no fascination for him, so long as he had enough to buy another drink.

At any rate, it's doubtful that even Waddell would have made a difference for the Athletics in 1905. At the top of his form, Mathewson was virtually untouchable. In the ultimate pitchers' Series, the first best-of-seven, he was the best.

Even without Waddell, Connie Mack had solid pitching available. His pitcher for the opening game, for instance, was Eddie Plank, who had won 25 games that season and went on to win 327 in his career.

Christy Mathewson set a Series record by pitching three shutouts in the New York Giants' win over the Athletics in 1905. *(George Brace)*

There was an unusual touch to this pairing: Both Plank and Mathewson were college graduates, at a time when most players were lucky to have finished eighth grade.

Mathewson pitched an extraordinary game, yielding only four hits and allowing only five other balls to be hit to the outfield. In five innings, he set the A's down 1–2–3, and only an error prevented him from doing that in a sixth inning. Only twice did the Athletics have runners in scoring position.

Not until the third did Philadelphia get a base runner, when Donlin dropped Ossee Schreckengost's fly ball. Mathewson then got Plank to ground into an inning-ending double play.

In the fourth, the A's got their first hit, when Topsy Hartsel singled to center. But Hartsel was stranded when Mathewson got the next three hitters to ground out.

Philadelphia's first scoring threat came in the sixth when Schreckengost led off with a double and advanced to third as Plank struck out on a wild pitch, Bresnahan throwing to first for the out.

Mack tried to squeeze the run home, but Hartsel's bunt was fielded cleanly by Mathewson, who threw out Schreckengost at the plate. Bris Lord then grounded into a double play to end the inning.

Mathewson set down the next eight batters before Lord hit a two-out double in the ninth. Lord stayed at second as Mathewson induced Lave Cross to ground out to end the game.

The Giants got all the runs they needed in the fifth, and, fittingly, it was Mathewson who started the rally with a single. Bresnahan hit into a force-out but then stole second (he was the fastest catcher of his day and one of the fastest of all time) and scored on Donlin's single. Donlin scored the second run of the inning on a double by Mertes.

Mathewson also played a part in the Giants' third run, in the top of the ninth. After Gilbert had singled—his third hit of the game—Mathewson sacrificed him to second, and he scored on Bresnahan's single.

Philadelphia got revenge in the second game and by an identical 3–0 score, Chief Bender outdueling McGinnity in this one. Bender, whose nickname came from his Indian nationality, also matched Mathewson in yielding only four hits, though he walked three; Mathewson had not given up a walk in his shutout.

Philadelphia got one run in the third when Schreckengost reached base on an error, was advanced to second by a sacrifice, and moved to third on a ground out; he scored on Lord's single.

Schreckengost, a typographer's nightmare, also started the rally that got the A's last two runs in the eighth, with a single. He scored on Hartsel's double, and Hartsel then scored on a single by Lord.

Mark those runs well. They were the last the A's were to score in the Series.

In World Series play nowadays, the first two games and the last two are played in one city and the middle three games in the other. In 1905, the Series had opened in Philadelphia, moved to New York for the second game, and now returned to Philadelphia for the third.

The visitors had won each game so far, and the pattern remained intact in the third game, the Giants overwhelming the host A's by 9–0. Coakley pitched the entire nine innings for the A's. This would seem to be cruel and unusual punishment, but perhaps the manager, Mack, was angry with him because he had been involved in the horseplay that had cost the A's the services of Waddell.

Or, perhaps, Mack realized there was no sense in wasting other pitchers against Mathewson. Christy pitched a carbon copy of his first game, yielding only four hits, though he did walk one batter in this one.

Sometimes pitchers with a big lead will unconsciously let up a bit on the other team, but if Mathewson relaxed at all, nobody noticed: the A's never got a runner past first base.

The Giants got two runs in the first and turned the game into a runaway with a five-run fifth. That was the one big inning of the Series, but not because of the Giants' great hitting; they got only three hits in the inning.

With one out, Bresnahan started the rally by walking. Browne followed with a single, and Donlin walked to load the bases. Bresnahan scored when McGann was safe on an error, and Browne came in on a single by Mertes.

Donlin scored the third run when Dahlen hit into a force play, McGann going to third. Dahlen stole second, and McGann scored as Devlin singled, Dahlen going to third. Then, the Giants pulled off a delayed double steal for their fifth run. Devlin stole second, and, when the throw went to second, Dahlen came home from third.

It was back to New York for the fourth game, and the Giants took command of the Series with the best-pitched game yet, McGinnity outdueling the unlucky Plank, 1–0. McGinnity gave up five hits, Plank only four.

The one run in the game was unearned. In the bottom of the fourth, Mertes reached base on an error for the Giants, went to second on a ground out, and scored on Gilbert's single.

Still in New York, Mathewson applied the coup de grace to the A's with a 2–0 win over Bender in the fifth game.

Mathewson was uncommonly generous in this game, yielding six hits to the A's. But only in the fifth inning did the A's get a runner to second, when Mike Powers hit a two-out double, and Mathewson retired the last ten batters of the game—and Series.

The Giants got a single run in the fifth without a hit. Mertes and Dahlen walked and advanced on a sacrifice, and Mertes then scored on Gilbert's fly to left.

The final run of the Series was scored in the eighth inning by Mathewson who walked, went to third on Bresnahan's double, and scored on Browne's ground out.

That was only fitting, because it was Mathewson's Series. His performance has never been equaled and probably never will be: three shutouts, only 14 hits in 27 innings, 18 strikeouts, and one walk.

It was also, of course, the best-pitched Series ever, with all five games ending in a shutout. Not a triple or home run was hit in the five games. The Giants hit just .203 as a team, the A's a sickly .161. Bresnahan was the only hitter to top .300, with a .313 mark, and one of only three regulars on both teams to top .250. (Interestingly, Mathewson hit .250 himself, the third-best average on his team.)

It was an important win for the National League, whose reputation had suffered because of the first Series loss and the Giants' refusal to play in 1904.

As for the Giants' fans . . . well, their sentiments were summed up in a poem by W. E. Kirk on the sports pages of the *New York American,* which concluded with this stanza:

> Far from the madding crowd's ferocious yells
> The Polo Grounds will miss the Giants' tricks.
> Until a crowd of thirty thousand tells
> That we have started Season Nineteen-Six.

Joe Tinker, Johnny Evers, and Frank Chance were the most famous double-play combination in baseball history and the leaders of a Cubs' team that was in four World Series in five years. *(George Brace)*

3. Who's Afraid of the Big Bad Cubs

The World Series, dramatic as it may be, is not always the best test of baseball. In a short series, strange things can happen. One team may come in hot, another cold. A good team may be overconfident. A star pitcher can start as many as three games out of seven and have a disproportionate effect on the outcome. Star players may slump, weak ones may hit a hot streak.

For all these reasons, the better team does not always win, a fact baseball fans surely realized in 1906 after the third World Series, one that matched two Chicago teams, the National League Cubs and the American League White Sox.

This was the first one-city World Series and, given the history of the Cubs since their last pennant in 1945, may be the last ever between two Chicago teams.

It was also the first great upset. The experts figured it would be a short Series, no more than 5–6 games. They were right about that, but wrong about the outcome.

Finally, it was the first Series with a surprise star. Utility White Sox infielder George Rohe had an otherwise undistinguished career that ended after the 1907 season, but in a Series that had five future Hall of Fame players, it was Rohe who made the difference.

The 1906 Cubs were, says baseball historian Donald Honig, one of the ten best teams of all time. The team became the first twentieth century dynasty, winning three straight National League pennants and four in a five-year stretch.

At the start of the year, it had seemed that John McGraw's New York Giants would be the first dynasty. The Giants had won two straight pennants and had won the 1905 Series in five games; with Christy Mathewson as the team's physical and spiritual leader, the Giants seemed poised for their third straight pennant in 1906.

That hope evaporated early. The 1906 pennant was in doubt only for the first third of the season. The Giants and Cubs moved back and forth between first and second in April and most of May, but on May 28, the Cubs took over first place and kept it.

Their season statistics were awesome. Although they played only 152 games (two games were rained out and never rescheduled), the Cubs won 116 games, a major league record that has never been seriously challenged, even though the schedule has been lengthened to 162 games. Their winning margin over the second-place Giants was a whopping 20 games.

The trademark of the 1906 Cubs was consistency. Several clubs have had longer winning streaks than the Cubs' high of 14 that year (the 1916 Giants won 26 straight but finished fourth!), but the Cubs had no long losing streaks.

Remarkably, they won even more frequently on the road than at home. In home games, they were 56–21, a good record but one which has been surpassed by other teams. On the road, they were 60–15, a major league record that would probably be more difficult to beat than even their overall season mark.

In winning their three straight pennants, 1906–08, the Cubs won 322 games. That, too, is a major league record.

Despite all those impressive statistics, the Cubs of that era are best known for three of their players—shortstop Joe Tinker, second baseman John Evers, and first baseman Frank Chance, the most famous double-play combination in baseball history.

The story behind the trio remains one of baseball's most interesting. *New York Mail* columnist Franklin P. Adams was a great baseball fan. In a hurry one day because he wanted to finish his column and get out to the Giants' game, he dashed off this little verse:

> These are the saddest of possible words—
>   "Tinker to Evers to Chance."
> Trio of Bear Cubs and fleeter than birds—
>   "Tinker to Evers to Chance."
> Ruthlessly pricking our gonfalon bubble,
>   Making a Giant hit into a double,
> Words that are weighty with nothing but trouble—
>   "Tinker to Evers to Chance."

Although Adams himself never thought of the verse as anything but the column filler it was, the words became so much a part of baseball lore that "Tinker to Evers to Chance" became synonymous with double plays. The trio was even inducted into the Hall of Fame together in 1946.

There were some interesting sidelights to the story. For at least two years, Tinker and Evers didn't speak to each other. Tinker was upset over an incident off the field—Evers had taken a cab away from the park and left Tinker and a couple of other players standing—and told Evers, "If you and I talk to each other, we're only going to be fighting all the time. So, don't talk to me, and I won't talk to you. You play your position and I'll play mine, and let it go at that."

There were times when Chance, nearly driven crazy by Evers's incessant chattering, wished he had made a similar arrangement.

None of the three started at the positions that made them famous. Chance came up to the Cubs as a catcher; he was switched to first to take advantage of his hitting when it became clear that he wasn't good enough to be the starting catcher. Tinker came up as a third baseman, Evers as a shortstop; both were switched by Frank Selee, then the Cubs' manager.

Chance was probably the best player of the three. Starting in 1903, he hit more than .300 for four straight years (.319 in 1906 and even higher in other seasons) in a pitcher-dominated era. He was also an excellent base stealer, with a high of 67 in 1903 (57 in 1906); he holds the Cubs' career mark of 405 stolen bases.

Chance's leadership qualities were evident from the moment he became a starter, and when Selee contracted pneumonia in mid-1905, Chance was named playing manager. Chicago writer Charles Dryden soon nicknamed him "The Peerless Leader."

Tinker was a good-fielding shortstop with a lifetime batting average of .263, adequate at a position where fielding is prized more than hitting. Evers hit .270 lifetime and was the team's spark plug.

How good were they as a unit? Then and now, that has been the subject of an often bitter debate. McGraw once called a press conference to tell writers they had created "a fake," though it was a nonsportswriter, Adams, who had written the famous verse.

McGraw thought the Pittsburgh combination of Honus Wagner, Dots Miller, and Bill Abstein was at least as good as the Cubs' combination, and he was also high on his own combination of Dave Bancroft, Frankie Frisch, and George Kelly. Although the Giants' manager didn't like to admit that the other league ever did anything right, he also felt the Philadelphia Athletics' combination of Jack Barry, Eddie Collins, and Stuffy McInnis was better than "Tinker to Evers to Chance."

By modern standards, the trio did not turn a lot of double plays, notwithstanding Adams's lament. The most double plays Tinker was ever involved in during a season was 55 in 1906; Evers's high mark was 58 the following season.

Former New York sportswriter Charlie Segar came up with even more critical statistics. According to Segar, the number of double plays that went either from Tinker to Evers to Chance or Evers to Tinker to Chance was only 56 in a four-year period, 1906–09.

Segar's findings seem questionable. In 1906, for instance, the official statistics showed Tinker involved in 55 double plays, Evers in 51, and Chance in 71; according to Segar, only 17 double plays involved all three. That leaves an incredible number that would have had to have been made in unusual combinations.

It is impossible, too, to compare double play figures from that era with this one. In that low-hitting era, teams were much more likely to bunt runners along, removing the chance of a double play. And fielders wore tiny gloves, which made it more difficult to come up with ground balls.

Even so, there is no question that the reputation of Tinker, Evers, and Chance was inflated by Adams's little verse. In fact, they might have been inferior to the fourth member of that infield, third baseman Harry Steinfeldt. An excellent fielder, Steinfeldt hit .327 for the Cubs in 1906 and led the league with 83 RBIs and 176 hits. Steinfeldt played 14 years in the majors, his last four seasons coming during the Cubs' dynasty years, but he isn't in the Hall of Fame. He should have introduced himself to Adams.

The 1906 Cubs also had one of the league's top catchers, Johnny Kling, who was especially known for his throwing ability. He hit a solid .312 that year.

Another Cub star was Frank (Wildfire) Schulte; in only his second full major league season, the 23-year-old Schulte hit .281 and tied for the league lead with 13 triples. Five seasons later, in 1911, Schulte became the first major leaguer in the twentieth century to hit more than 20 home runs, with a total of 21.

The Cubs were also an excellent fielding team, as Tinker, Steinfeldt, and Kling all led their positions in fielding percentage. But it was the pitching staff that really made the Cubs a great team.

The staff leader was Mordecai "Three-Finger" Brown, who eventually joined Tinker, Evers, and Chance in the Hall of Fame.

Brown got his nickname because of a childhood accident; at the age of seven, he had put his hand into a feed cutter, and his index finger had to be amputated at the knuckle. While his hand was still in a splint, he started chasing a hog one day and fell and broke the third and fourth fingers on the same hand. Although they healed, they were grotesquely twisted throughout his life. But what Brown lost in beauty, he gained in effectiveness; the gnarled fingers allowed him to put unusual curves on his pitches.

Brown won 239 games in his major league career, and he earned them. Because he was the Cubs' ace, he often had to pitch against the great Mathewson, but he bested Christy on a career basis, winning 13 times while losing 11. Between July 12, 1905, and October 8, 1908, he won nine in a row against Mathewson.

Starting in 1906, Brown won 20 or more games for six straight seasons (a total of 148 wins), including 26 in 1906. In that season, he had the lowest ERA in National League history, 1.04.

Brown was hardly the only outstanding Chicago pitcher. Jack Pfiester, the only left-hander on the staff, was 20–8 with an ERA of 1.56. Ed Reulbach was 20–4 with an ERA of 1.65. Carl Lundgren was 17–6 with an ERA of 2.21.

To complete the staff, the Cubs made a mid-season trade with Cincinnati to get Orval Overall, who was 12–3 with the Cubs and became the fourth member of the staff to allow fewer than two earned runs a game, with an ERA of 1.88.

To put those earned run averages into perspective, only two other National League pitchers—Vic Willis and Lefty Leifeld—finished under two earned runs a game that season. Mathewson, always the standard for National League pitchers, had a 2.97 ERA that year.

In contrast to the Cubs' easy march to the National League pennant, their crosstown rivals, the White Sox, had had a long and strenuous battle to win the American League title.

In early August, the White Sox had actually been in fourth place, behind Philadelphia, New York, and Cleveland. Getting hot at the right time, the White Sox won 19 straight to move into first place, and they held on to win by three games over New York.

But compared to the Cubs, the White Sox win was unimpressive. The White Sox won only 93 games, three fewer than the runner-up Giants had won in the National League. This was certainly no dynasty team, as was proved when the White Sox finished third, third, and fourth in the next three years in the American League.

Like the Cubs, the White Sox had solid pitching. Nick Altrock won 21 games, Doc White 18, and Ed Walsh (who would win 40 games two seasons later) 17. White led the league with a 1.52 ERA and the White Sox' team average was a good 2.13.

However, the White Sox were known as the "Hitless Wonders." They hit only .230 as a team and had merely six homers; Schulte had one more by himself for the Cubs.

Looking at these statistics, the oddsmakers made the Cubs a 3–1 favorite in the Series. The only real question seemed to be how long it would take the Cubs to win. They reckoned without George Rohe.

Rohe was in the lineup only because of an injury to shortstop George Davis. White Sox manager Fielder Jones moved third baseman Lee Tannehill to shortstop and put Rohe at third base.

Rohe had an impact almost immediately, tripling in the fifth inning of the first game off Three-Finger Brown. Jiggs Donahue struck out, and Patsy Dougherty grounded back to the mound, but Johnny Kling dropped Brown's throw to the plate and Rohe scored.

The White Sox added another run in the sixth when Frank Isbell singled in playing manager Jones. The Cubs finally scored in the bottom of the inning on a walk to Kling, a single by Brown, a sacrifice, and a wild pitch.

That was it, as Nick Altrock won a battle of four-hitters with Brown.

Although it was not yet mid-October (the Series started on October 9), the weather for most of this Series was more like mid-December in Chicago. Snow flurries had fallen for the first game and freezing winds cut across the field for the second game, making it painful for hitters when they connected.

That didn't matter much to the White Sox, who got only one hit, a seventh-inning single by Donahue. Oddly, they had scored a run before that in the fifth inning on a walk, wild pitch, and error by Tinker.

This was the one game of the Series that went the way most people had expected. The White Sox were almost literally "Hitless Wonders" as Ed Reulbach came within the one pitch to Donahue of becoming the first pitcher to throw a no-hit game in the World Series.

The Cubs got to Doc White for three runs in the second inning, more than enough to win this game. With one out, Steinfeldt singled and Tinker beat out a bunt.

Evers laid down a sacrifice bunt, and when Isbell threw wide to second base, Steinfeldt scored and Tinker went to third. Kling was intentionally walked to load the bases.

Reulbach's bunt got Tinker home and moved up Evers and Kling, and Evers then scored on an infield hit by Solly Hofman.

The Cubs scored single runs in the third and sixth, and then added two more in the eighth to coast home as 7–1 winners.

Very often, there is one key play in a World Series that determines not only who will win that game but who will win the Series. In 1906, that play came in the sixth inning of the third game and it was Rohe who made it.

For five innings, the Cubs' Jack Pfiester and the Sox' Ed Walsh were locked in a scoreless battle; Walsh had yielded just one hit, Pfiester two.

In the top of the sixth, Lee Tannehill led off for the Sox with a single. Pfiester was determined not to give Walsh a ball he could bunt for a sacrifice, and he ended up walking his pitching counterpart and then loaded the bases by hitting Eddie Hahn.

Pfiester settled down to get Jones on a pop foul and then struck out Isbell on three straight pitches. He was almost out of it—but then, up came Rohe.

The first pitch to Rohe was a curve ball that dipped out of the strike zone. Cubs' catcher Johnny Kling said to Rohe, "so you're the guy who likes fastballs. That was a fastball you hit off Brownie in the first game. Well, you won't see any more."

Rohe figured, correctly, that Kling was trying to use a little psychology on him. "I figured Kling was trying to confuse me," he said. "I looked for the fast one and got it. The ball was a fast inside pitch, shoulder high, and I hit it right on a line."

Rohe's liner went into the crowd in left-center; he got a triple that unloaded the bases in a hurry, and Walsh was virtually untouchable the rest of the way. Only one Cub reached base in the last four innings, on an Isbell error, and the White Sox had taken a 2–1 lead in the Series on the strength of Walsh's 2–0 two-hit masterpiece.

The Cubs weren't through, as Brown got revenge for his first game loss with a 1–0 win over Altrock in the fourth game. Brown was magnificent in this one, not yielding a hit until the sixth and only two overall. Only twice did the White Sox get a runner in scoring position.

Altrock wasn't so overpowering, yielding seven hits, but it wasn't until the seventh that the Cubs could score their one run, and it was scored in a fashion that shows the

d Walsh was the leader of the Chicago White
ox pitching staff in 1906 when the "Hitless
Vonders" upset their crosstown rivals in the
Vorld Series. *(George Brace)*

strategy of that dead ball era. Chance led off with a single, and then the Cubs sacrificed twice to get him to third. Evers then followed with a single.

Warm weather returned for the fifth game, and, with it, the White Sox bats came out of hibernation. Incredibly, the weak-hitting Sox started treating the star Cub pitchers like batting practice pitchers.

Manager Jones had played a hunch the game before: With Davis ready to play, he had moved Rohe to third and taken Tannehill out of the lineup. It hadn't mattered against Brown in that game, but the hunch paid off in the fifth game. Rohe continued his effective hitting with three hits in four at-bats (plus a walk), including a double and a run batted in. Davis was even more effective, as his two hits knocked in three runs.

The tone of this game was set early, when the Sox scored a run in the top of the first and the Cubs came back with three in the bottom of the inning. The White Sox tied the score with two runs in the third and then took command of the game, and the Series, with a four-run fourth inning.

It was no fluke, either, as some White Sox rallies tended to be. Walsh led off with a walk and, after he was forced at second, Jones singled and Isbell, Davis, and Donahue all doubled. Although it was only the fourth inning, the double was Isbell's third of the game, and he got a fourth in the eighth inning.

As much as anything, the game showed the unpredictability that is the heart of baseball's appeal. Reulbach, who had almost pitched a no-hitter in the second game, was knocked out in the third inning of this one. Walsh, who had pitched a two-hit shutout in the second game, was hammered for six runs and knocked out in the sixth inning, though he did get the win.

And the final score was an improbable 8–6 win for the White Sox, a team that had scored only six runs total in the first four games of the Series.

Chance sent his ace, Brown, back to the mound in a desperate attempt to salvage the Series in the sixth game. Perhaps that might have worked if the Cubs had been playing a team from the east, because there would have been travel days. But with both teams being from the same city—and no television executives to tell owners the games must be postponed to be played in prime time—there was no need for days off, so Brown was pitching with only one day rest. It wasn't enough.

An overflow crowd had packed South Side Park (the official attendance was 19,249, but gate-crashers swelled the attendance to more than 25,000) to cheer the White Sox on, and the fans weren't disappointed. This one was a cakewalk for the Sox, who scored seven runs in the first two innings and cruised to an 8–3 win. White went all the way for the victory.

Isbell got three more hits in this game, and Davis knocked in three runs. Rohe went two-for-five, giving him five hits in the last two games. For the Series, he tied with Donahue for the leading batting average with .333 and topped everyone with a slugging average of .571.

More significant than Rohe's statistics was the fact that he got the key hits in the early part of the Series that convinced the White Sox the mighty Cubs could be had.

For the Cubs, it was a very bitter loss. Many of them had bet more than their Series share on themselves, and who could have blamed them? Manager Chance took the loss philosophically. "It was a hard Series to lose," he said, "but you can't win all the time."

Good teams bounce back, and the Cubs proved their greatness by winning the next two National League pennants and atoning for their 1906 loss by winning the next two World Series, both from Detroit, shutting out the Tigers in 1907 and winning, 4–1, in 1908.

And George Rohe? He batted only .213 the next season and was sold after that to New Orleans in the minors. He never played another major league game—but he had some memories that many better players could never match.

4. Home Run Baker?

There is no better example of how the World Series can magnify accomplishments than the case of Frank "Home Run" Baker.

Baker was a solid player for the Philadelphia Athletics and New York Yankees, a strong-fielding third baseman who was also a solid hitter, with a .307 average for his 13-year career. He earned his spot in the Hall of Fame.

But, Home Run Baker? Playing in an era when home runs were rare, Baker four times led the American League in homers but never hit more than 12 in any one season. His lifetime total of 93 is actually ten fewer than his lifetime total of triples.

But Baker picked his spots. In the 1911 Series, he hit two crucial home runs, and his reputation was made. He was known as Home Run Baker from that point on.

Baker's heroics were only one of many notable aspects of a remarkable span of four World Series, 1911–14.

The first and third in that string matched the two most famous managers in the game, John McGraw of the New York Giants and Connie Mack of the A's, and never has there been a more disparate matching.

McGraw was gruff, profane, combative, and willing to do anything that would give him an edge. He was a very superstitious man, dressing his 1911 Giants in the same black uniforms that had made such an impression on players and spectators alike as the Giants had won the 1905 Series.

Mack was a gentleman in a ruffian's game. He was never quite the saint he was made out to be, but his habit of wearing a business suit with high-collared dress shirts, instead of a uniform, and his manner of speaking, addressing players by their full names, set him apart from everybody else in the game.

Even their baseball philosophies differed. Mack believed in bringing his team around slowly, because he feared that too fast a start would cause a team to collapse late in the long season. McGraw believed in getting off to a fast start, thinking that would demoralize would-be contenders.

Connie Mack managed the first
American League dynasty team,
the Philadelphia Athletics of
1910–14, who were in four
World Series in five years.
(George Brace)

Both men were, of course, highly successful. McGraw won ten pennants in 33 years of managing, all of them in his first 25 seasons, and many still regard him as the best manager of all time. Mack won one less pennant, but he was even smarter than McGraw because he bought a part of the A's immediately and eventually became the full owner. For 53 years, owner Mack could not bring himself to fire manager Mack.

The managers were almost a sideshow, though, as that four-year run of Series produced disputed plays, incredible results, astounding errors, a great upset, and even a newspaper feud between Giant pitchers Christy Mathewson and Rube Marquard.

There was one game that ended in such a confusing fashion that few even knew who had won the game. There was a historic muff of a fly ball that forever tainted the career of a fine player. In one game, the player who scored the winning run didn't touch home plate, but the opposing manager was afraid a protest would spark a riot.

In 1911, McGraw was riding high again, his club having dethroned the Chicago Cubs, who were fading after the run of four pennants in five years. The Giants were probably the most famous club of the day, partly because of McGraw and partly because the team attracted more attention by playing in New York.

Although some said he had lost a little off his fastball, Mathewson was still a great pitcher for the Giants, winning 26 of 39 decisions in 1911 and posting a league-leading 1.99 earned run average.

He was backed up by Rube Marquard with a 24–7 record. McGraw had bought Marquard in 1908 from Indianapolis for the then unheard-of sum of $11,000, and when Rube won only nine games in his first three seasons, he became known as the "$11,000 Lemon." But he shed that tag, and vindicated McGraw's judgment, by winning 73 games as the Giants won three straight pennants, 1911–13.

That 1911 Giants team was an outstanding one, with an infield of Fred Merkle at first, Larry Doyle at second, Art Fletcher at shortstop, and Buck Herzog at third. Chief Meyers was the catcher, and Josh Devore, Fred Snodgrass, and John "Red" Murray the outfielders. (McGraw moved his outfielders around; in the 1912 Series, for instance, Devore and Snodgrass alternated in center field, and each figured in spectacular plays.)

As a team, the 1911 Giants stole 347 bases, still a National League record. But as formidable as they were, they were not as good as the Athletics.

The 1910–14 Athletics won four pennants in five years and three World Series, and Mack thought the 1911 team was the best he ever had.

The heart of the team was the infield, with Baker at third, Jack Barry at short, and Eddie Collins at second. Baker and Collins are in the Hall of Fame, and there are many who believe Collins was the best second baseman of all time.

When Stuffy McInnis took over at first base for Harry Davis later in the dynasty run, the infield became known as the "$100,000 infield," at a time when $100,000 was as much money as fans and writers could imagine. The nickname came because a writer

Rube Marquard was victimized by "Home Run" Baker in the 1911 World Series—and by teammate Christy Mathewson in a newspaper column. *(George Brace)*

Eddie Collins starred for the Athletics in the World Series and then for the "Black Sox" of 1919. *(George Brace)*

asked Mack if he would sell the infield for $100,000 and Mack replied, laughing, "No, not even for that much."

As munificent as that sum seemed at the time, the infield was probably underpriced. When financial woes later caused Mack to break up his great team, Collins went for $50,000 by himself, and Baker brought another $35,000. Barry was also sold, but the sale figure was not announced.

That Athletics team had great pitching, too. Jack Coombs, famed for his big curve ball, won 28 games, almost matching the 31 he had won the year before.

Coombs' great success was brought to an untimely end by arm trouble—he won 20 games in 1912 but only 42 more in a career that stretched into 1920—but the other great pitchers on that team, Eddie Plank and Chief Bender, had long-lasting success that eventually brought them both into the Hall of Fame.

Plank was a scholarly pitcher, as befitted one of the few college graduates (Gettysburg) in the majors at that time. He watched hitters closely to detect weaknesses and pitched to spots at a time when few pitchers bothered to do so. He won 20 or more games seven times in his career and finished with 327 career wins. In 1911, he was 22–8.

It was Bender, though, who was the most fascinating of the A's pitchers. A full-blooded Indian who came by his nickname legitimately, he was often heckled by fans who directed war chants in his direction. Not bothered at all, the Chief would occasionally turn around and yell back at them: "Foreigners!"

Bender was not as big a winner as Plank, either in 1911, when he won 17, or in his career, when he won 210. But he was always a high percentage pitcher (in 1911, he lost only five games), and he was considered the A's "money pitcher." When there was an important game to be won, he wanted to pitch. As often as not, Mack obliged him.

Baseball historian Fred Lieb called the '11 and '12 Series the best back-to-back Series he ever saw. They were also, Lieb added, his first two Series, and that might have given them more importance in his mind. But, when you analyze those Series, you can understand Lieb's enthusiasm.

The 1911 Series started late because the regular season had been extended (in time, not in number of games) to allow Brooklyn owner Charley Ebbets to schedule a Columbus Day game to put some money into his nearly empty bank account. Thus, the Series started on the same day it had ended in 1905—and with the same pitchers opposing each other, Mathewson for the Giants and Bender for the A's.

Mathewson had won that final game in 1905, 2–0, and he won this one, too, 2–1. It was at least a moral victory for the A's, who finally scored on the great Matty after being shut out three times by him in the 1905 Series.

The A's run, the first of the game, came in the second inning when Baker singled, went to second on a sacrifice and to third on a passed ball, and then scored on a single by Harry Davis.

The Giants tied it in the fourth when Fred Snodgrass walked and then came all the way around when the usually reliable Collins fumbled a ground ball by Buck Herzog on a hit-and-run play.

In the seventh, Chief Meyers doubled and scored on a single by Josh Devore, and that was all the margin Mathewson needed.

The next day, left-handers Plank and Marquard were locked in a 1–1 pitching duel in the sixth inning. Collins doubled with two outs, bringing Baker to the plate. Baker took a ball and a strike and then saw a pitch he liked, a fastball over the inside of the plate that he lined over the right field fence to give the A's a 3–1 lead they maintained for the rest of the game.

Both Mathewson and Marquard had bylined stories in New York newspapers during this Series, Jack Wheeler doing the ghostwriting for Mathewson and Frank Menke writing for Marquard. The next day, this appeared under Mathewson's name in the *New York Herald*:

> Marquard made a poor pitch to Frank Baker on the latter's sixth-inning home run. There was no excuse for it. In a clubhouse talk with his players, Manager McGraw went over the entire Athletics' batting order, paying special attention to the left-handed hitter, Frank Baker. We had scouted Baker, knew what pitches were difficult for him to hit, and those he could hit for extra bases. Well, Rube threw him the kind of ball that Baker likes.

Were those actually Mathewson's thoughts, or was Wheeler putting words in his mouth (or typewriter)? Most likely, it was the latter; they hardly seemed in keeping with Mathewson's image. At any rate, Christy had reason to regret those words, because he fell victim to Baker himself in the very next game.

This was another pitching duel, this time between Matty and Coombs, who had won three games against the Cubs in the 1910 World Series. Going into the ninth inning, the Giants held a 1–0 lead.

Mathewson got the dangerous Collins for the first out of the inning and then worked very carefully to Baker, determined not to make the same kind of mistake Marquard had made. But, if it wasn't the same kind of mistake, it was nonetheless the same result. On a 2–1 count, Baker swung at a low curve and lofted it over the right field fence to tie the score. Giant fans were stunned, not just that Baker had hit home runs in successive games but that the second had come off the great Mathewson. "It was so quiet," wrote Lieb, "that those with especially good hearing could pick up the patter of Baker's feet as he romped joyfully around the bases."

The A's broke the tie in the 11th, and Baker was again a part of the rally, though his effort was not so spectacular this time. With one out, Collins singled and then Baker beat out a slow roller to third base. When Herzog threw wildly trying to get Baker, Collins advanced to third and Baker to second.

Collins scored when Larry Doyle muffed Danny Murphy's grounder, and Baker added the third run on a single by Davis.

The Giants nearly tied the score in the bottom of the inning. Herzog doubled and Meyers drove a ball deep into the left field bleachers that was just foul. But then Meyers grounded out and, though Herzog scored on an error by Collins, that was all for the Giants.

Coombs, the winner, had given up only three hits in 11 innings. Mathewson had given up nine but hadn't walked a man. In fact, he had had only 28 pitches called balls in 11 innings!

But he had given up that home run to Baker, and that was as embarrassing as it was critical. In the paper the next day, under Marquard's byline, Mathewson was thoroughly roasted.

Years later, Menke told Lieb the roasting was primarily his idea. "Marquard was interested mostly in the money," said Menke. "He was pretty mad at Mathewson's blast at him. So, I told Rube, 'Now is our chance to get even.' He agreed."

Ironically, the two pitchers roomed together while Marquard was with the Giants. Although they may have been mad at each other for a time during this Series—professional jealousy is possible with the best of friends—Marquard admired Mathewson as much as anybody else did. "What a grand guy he was!" he told Lawrence Ritter a half century later.

There was another incident during this game, and again it involved Baker. In the eighth inning, Snodgrass tried to go to third on a short passed ball and spiked Baker in the thigh, ripping a foot-long hole in Baker's uniform pants.

The play was compared to a similar one involving Ty Cobb during the 1909 American League season, and some of the A's players thought Snodgrass was trying to put Baker out of the Series. Even the usually calm Mack called it a needlessly high slide. McGraw, a former third baseman, said Baker had an awkward way of defending the bag.

Tempers, and everything else, had a chance to cool as it rained for five successive days. The sixth day, the rains stopped, but the field was still soaked, so Philadelphia owner Ben Shibe had his groundskeeper burn gasoline to dry out the soggy turf.

Because of the long layoff, Mathewson was able to come back in the fourth game when the Series finally resumed, but he'd had too much rest. Like most pitchers who rely on their control, he needed to work frequently (every fourth day, in his case) to keep sharp. The A's battered him for ten hits and four runs in seven innings. Seven of the hits were doubles, including two each by Baker, Barry, and Murphy.

Meanwhile, after giving up two runs to the Giants in the first inning, Bender settled down to pitch shutout ball the rest of the way in the 4–2 Philadelphia win, and he impressed Devore, the Giants' leadoff hitter. "The Chief makes the baseball look like a pea," said Devore. "Who can hit a pea when it goes by with the speed of lightning?"

That win gave the A's a 3–1 Series lead, and it seemed Philadelphia would end the Series in the fifth game, at the Polo Grounds when they carried a 3–1 lead into the ninth inning, all their runs coming on a third-inning homer by Rube Oldring.

Coombs was pitching as well as he had in the third game of the Series, though he had torn a ligament in his groin in the sixth inning when his spikes had gotten caught in the pitching rubber as he was pitching to Fletcher.

It was obvious that Coombs was in pain, but he stayed in the game and seemed to have the situation under control. In the ninth, he got Herzog to ground out to open the inning. Fletcher blooped a double to left, but when Meyers grounded out, Coombs and the A's were only one out away from a Series triumph.

McGraw sent up Otey "Doc" Crandall as a pinch hitter. Crandall was a pitcher, believed to be the first relief specialist (26 of his 41 pitching appearances during the 1911 season had been in relief), but he could also hit as he proved by doubling to left and scoring Fletcher.

Mack considered relieving Coombs at that point, but the pitcher begged to be allowed to continue. He was certain he could get Devore, who had had just three hits in the Series. He was wrong. Devore singled to score Crandall with the tying run.

The hit triggered a roar from the Giants' fans that Lieb compared to the outburst that followed Bobby Thomson's home run in the 1951 National League playoffs against the Dodgers.

The inning ended with Devore being thrown out trying to steal, but the Giants came right back in the bottom of the tenth, after the A's had been held scoreless in the top of the inning. By this time, Plank was pitching. Doyle opened with a double and went to third on a sacrifice by Snodgrass. Merkle flied to right field and Murphy made a good throw to the plate, but Doyle beat it. Players from both teams, including A's catcher Jack Lapp, left the field. Only plate umpire Bill Klem remained in place. He had seen that Doyle hadn't touched home plate.

"I stood there, awaiting an Athletics protest, but none came," Klem told reporters that night. "If Lapp or any other Philadelphia player had tagged Doyle with the ball before Larry left the park, I would have called Doyle out and ordered the 11th inning to begin."

Mack told Lieb years later that he, too, knew that Doyle had not touched home plate, and he was upset because his players, especially Lapp, rushed off the field to get away from the fans.

But Mack did not make a protest because he remembered that the Giants had lost a pennant in 1908 as a result of a disputed play, the famed "Fred Merkle boner." Merkle had failed to run from first to second on the winning hit and was declared out on a force play long after the winning run had crossed the plate. The game was replayed and the Giants lost it, and the pennant, to the Chicago Cubs.

"While I knew no legal run had scored," said Mack, "Lapp was running away. I had to consider the moment. I knew that within three minutes, there would be 20,000 shouting fans on the field. The Giants had snatched a victory from us. Had someone then tried to tell the Giants that they had not won that fifth game, I believe they would have torn down the place. That's why I didn't send someone after Lapp or lodge an immediate protest. Also, I was confident we would get them the next day."

Mack was right. The A's ended the Series conclusively the next day, hammering the Giants, 13–2.

The Giants were back in the Series the next year, 1912, but the Athletics weren't, the only time in a five-year stretch when they were beaten out for the American League pennant. In fact, the A's finished third that year, just behind Washington and 15 games in back of Boston, by now playing in Fenway Park and under the nickname of Red Sox.

The Red Sox were very good, especially in the outfield; Duffy Lewis, Tris Speaker, and Harry Hooper are generally regarded as the best-fielding outfield of all time. Speaker and Hooper are in the Hall of Fame, and old-time Red Sox fans used to say that, if the Hall could take in Joe Tinker, Johnny Evers, and Frank Chance as a unit, Lewis should have gone in with Speaker and Hooper, too.

It was, in fact, Lewis who had the most difficult job, covering left field in Fenway. At that time, the ground sloped upward from about 25 feet in front of the fence, rising perhaps about eight feet by the time the fence was reached. Outfielders had to simultaneously make sure they didn't stumble going up the incline and judge the ball perfectly; it was disastrous if they reached the top of the incline and found the ball was falling short.

Lewis managed this feat so well that the area became known as "Duffy's Cliff."

No less an authority than Babe Ruth called Hooper the best outfielder he had ever seen. "He would take one squint, then turn his back and run to the place where the ball was headed," said the Babe. "And in all his career, I don't believe he misjudged a dozen fly balls."

The star of the team, however, was Speaker, who is still often named to the all-time All-Star teams as the center fielder, though Joe DiMaggio and Willie Mays have their supporters from other eras.

Speaker played in so far that he was almost a fifth infielder, and it was virtually impossible to drop a ball in front of him. Yet he could go back on a fly ball with such swiftness that it was rare to see a ball hit over his head.

The "Gray Eagle," as he became known, was also a feared hitter, with a lifetime average of .344 and a major league career record 793 doubles. He had probably his best all-round year in 1912 when he hit .383 with a league-leading 53 doubles, while scoring 136 runs, driving in 98 runs, and stealing 52 bases. He won the Chalmers Award as the league's Most Valuable Player.

Speaker had to be awfully good to beat out teammate Joe Wood, an awesome pitcher that year who led the league in wins (34), winning percentage (.872), complete games (35), and shutouts (10). Wood, who compiled a 1.91 earned run average, also tied the American League record by reeling off 16 straight wins on the way to a 34–5 year.

Wood hurt his arm the next year and was never the same pitcher again. Eventually, he switched to the outfield to extend his career. But for a brief period, he was probably as dominant a pitcher as any of the great ones.

He became known as "Smokey Joe" early in his career when a teammate, watching him warm up, commented, "He sure can smoke 'em."

Indeed he could. Lieb, who saw all the power pitchers from Walter Johnson to Nolan Ryan, thought Wood was as fast as any of them. Johnson concurred. Asked one time if he could throw harder than Wood, Johnson said, "Listen, my friend, there's no man alive can throw harder than Smokey Joe Wood."

Wood, of course, started the 1912 Series for the Red Sox. The Giants were expected to counter with Mathewson. Instead, McGraw pitched rookie spitballer Jeff Tesreau, who had won 16 games in the regular season.

Why? McGraw hinted that he wanted Mathewson to pitch the second game, which would be played in Boston; there wouldn't be as much pressure for Tesreau pitching before the home crowd in New York.

But McGraw also had another ace he didn't use in that opener, Marquard, who had won a record 19 straight games to open the National League season that year. (Actually, he would have had 20 straight under modern scoring rules, because he came on in relief in a game the Giants rallied to win.) McGraw could still have pitched Marquard in the opener and had Mathewson available for the second year.

A more likely explanation is that McGraw didn't want to waste either Mathewson or Marquard against Wood, who was so overpowering. If they didn't have to pitch against Wood, it was possible Mathewson and Marquard could each win two games in the Series.

Wood wasn't overpowering in that game, yielding eight hits and three runs, but he struck out 11 Giants and rose to the occasion when he had to.

In the ninth, the Giants had drawn to within 4–3 and had runners on second and third with one out, with Fletcher up. "Well, I threw so hard I thought my arm would fly right off my body," Wood said later. "I struck Fletcher out."

That brought up Crandall, who had come in to relieve Tesreau. Wood feared that McGraw would use Beals Becker, who had hit Wood well in the Western Association, as a pinch hitter, but the Giants' manager wasn't aware of Becker's success against Wood.

Wood ran the count on Crandall to three-and-two. "Fastballs, that's what I was throwing," he said. "Just burning them in and hoping for the best. . . . I threw one right by him for strike three. That was the biggest thrill I ever had in baseball, those two strikeouts."

Significantly, the Giants were betrayed by their defense in this game, a pattern that would last throughout the Series and ultimately destroy them. Outfielders Devore and Snodgrass allowed a fly ball to drop between them, and second baseman Doyle muffed a double-play ball.

As they had in the first World Series in 1903, the Royal Rooters were again leading the cheers for Boston. The group, led by Boston mayor John "Honey Fitz" Fitzgerald, grandfather of John F. Kennedy, had traveled to New York, and Honey Fitz presided over ceremonies at the second game in Boston, presenting a new car to manager Jake Stahl.

Perhaps unnerved by all the ceremony and the boisterous Boston crowd, the Giants committed five errors behind Mathewson. The usually sure-fielding Lewis dropped a fly ball in the ninth for the Red Sox, who would otherwise have won the game in regulation time.

The game went another two innings, at which point umpire Silk O'Loughlin called it because of darkness, a 6–6 tie. That would ultimately cause the Series to last through eight games, which became a factor in a classic ticket snafu involving the Royal Rooters.

Joe Wood starred in the 1912 World Series for the Boston Red Sox before his arm went bad. (George Brace)

The third game of the Series was also played in Boston, because there had been no result with the second game; otherwise, games were alternated between the cities.

This game featured one of the most controversial plays of this or any Series, as Marquard won a pitching duel with Bucky O'Brien.

With one out in the bottom of the ninth and the Giants leading, 2–0, Lewis beat out an infield hit and scored when Larry Gardner doubled to right. Stahl's grounder was knocked down by Marquard, who threw to third to get Gardner.

Heinie Wagner beat out an infield hit, with Stahl going to third, and then stole second on the first pitch to Forrest Cady. The winning runs were now in scoring position.

World Series games then started at 3:00 P.M. and parks, of course, had no lights, this being long before the era of night baseball. The Fenway Park field was enshrouded in mist, and it was becoming more and more difficult to see.

Cady drove a long fly to right center. Stahl and Wagner, with two outs, were both running on the hit and had crossed home plate by the time Devore dove for the ball. The Giants' center fielder picked himself up and ran through the center field gate into the clubhouse.

Confusion reigned. Had Devore caught the ball or not? If he had, the Giants had won. If he had not, the Red Sox were the winners. Nobody could tell from Devore's actions since the Giants' outfielder would have run off the field whether he had caught the ball or not, because the play ended the game.

Finally, writers got a call from the umpiring crew: Devore had caught the ball and the Giants had won the game, 2–1. But many Red Sox fans left the park thinking their team had won. Three of them even showed up the next day claiming Devore could not have caught the ball because they had it, each fan showing a different baseball, of course. But the decision stood; the Giants had won the game.

The Red Sox bounced back to win the next game, 3–1, with Wood again beating Tesreau, who was beginning to understand what the term "sacrificial lamb" meant. Gardner tripled, singled, and walked for the Red Sox and figured in the scoring of all three runs.

The next game matched Mathewson against Boston rookie Hugh Bedient, a right-hander from Falconer, New York, who as a boy had been a hero-worshiper of Mathewson.

Bedient, who had had a 20–9 record during the regular season, didn't let Mathewson's presence awe him, though, giving up only three hits to the Giants.

Mathewson yielded only five himself, but all of them came in the first three innings. Hooper and Steve Yerkes hit back-to-back triples in the third to score the first Boston run, and then Doyle fumbled Speaker's grounder to allow Yerkes to score the run that was the decider in the 2–1 Boston win.

Everybody assumed Wood would start the next game, because if he won, as expected, the Red Sox would cop the Series. But Red Sox owner Jim McAleer had different ideas. On the Sunday train to New York (the teams had the day off because Sunday baseball was not allowed in New York at the time), McAleer told Stahl he wanted O'Brien to pitch.

"Joe is all geared up for the game," said Stahl. "I can't change now."

"You can and you will," said McAleer. "I'm still the president of this club. Give Wood another day of rest."

What was McAleer's reasoning? A former player, he may simply have been following Owner Rule No. 1: that he always knows better than the manager. He may also have wanted O'Brien to have another shot. O'Brien, a late bloomer who was already 30 but only in his second major league season, had won 19 games for the Red Sox and was immensely popular with the Irish fans in Boston, particularly since he had been born and raised in nearby Brockton.

Most likely, though, McAleer reasoned that, even if the Red Sox lost, they could still wrap up the Series with a win in Boston in the next game and he'd have another payday.

Whatever the reasoning, the game was a disaster for the Red Sox. O'Brien gave up five runs in the first inning before he was relieved, and the Giants went on to win behind Marquard, 5–2.

The train ride back to Boston was more exciting than the game. Tiring of the barbed comments tossed his way by teammates, O'Brien yelled, "For Christ's sake, I did the best I could."

Wood's brother, Paul, who had lost $100 betting on the game, yelled back, "Go to hell!" and the two men started fighting in the train aisle. O'Brien wound up with a black eye.

That was nothing, though, compared to what happened before the next game when the Royal Rooters discovered they had no seats. The group had had tickets for the three games scheduled at Fenway Park (the site of the seventh game, if necessary, was to be decided by another coin flip). But, because the second game was a tie, there had been an extra game played in Boston. This would be the fourth game. The Royal Rooters, thinking their seat locations were automatically fixed, had not made ticket reservations for the game, and a clerk in the ticket office had sold the seats on a first come, first served basis.

The Rooters refused to leave the park until they got seats, sitting in the aisles during pregame warmups. Just as the game was scheduled to start, they marched on the field, about 500 of them, with their band playing their fight song. Honey Fitz was at their head.

Mounted police were called to herd the group off the field. They left, trampling the outfield fence and cursing the Red Sox management and John McGraw. One of them yelled, "To hell with Queen Victoria," though what the queen, dead many years, had to do with American baseball was not clear.

Wood had waited around for the demonstration to end, and his arm seemed to stiffen during that period. The Giants treated him like a batting practice pitcher, scoring six runs in the first inning and going on to win, 11–4.

The momentum seemed to have turned. The Giants had won two straight to tie the Series and had Mathewson ready to go in the deciding game, again facing Bedient. The only edge the Red Sox had was that the game would be played at Fenway; in the coin flip, American League president Ban Johnson had correctly called tails.

The Giants scored a run in the third on Devore's walk, two infield outs, and a double by Murray. They lost what seemed another run in the sixth when Hooper leaped above the right field fence to grab a drive by Doyle, falling into the crowd after he did. The umpires ruled it a catch, though Doyle disputed it. "I still think Hooper was off the playing field when he caught it," said Doyle later.

The Red Sox tied it in the seventh with a pop fly double by Stahl that fell between three Giant fielders and a pinch-hit double by Olaf Henriksen, in his only at-bat in the Series.

Wood came in to pitch in the eighth, so the premier pitchers of the Series, Mathewson and Wood, were matched for the first time, in the deciding game. That's what the World Series is all about.

Wood shut out the Giants in the eighth and ninth, but the Giants got a run off him in the tenth, with doubles by Murray and Merkle. Wood ended the inning by knocking down a line drive by Meyers with his pitching hand and throwing him out, but his hand started swelling up, so he wouldn't be able to pitch any more on this day.

That didn't worry the Red Sox. "We were more angry than nervous," remembered Gardner. "We knew what we had to do and set out to do it." But they needed help from the Giants—which they got.

Wood should have been the lead-off hitter but, because of his swollen hand, he was replaced by pinch hitter Clyde Engle, who lofted a soft fly to Snodgrass in center. Incredibly, Snodgrass dropped the ball and Engle reached second.

Hooper then drove a ball to deep left center. This time, Snodgrass made what he considered one of the finest catches of his career. Engle, so sure the ball was a hit, had passed third base and was nearly doubled off.

Mathewson walked the next batter, Yerkes, and then got Speaker to hit a pop foul down the first base line. The ball should have been caught by the first baseman, Merkle, because it was almost in the coaching box. Matty could have caught it himself. But neither Merkle nor Mathewson went for the ball, so the catcher, Meyer, had to make a desperate lunge for it. He missed, and Speaker had another chance.

The play will be forever shrouded in mystery. Wood thought Mathewson had called for Meyer to go for it. Others thought Speaker or somebody from the Boston bench had "coached" Merkle off the play.

Speaker took advantage of his second chance and singled to right, scoring Engle with the tying run and sending Yerkes to third. Lewis was walked to set up a force at the plate, but then Gardner flied to deep right and Yerkes came home easily with the winning run.

McGraw, asked what he did to Snodgrass for dropping the fly ball, said later, "I raised his salary $1,000!" History hasn't been so kind. His muff is remembered, his great play on the next drive forgotten. He was only 25 and should have been at his peak, but the incident haunted him and no doubt contributed to his leaving the game only four years later, his early promise never fully realized.

The next year the Giants again won the National League pennant, and the Athletics took it in the American League. The 1913 Series did not match the extraordinary excitement of those of the previous two years, but it was noteworthy for some personal factors.

Although nobody realized it at the time, the Series was the last for Mathewson. Christy pitched a ten-inning shutout in the second game of the Series, won by the Giants, 3–0. In the fifth game, the Athletics and Plank triumphed, 3–1, to wrap up the Series; only two of the Philadelphia runs against Matty were earned.

Disappointing as it was, that final game was indicative of the bad luck in which Mathewson had pitched since his spectacular Series in 1905. Although he had a cumulative earned run average of 1.15 in World Series play, he was only 5–5 overall. He had made 11 starts and completed ten of them. Three of his defeats had been by a single run.

When the final game was over, he walked slowly to the Polo Grounds clubhouse in center field. Another Giants pitcher, Art Fromme, tried to put a mackinaw jacket over his shoulders, but he let it drop to the ground as he disappeared from sight.

The Giants' reign in the National League was also coming to an end; McGraw would not win another pennant for four years, an eternity for a man who hated to lose the way he did. He had won three straight pennants but lost each year to the American League winner; however, he was gracious in defeat this third time. He told Mack, "You've got the greatest infield I've ever seen. You deserved to beat us."

In the clubhouse, though, he quarreled with Wilbert Robinson, his first base coach, accusing Robinson of missing a sign. The two had been close friends for years, starting with the old Baltimore Orioles in the 1890s, but this one incident ended their friendship. Robinson became manager of the Brooklyn Dodgers, and they became bitter managerial rivals for the length of Robinson's 18-year career.

Only a game? Not to John McGraw.

5. Those Miracle Braves

On its face, the 1914 World Series appeared to be the worst mismatch since the Series had begun in 1903. Some dared to predict that it would be the first Series to end in a four-game sweep. And so it was—but not in the way that had been anticipated.

For the fourth time in five years, the Philadelphia Athletics were the American League champions. The A's seemed as strong as ever in winning the pennant by 8½ games over a good Boston Red Sox team.

Jack Coombs, who had been the staff leader when the A's started their string of pennants, had fallen victim to arm problems and was not a factor, but he was hardly missed. This A's team had remarkable pitching balance, with seven pitchers winning at least ten games.

The staff leader was Chief Bender, who won 17 and lost but three games; Bullet Joe Bush also won 17 games for the A's. Bob Shawkey added 16 and Eddie Plank 15.

The A's hitting was equally potent; the team led the league in runs, with 749. Everywhere you looked, the A's had all-stars, most notably in the "$100,000 Infield," anchored by future Hall-of-Famers Eddie Collins and Frank (Home Run) Baker.

In contrast, the Boston Braves were clearly the weakest National League champion since the Series had begun. For years, the league had been dominated by the New York Giants and Chicago Cubs, two dynasty teams. From 1904 through 1913, the Cubs and the Giants had won every pennant but one. When the Braves surprised everybody, probably including themselves, by breaking through the Giants–Cubs monopoly to win in 1914, the main question was: Who are these guys?

In the early years of the National League, the Braves had been a strong franchise, winning five pennants in the 1890s, for instance. But the competition from the American League had proven deadly in the early part of the twentieth century, top stars being lured from the Braves and fans being wooed away by the rival Red

Sox/Pilgrims, a pattern which was to eventually cause the Braves to move from Boston (for Milwaukee after the 1952 season and for Atlanta after the 1965 season).

The team nickname had been changed three times, from the Beaneaters of the 1890s to the Doves, then Rustlers, and finally Braves, the nickname that has remained to this day. The team played at a rundown park, at the South End Grounds.

In 1913, the pattern of decay began to change, when George Stallings was brought in to manage the club. Stallings was a contradictory man. He was well-educated, a graduate of Virginia Military Institute, and a medical student at the College of Physicians and Surgeons in Baltimore. Off the field, he was a courtly gentleman.

On the field, though, he was a profane, superstitious man, given to explosions of temper, most of which were directed at pitchers. He once said that his epitaph should be: "Oh, those bases on balls!" At the start of the 1914 season, he declared, "I've got 16 pitchers and they're all rotten."

But Stallings had the one gift common to all good managers: He could make players believe in themselves and play to the best of their abilities. His personality was the key for a club that became known as the "Miracle Braves."

Equally important, Stallings acquired the on-field leader he needed through a strange series of events that started in Chicago, where owner Charles Webb Murphy was presiding none too quietly over the demise of the Cubs' dynasty.

In 1912, Murphy had fired Frank Chance as manager of the Cubs and replaced him with Johnny Evers. When Evers had finished third in his one year as manager, Murphy had fired him. Evers then threatened to jump to the outlaw Federal League, which was being formed for the 1914 season.

National League president John K. Tener, who had just taken office, put pressure on Murphy to sell his stock in the Cubs to Charles P. Taft, Murphy's original backer. A deal was then arranged with the Braves that sent Evers to Boston in exchange for infielder Bill Sweeney and cash; Evers got a $25,000 bonus to keep him from jumping to the Federal League.

Evers teamed with Rabbit Maranville to form a double-play combination that was probably better than the celebrated one in which he had paired with Joe Tinker at Chicago, but that didn't seem to help the Braves in the early part of the 1914 season. As late as July 19, they were last, with a 35–43 record.

But the National League race was an unusually close one that year. Only 11 games separated the Braves from the first place Giants, and as early as July 21, the Braves had leapfrogged to fourth place.

Once they got the hang of it, the Braves just kept winning and winning and winning, 34 of 44 in one stretch. They reached the .500 mark on August 1 but were still fourth, behind the Giants, Cubs, and Cardinals. By August 10, they had climbed past the Cubs and Cardinals, but the Giants were still ahead, by 6½ games.

Still, the Braves kept winning. They tied for the lead for the first time on August 23 and got undisputed possession of first on September 2. They slumped mildly and fell back briefly to third, but by September 8 they were in first place to stay.

The Braves' drive for the pennant is generally regarded as one of the three great stretch drives in National League history, ranking with those of the 1942 St. Louis Cardinals and 1951 New York Giants.

In two respects, though, it's the greatest: (1) it is the only time in baseball history a team has come from last place on the Fourth of July to win; and (2) the Braves not only won, they won in a runaway, 10½ games over the second-place Giants. From July 19 to the end of the season, they had gained 21½ games on the Giants!

As impressive as that was, it didn't sway the experts, who felt the Braves had no chance in the World Series. The A's were made 3–1 favorites, and Giants' coach Hughey Jennings told writer Fred Lieb, "They ought to be 10–1."

Veteran baseball writer Francis Richter had this pre-Series analysis of the Boston team: "It is in all respects a surprise, a wonder, and a problem. It furnished the sensation of the season by winning a major league championship, under exceptional conditions, contrary to every law of averages and form, and thereon rests their sole hope of World's Series capture. It is composed entirely of players with either too little or too much major league experience. The records show the team to be mediocre in batting, inferior in base running, and superior only in infielders and batteries."

Stallings did have superior pitching with Dick Rudolph (27–10 and a 2.35 ERA), Bill James (26–7 and 1.90 ERA), and Lefty Tyler (16–14 and a 2.69 ERA).

The infield was solid, anchored by Evers and Maranville. But the outfield was weak. Stallings used as many as 11 different outfielders, platooning at a time when that was virtually unheard of. No one outfielder got as many as 400 at-bats in the season. The Braves' only .300 hitter was Joe Connolly at .306—but with only 399 at-bats.

Those who had watched the Braves during the regular season were contemptuous of their chances. Hank O'Day, the former umpire who had been named manager of the Cubs, said he expected the A's to sweep the Series.

But there were forces operating that made the A's ripe for an upset. One was the Braves' obvious momentum. They were playing at their peak and had the confidence that a hot streak instills in players.

Another factor was overconfidence by the A's, who believed what the experts were saying about the relative merits of the two teams. Before the end of the season, Connie Mack had given his ace, Bender, some time off to scout the Braves. Instead, Bender took a vacation. When Mack learned his pitcher was not scouting, Bender told him, "What's the use of wasting time looking over that bunch of banjo hitters?"

The most important factor, though, was the presence of the Federal League. As an entity, the league had a very short life, lasting only the 1914 and 1915 seasons before disbanding. But it had a great influence on the A's.

The new league was trying to entice veteran stars with big contract offers. The A's were vulnerable to this kind of pitch because Mack had never had much operating capital. His stars were playing for shockingly low salaries. Bender's salary was $5,000, Plank's only $4,000. Both had already signed contracts to play the following year in the Federal League, and the A's team morale was very low.

On the eve of the Series, Stallings scoffed at the odds against his team and predicted that the Braves would win four straight, a feat that had not yet been accomplished in the Series. Perhaps he knew something.

The Braves took command of the first game, and the Series, in the second inning, scoring twice off Bender, the A's famed "money pitcher."

The amusingly nicknamed "Possum" Whitted led off with a walk and, after Butch Schmidt had flied out, Hank Gowdy doubled to left to score Whitted with the game's first run.

It was the first of six hits in the Series for Gowdy, the biggest Series surprise since George Rohe in 1906. A .243 hitter during the regular season, Gowdy hit .545 in the Series, a mark surpassed only by Babe Ruth (.625 in 1928) in the history of the Series. Five of Gowdy's hits were for extra bases—three doubles, a triple, and a home run—as he scored three runs and knocked in another three. Bender should have scouted him, at least.

The Braves sewed it up with a three-run sixth in which they knocked out Bender, the only time the Chief was ever knocked out in a Series game.

With one out, Evers singled and Connolly walked. Whitted tripled to right center and Schmidt singled in Whitted. Weldon Wyckoff relieved Bender, but the damage was done and the Braves went on to a 7–1 win.

Rudolph had pitched a five-hitter in winning the first game for the Braves. James was even better in the second game, yielding only two hits, a double by Wally Schang and an infield hit by Collins. Until Schang's double with one out in the sixth, James had a no-hitter.

Plank was almost as effective for the A's. Although he yielded seven hits, he was locked in a scoreless duel with James until the ninth.

Then, with one out in the top of the ninth, the Braves got the only break they needed in the Series: Amos Strunk lost Charlie Deal's fly in the sun, and it fell in for a double. Deal then stole third and, though James struck out for the fourth time in the game, Les Mann followed with a single to score Deal. The A's threatened in the top of the ninth when Jack Barry and pinch hitter Jimmy Walsh walked, to put the tying and winning runs on base with one out. But then James got Danny Murphy to hit into a double play, and the Braves had won, 1–0.

The Series then switched from Philadelphia to Boston (where the Braves were using Fenway Park instead of their dilapidated park), but the result remained the same, the Braves winning again, 5–4.

This was the only game in the Series in which the A's ever led. Their single run in the top of the first gave them a lead which lasted until the Braves tied the score in the bottom of the second. In the fourth, the A's went ahead again with a run, but the Braves tied the score in the bottom of the inning.

The most crushing blow for the A's, though, came in the tenth inning, when it seemed they might finally break through for their first win of the Series.

Schang opened the inning with a single. Pitcher Joe Bush struck out trying to sacrifice. Murphy hit back to Braves' starter Tyler, whose throw to second was too late to get Schang. Rube Oldring grounded out, the runners advancing, and Collins walked to load the bases.

Baker then lined a single off the shins of Evers at second base and Schang and Murphy, both running with the pitch, scored. It was cause for jubilation for the A's who, in one inning, had scored twice as many runs as they had managed in the first two games combined.

Their jubilation was short-lived, however. Gowdy led off the bottom of the tenth with a long fly that went over Walsh's head in center, bouncing into the stands. Under today's rules, that would have been a ground-rule double; then, it was counted as a home run.

That difference matters only in the statistics, not the scoring, because Gowdy would eventually have scored, anyway. Josh Devore struck out following Gowdy, but then Herbie Moran walked, Evers singled him to third, and Connolly's fly ball scored him to tie the game.

In the 12th, Gowdy started another Boston rally with a double, and Mann ran for him. Pinch hitter Larry Gilbert (hitting for James, who had relieved Tyler in the 11th), was intentionally walked.

Moran bunted to A's pitcher Joe Bush, who threw wildly to third trying to get Mann, who came in to score the winning run.

The Series could have been called at that point; the demoralized A's went down quietly, 3–1, in the fourth game the next day with Rudolph getting his second win of the Series. Rudolph gave up seven hits but walked only one batter, which no doubt made Stallings happy.

Among other things, the Series showed how star pitchers can be more important even than in the regular season. Stallings used only his top three pitchers, Rudolph, James, and Tyler. The A's may have had better balance for a season, but it didn't matter in this short Series, where Rudolph and James were simply overpowering: James shut out the A's in 11 innings, the last two in relief, and Rudolph yielded only one earned run in 18 innings.

It also showed how season batting averages aren't necessarily an indication of Series' success. The hard-hitting A's hit only .172 as a team in the Series, and Baker's .250 topped the regulars (Strunk hit .286 but on only seven at-bats in two games).

Meanwhile, Gowdy hit .545, Evers .438, and Maranville .308 for the supposedly punchless Braves; none of the three approached those averages in the regular season.

Neither team fared well in the aftermath of this Series. Losing Bender and Plank to the Federal League, Mack also sold Collins for $50,000 to the White Sox, in a deal engineered by American League president Ban Johnson, and also sold Coombs, Pennock, Barry, and Shawkey to other teams. The A's sank to last place in the 1915 season.

After that season, Mack also sold Strang, Bush, Strunk, and first baseman Stuffy McInnis, and the A's did not climb out of the American League cellar until 1922.

The Braves' story lacked a happy ending, too, as they slowly sank to second, third, and then sixth in successive seasons. Their inability to follow up on their dramatic success in 1914 cost them their chance to become the dominant team in Boston; the Red Sox, with a young pitcher named Babe Ruth, won successive pennants in 1915 and 1916 and eclipsed the Braves in the affection of the fans.

But nothing that happened in subsequent years can take away the brilliance of the Braves' accomplishments in 1914. They were indeed the Miracle Braves.

6. The Sox Were Black

It was the 1919 World Series and strange things were happening to the Chicago White Sox, who were considered possibly the best team of the twentieth century at that time.

Eddie Cicotte, a 29-game winner in the regular season, was hammered for five runs in one inning by the Cincinnati Reds on six hits, one of them a triple by opposing pitcher Dutch Reuther. In his second start, Cicotte, known as a fine-fielding pitcher, deflected a throw from the outfield that allowed a key run to score.

Fine-fielding White Sox center fielder Oscar "Happy" Felsch dropped a fly ball. Claude "Lefty" Williams, known as a control pitcher, walked three batters in one inning as the White Sox lost another game.

What was going on? Many of the star White Sox players were throwing the World Series.

The 1919 World Series, which came to be known as the Black Sox Series, is the only World Series that was fixed. To modern fans, the thought is simply incomprehensible. But the thought was not incomprehensible to the White Sox players who participated in the fix. What they were doing was different only in scope from what others were doing at the time, when the atmosphere surrounding the game was much different than it is now.

Fixed games were no rarity in baseball in the early part of the century. There had even been rumors earlier of a fixed World Series: The "smart guys" said the 1912 Series would be fixed so the Giants could win, a theory that went up like smoke when the Red Sox won the Series.

Indirectly, the Reds were in the 1919 World Series because of fixed games. The Giants had a first baseman, Hal Chase, who was a great player but who had long had the reputation of throwing games. Even one of his own managers, Frank Chance, had made the accusation to newspapermen when Chase was with the Cubs.

In 1918, Chase had been with Cincinnati. Former Giants pitching great Christy Mathewson was managing the Reds, and he, too, suspected Chase of throwing games. Just before Mathewson went into the army and was sent overseas, he made charges to the Cincinnati newspapers and National League president John Heydler.

Heydler tried to make a full scale investigation, and he told writers off the record that he felt Chase was guilty. But he could not communicate with Mathewson, and he lacked the proof for a case against Chase. He declared the first baseman not guilty of the charges, and Chase was picked up by John McGraw and the Giants.

In 1919, the Giants and Reds were in a tight battle for the pennant in mid-August when McGraw announced that Chase and third baseman Heinie Zimmerman were "suspended indefinitely"—which turned out to mean that their baseball careers were ended. Without Chase and Zimmerman, the Giants could not stay with the Reds, who went on to win the pennant by nine games.

Lieb later said that Heydler had told him he got a signed affidavit from a Boston gambler in 1919 and a photographic copy of Chase's canceled check for $500 given him for throwing a game in 1918. Armed with that evidence, he went to Giants owner Charles Stoneham and told him that Chase could not play in any more games. Stoneham, according to Heydler via Lieb, said, "If that's the way it is, that's it. John, you had no other choice."

(Zimmerman's dismissal was less straightforward. No charges were ever filed against him, and McGraw said he had been released because "I was disgusted with his play." Perhaps. Zimmerman, a lifetime .295 hitter, was hitting only .255. He never contested McGraw's move.)

There were other cases and rumors. Lee Magee, a Cincinnati second baseman, had apparently worked with Chase; eventually, he was declared out of baseball by Judge Kenesaw Landis, when Landis was named commissioner in 1920. Rumors surrounded Chicago Cubs pitcher Claude Hendrix and infielder Gene Paulette of the Philadelphia Phillies, and St. Louis Browns second baseman Joe Gedeon; all would eventually be thrown out of baseball by Judge Landis. McGraw told Lieb that Buck Herzog had consistently played out of position in the 1917 World Series, but he could not prove that Herzog was trying to throw games and so filed no charges, though he traded Herzog to the Boston Braves.

In such an environment, it was probably inevitable that an attempt would be made to fix a World Series. After all, the amount of money to be made betting on a regular season game was relatively small compared to what could be made on a Series.

This particular Series was also a natural, for a couple of reasons. One reason was that the White Sox seemed to be much the stronger team, and so the odds would be good for a killing.

The other, more important, reason was that the White Sox needed the money. Except for Eddie Collins, the great second baseman who had come over from

Philadelphia, the players were woefully underpaid; Collins had been able to work out a good contract because he negotiated at a time when the Federal League was competing for his services.

Cicotte, for instance, was getting only $5,500 a year. Shoeless Joe Jackson, second only to Ty Cobb as a hitter, and the great Chicago third baseman Buck Weaver were getting $6,000. But first baseman Chick Gandil and center fielder Felsch got just $4,000 and pitcher Williams was under $3,000!

As a comparison, Roush got $10,000 that season for Cincinnati, Jack Daubert $9,000, and Heinie Groh $8,000.

White Sox owner Charles Comiskey also cut corners elsewhere. Players got only $3 a day meal money, for instance, compared to $4 on other teams. He reportedly promised Cicotte a $10,000 bonus if the pitcher won 30 games, but Cicotte wasn't allowed to pitch again after he won 29 games, supposedly because he needed to rest for the Series.

Ironically, Comiskey had once resigned as manager of the St. Louis club of the National League to join the newly formed Players League (and at a cut in salary) because he didn't think St. Louis was paying his players decent salaries. "I couldn't do anything else and still play square with the boys!" he was reported to have said at the time.

He was willing to spend money in other ways. He had spent $65,000 to get Jackson from Cleveland, $50,000 to buy Collins from the A's, $12,000 to get Felsch from Milwaukee, a minor league club; those were impressive sums in those days. He had spent $500,000 after the 1909 season to expand his park to a capacity of 33,000, and he had reportedly been rewarded for his foresight; he was thought to be a millionaire.

But he drew the line when it came to paying his players, and that penuriousness was to cost both him and his players greatly.

In hindsight, what is most striking about the whole affair was the naivete of the players. They seemed to give no thought to what would happen if they were caught; they were blatant in their moves during the games and made no special effort to keep their meetings with gamblers secret. Weaver, who apparently had no intention of ever taking part in the fix and never got any money, nevertheless sat in on two meetings and never told anybody about them. Finally, it was one of the players who made the approach to the gamblers, not vice versa as is usually assumed.

One can only assume that the players thought they were not doing anything wrong. They probably had a better idea of how many fixed games there actually were than an outsider could, and they knew that, until the Chase case came up, no player had been punished.

According to Eliot Asinof, whose *Eight Men Out* is a very comprehensive view of the Black Sox Series, it was Gandil who approached gambler Joseph (Sport) Sullivan and told him, "I think we can put it in the bag!"

Chick Gandil first approached gamblers about fixing the World Series. *(George Brace)*

Buck Weaver had a great Series in 1919 and was not part of the fix, but because he attended one meeting of the conspirators, he was banned from baseball. *(George Brace)*

Gandil then sought out the players he thought would listen to him. Some he didn't even talk to—Collins, catcher Ray Schalk, pitcher Dick Kerr—because they were in a different clique. The White Sox were a living denial of the old cliche that winning teams have togetherness; some players didn't talk to other players for years.

First, Gandil recruited Cicotte, the key man because he would pitch most frequently for the White Sox. Cicotte, then 35, was worried about his future and agreed, if he could get $10,000. Then, Gandil got Williams, Felsch, and shortstop Swede Risberg; reserve infielder Fred McMullin was included because he overheard Gandil and Risberg talking.

Those six were active in the fix, though McMullin's role in the Series was too minor to affect anything. But Jackson, though he eventually got $5,000, never played like a man trying to fix anything; he hit .375 and got 12 hits during the Series. Weaver got no money and never asked for any, and he had a great Series, hitting .324.

The motives of the six active conspirators were plain enough; those of Jackson and Weaver are confusing. Most likely Jackson, an uneducated country boy, was just going along with his friends but was too competitive to hold back once he was on the field. Weaver? He obviously didn't intend to be a part of the fix but, given the climate of the times, probably didn't want to "squeal" on his teammates, either.

Sullivan was a front man for a big-time gambler, Arnold Rothstein. He got approval from Rothstein to go ahead with the fix, but the plan didn't work out as smoothly as Gandil thought it would. The players were supposed to get $80,000 to split before the first game but only Cicotte and Gandil got any money, $10,000 for each. Nevertheless, the players decided to go along with the fix.

The odds were not quite as good as they should have been, either, because rumors of a fix had leaked out in too many places. Originally, the White Sox had been heavy favorites, but all of a sudden, everybody wanted to bet on Cincinnati. There was virtually no Chicago money around. Fred Lieb reported that, in the lobby of the Metropole Hotel in Cincinnati, he was approached by a gambler offering 6–5 if he'd take the White Sox. That surprised Lieb, who assumed the White Sox would be favored. "Has Cicotte come up with a lame arm?" he asked fellow baseball writer Dan Daniel.

Cicotte took a pounding in that first game, with the Reds winning easily, 9–1, and the odds on the Reds jumped even higher. Baseball writers like Hugh Fullerton, who had picked the White Sox, were very suspicious; the Cicotte who was hammered in this game had had a 1.82 earned run average during the regular season.

The second game was even stranger, as Cincinnati won, 4–2. Williams gave up only four hits while winning pitcher Slim Salee gave up ten, but Williams walked three batters in the fourth and then gave up a triple to weak-hitting Larry Kopf.

For the rest of the game, Williams had the Reds under control and White Sox fans thought he was only pitching in bad luck, with one bad inning. Others knew better.

White Sox manager Kid Gleason told his owner, Comiskey, "There's something funny going on here."

According to one account, Comiskey went to National League president John Heydler and asked him to talk to American League president Ban Johnson about it. (Comiskey and Johnson, once great friends, had become bitter enemies and no longer spoke.)

It seems more likely, though, that Comiskey tried to ignore the evidence that the Series was fixed, because he had a large financial interest in the players involved. Certainly, he did nothing to speed along the investigation that finally started after the Series.

The White Sox won the next game, 2–0, behind Kerr, the one frontline pitcher who was not in on the fix. Kerr was a solid pitcher who won 21 games in 1920 and 19 in 1921 before he had arm problems, but his fame has always rested on the fact that he won two games in the Black Sox Series—and that, as a minor league manager, he turned Stan Musial into an outfielder.

Despite his suspicions, Gleason went back to Cicotte in the third game. "We've got to look good in losing," Cicotte reportedly told one of his fellow conspirators. "We must think of our 1920 contracts."

Jimmy Ring helped him by pitching shutout ball for Cincinnati. The only runs of the game came in the fifth when Cicotte made two fielding errors. The first was on a throw; Cicotte fielded a grounder by Pat Duncan and threw wildly to first, the error enabling Duncan to go to second. Then Kopf singled to right. Jackson made a throw to the plate that looked as if it would get Duncan easily, but Cicotte deflected it into foul territory. That caused knowledgeable observers to become even more suspicious because Cicotte was known for his fine fielding.

Greasy Neale then doubled to score Kopf, and Cincinnati had a 3–1 lead in the Series.

It was Williams's turn in the next game, and he followed the same pattern he had in his first start, pitching effectively except in the sixth inning, when the Reds scored four times en route to their 5–0 win. Williams' effort was aided by Felsch's dropping of Roush's long fly ball in that inning, scored as a triple though many thought it should have been caught.

In a normal Series, that would have been it, because the Reds had taken four games to one. But the Series had been expanded to a best-of-nine format in 1919. Ironically, baseball's leaders thought this would be the year, the first after World War I, to really capitalize on the sport's interest. They couldn't have known, of course, that some of the White Sox would try to throw the Series.

To those who suspected the Series was being thrown, the next two games were strange ones indeed. In the sixth game, the White Sox won behind Kerr, 5–4; it was no

A great pitcher, Ed Cicotte was one of the ring-leaders in the fixed World Series of 1919. *(George Brace)*

surprise that Kerr pitched his best, but the winning run was knocked in by Gandil, the leader of the conspiring players. The next day, Cicotte pitched a 4–1 win over the Reds, and Cincinnati's edge was narrowed to 4–3.

Now rumors began circulating that there was a counterfix, that another group of gamblers had gotten to the Reds and bribed them to throw games to the White Sox once Cincinnati, with a 4–1 Series edge, had become the strong betting favorite.

White Sox fans, on the contrary, thought their heroes had merely been cursed by bad luck in the first five games of the Series and that class was beginning to tell.

Neither theory was correct. In reality, what had happened was that the Black Sox were angry because they had gotten only a portion of what they had been promised. If they weren't getting paid, they weren't going to throw any more games.

That rebellion ended quickly the next day. Rothstein told Sullivan the Series should end with the eighth game, and Sullivan contacted a hoodlum, who threatened Williams. The way Fred Lieb heard it later, Williams was told that if he didn't cooperate, he'd be shot right on the pitcher's mound.

As Hugh Fullerton was making his way to the press box the next day, a gambler he knew told him, "All the betting's on Cincinnati. It's going to be the biggest first inning you ever saw."

Whatever Williams was told—he never said—he certainly pitched like a man fearful for his life. He got the lead-off hitter, Morrie Rath, to pop up, but then Jake Daubert singled, Groh singled, Roush doubled to score Daubert, and Duncan doubled to score Groh and Roush.

That was enough for Gleason, who was already suspicious of Williams, and he brought in Bill James in relief. It was too late. The Reds never looked back as they rolled to a 10–5 win. It wasn't even that close. Only a four-run eighth inning rally by the White Sox, when the game was long decided, made it halfway respectable. (Jackson and Weaver doubled in the inning and Felsch tripled, although Felsch's hit came when right fielder Greasy Neale lost the ball in the sun.)

Was it worth it for the players? Only for Gandil, who collected $35,000 and retired to California; that was certainly more than he would have made in the rest of his career, had he continued to play.

Risberg collected $15,000, Cicotte $10,000, Felsch, Williams, Jackson, and McMullin $5,000 each, according to Asinof.

Recriminations began immediately after the end of the Series. White Sox catcher Ray Schalk told reporters that neither Cicotte nor Williams paid any attention to the signs he flashed, continually crossing him up by delivering different pitches, presumably ones that would be easier to hit. It was the first time Schalk had gone public with his complaints, but he had told the same thing to manager Gleason earlier in the Series.

Nonetheless, Comiskey tried to gloss over the affair, telling the press the day after the Series had ended: "There is always a scandal of some kind following a big sporting event like the World Series. These yarns are manufactured out of whole cloth and grow out of bitterness due to losing wagers. I believe my boys fought the battles of the recent World Series on the level, as they have always done. And I would be the first to want information to the contrary—if there be any. I would give $20,000 to anyone unearthing any information to that effect. . . ."

By this time, Comiskey almost certainly knew exactly what had happened. Joe Gedeon had talked to him and implicated Risberg. Harry Redmon, a St. Louis theater operator, told of conversations with Abe Attell, who was in on the fix. Comiskey had heard that Jackson was willing to talk about it, but he made no attempt to talk to his star outfielder.

Any attempts at a coverup were doomed, however, because too many people knew about the fix. Johnson was conducting an investigation for the American League as the 1920 season was playing out, and a Chicago grand jury was also investigating. Johnson gave the names of potential witnesses to the grand jury.

Finally, on September 27, 1920, Jimmy Isaminger in the *Philadelphia North American* reported an interview with gambler Billy Maharg that implicated the players, who then confessed.

The seven who were still playing were suspended by Johnson and indicted by the grand jury. They had apparently thrown more games during the 1920 season, including a three-game series with Cleveland in August that had kept the race close. With their suspension, the White Sox fell to second behind Cleveland, which won the pennant by two games.

The case did not come to trial until June 27, 1921, and the players were acquitted by the grand jury. But Judge Landis quickly announced:

> ... Regardless of the verdict of juries, no player who throws a ball game, no player that undertakes or promises to throw a ball game, no player that sits in conference with a bunch of crooked players and gamblers, where the ways and means of throwing a game are discussed and does not promptly tell his club about it, will ever play professional baseball!

So Cicotte, Williams, Felsch, Jackson, Risberg, McMullin, and Weaver were banned from baseball.

It was a sad ending to a sad story, especially for Weaver and Jackson, who had played their best. In retrospect, justice would have been served and the message to other players delivered just as clearly if their punishment had been limited to a year's suspension.

But that was not Judge Landis's way. He was never a man who could resist the grandstanding gesture. As Heywood Broun wrote, "His career typifies the heights to which dramatic talent may carry a man in America if only he has the foresight not to go on stage."

So, what may have been as good a team as ever played baseball was broken up by the scandal, its true greatness never given a chance to flourish.

Three men from that team—Collins, Schalk, and pitcher Red Faber—made the Hall of Fame. Others would have but for the scandal. Jackson, for instance, was a lifetime .356 hitter (ranking third on the all-time list) who had hit as high as .408. Weaver was a great third baseman, so fast coming in that even Ty Cobb didn't bunt on him, and a solid hitter. Both would have been certain to have made the Hall.

Cicotte, who won 210 games in his career and five times had season earned run averages of under two runs a game, would likely have made it. Williams, only 27 when he was suspended, was just coming into his peak and had won 45 games in two seasons. He had more wins (82) at his age than had Hall of Fame left-handers Warren Spahn and Eddie Plank, who went on to win 363 and 327 games, respectively.

Even the winning Reds suffered because nobody has ever given them credit for winning the Series, assuming they won it only because the Black Sox were throwing it.

"One thing that's always overlooked in the whole mess," said Roush years later, "is that we could have beat them no matter what the circumstances!"

Perhaps, but we'll never know.

"Shoeless Joe" Jackson was a tragic figure, a great but naive player who was banned from baseball because of the 1919 Series—though he hit .375 in the Series. *(George Brace)*

7. The Babe vs. McGraw

Baseball came of age with the World Series of 1921, 1922, and 1923, its immense popularity justifying the claims of its supporters that it was truly the "national pastime."

These were classic battles between the Giants and the Yankees, the first time two New York teams had ever met in the World Series; all the games of the first two Series were even played in the same park, the Polo Grounds.

This was a fight not just for supremacy in New York and in baseball but between opposite baseball philosophies. John McGraw's Giants played "scientific" baseball, battling for one run at a time as baseball teams had been doing since the beginning. On the other side, Babe Ruth had shown that there was an easier way to get a run, or a cluster: with one sweeping swing that could put the ball in the seats.

In the end, Ruth's philosophy would prevail, with profound implications for the sport as a whole. The Yankees, who became identified with the long ball, big inning philosophy, went on to dominate the sport for the next six decades, and baseball players everywhere dropped their hands to the end of the bat and began swinging from their heels. McGraw's Giants lost the battle for the affection of the New York fans and fell into a subsidiary role to the Yankees that would last until they moved from New York to San Francisco in 1958.

But it didn't start that way. In 1921, in fact, it seemed that McGraw's philosophy was still the smart one and that it was the Giants who would be dominating baseball.

That was a great team McGraw had assembled in 1921, a team that would go on to become the first team in baseball history to win four straight pennants, a feat that had not been accomplished even by the dynasties of the 1906–10 Chicago Cubs, 1910–14 Philadelphia Athletics, and McGraw's own Giants of 1911–13.

Only one player remained from his 1917 National League champions, center fielder George Burns, who had actually joined the club as early as the 1911 season. With him in the outfield were Emil Meusel (called "Irish" for some mysterious reason, though he was actually of German heritage) and Ross Youngs, who would become one of the best Giants of all time, in right field.

The infield was probably as good, though hardly as famous, as the "$100,000 infield" of the 1914 A's. Sharp-fielding and good-hitting George Kelly was the first baseman; Johnnie Rawlings who, like Meusel, had been acquired in a trade with the Philadelphia Phillies, was the second baseman; Dave Bancroft was the shortstop, and probably the best in baseball; and peppery Frankie Frisch, a future Hall-of-Famer, was at third.

The pitching staff was well balanced, with Art Nehf its leader with a 20–10 mark; Fred Toney won 18 and Jesse Barnes and Phil Douglas 15 each.

The Giants, after finishing second for three straight years after their 1917 pennant, had finished four games ahead of second place Pittsburgh, and McGraw had his seventh pennant. He should have been happy but he wasn't, because he had been upstaged by the upstart Yankees and Ruth and a style of play with which he would never be comfortable.

The Yankees had been around since the forming of the American League, but they had long played second fiddle to McGraw and his Giants, the best-known team in baseball. The Yankees had been so insignificant, in fact, that the Giants had allowed them to play in the Polo Grounds since the 1913 season.

That all changed in 1920, when the Yankees bought Ruth from the Boston Red Sox. The deal was a huge one for those times: The Yankees paid $25,000 immediately and $25,000 plus 6 percent interest in three yearly installments; the total price came to $110,000. In addition, Boston owner Harry Frazee, whose theatrical ventures forced him to sell players to raise cash, was given a $300,000 loan. Interestingly, the collateral for the loan was Fenway Park, so the Yankees could actually have closed Fenway if Frazee had not repaid the loan.

In his final year in Boston, Ruth had eclipsed all home run records by hitting 29, but that was only a hint of what was to come.

In his first year in New York, 1920, Ruth hit 54 homes runs. That would be an astounding total even today; at that time, it was incomprehensible. No other player hit more than 19; no *team* hit as many as Ruth; the Red Sox team he had left hit only 22.

What could he do for an encore? Well, in 1921, Ruth hit 59 home runs, 44 doubles, 16 triples, a total of 119 extra base hits, out of 204 hits. He hit .378 with a slugging percentage of .847 and even stole 17 bases. He did all this in only 540 official at-bats (he averaged about one homer every nine at-bats) because pitchers walked him a league-leading 144 times. Even so, he scored 177 runs and knocked in 171, both league-leading figures.

Although Ruth later hit 60 home runs in one season, 1927, he never had a better overall season than either 1920 or '21. No other hitter has ever had one so good.

The fans responded wildly to this phenomenon. The Giants had held the single season attendance record of 910,000, set in 1908, but the Yankees soared past that in 1920 to 1,289,422. They fell off only a shade in 1921, to 1,230,696, as McGraw watched in impotent frustration.

Ruth wasn't the only Yankee star, either. Frazee had also sold two outstanding pitchers to New York, Waite Hoyt and Carl Mays, along with a solid catcher, Wally Schang, and third baseman Mike McNally.

The infield was solid with Wally Pipp at first, Aaron Ward at second, and Roger Peckinpaugh at short. Bob Shawkey was a solid pitcher, Bob Meusel an excellent right fielder.

The Yankees started strong in the Series, too, winning both of the first two games by a 3–0 score.

The controversial Mays was the winner in the first game. In the 1920 season, one of Mays' submarine deliveries had struck Cleveland shortstop Ray Chapman in the temple, and Chapman had died. Mays was known for pitching tight to batters who crowded the plate, and there were some who blamed him for Chapman's death. But the consensus was that Chapman had "frozen" at the plate and had not been able to move out of the way of the pitch, and Mays was allowed to continue pitching. The incident didn't seem to bother him; he had his two best years in 1920 and 1921, 26–11 and 27–9.

Mays allowed only five hits in the opener, and four of them were collected by Frisch. In the second game, Frisch got only one hit—and again, his teammates got only one more, as Hoyt pitched a two-hitter to top Nehf.

The second loss was all the more galling for McGraw, because Hoyt had started his major league career with the Giants in 1918, before being released. Only a few days past his 22nd birthday in this Series, Hoyt had won 19 games for the Yankees in 1921 and would go on to win 237 in a career that eventually landed him in the Hall of Fame.

In the third inning of the third game, the Yankees knocked out Toney, the Giants' starter, with a four-run outburst; though this Series was best-of-nine, the last scheduled to go that long, it seemed the Yankees were on their way to a sweep.

Just like that, though, the Series turned around. The Giants scored four times in the bottom of the inning to knock out Shawkey, the Yankee starter, and their once-quiet bats erupted for eight runs in the seventh and a Series record 20 hits overall en route to a 13–5 win.

Even more important, Ruth was hurt. He had damaged his arm while stealing second and third in one inning in the second game, and his injury had become infected. He hurt it again in the third game, and the Yankees announced that he might miss the rest of the Series.

Ruth was in the lineup for the fourth game, his arm bandaged and obviously bothering him. He still managed to hit his first Series home run in the fifth, a solo shot that gave his team a 1–0 lead in a pitching duel between Mays and Douglas, the opening game pitchers.

But Mays, who had shut out the Giants for 16 innings, lost his touch in the eighth inning. Irish Meusel tripled, Rawlings and Frank Snyder singled in front of a sacrifice bunt by Douglas, and Burns doubled to give the Giants a three-run inning. Both teams added a run in the ninth as the Giants won, 4–2, to square the Series.

His arm still bandaged and a tube draining from his wound, Ruth played again in the fifth game and was the hero in a surprising set of circumstances: He beat out a fourth inning bunt when the score was tied, 1–1, and came around to score on Bob Meusel's double.

Hoyt gave up only an unearned run and won his second game for the Yankees, 3–1. As it turned out, that would be their last win. Ruth did not even suit up for the next two games and could only pinch-hit unsuccessfully in the eighth game, and the Giants won all three against the suddenly punchless Yankees.

The final game, in which Nehf beat Hoyt, 1–0, was the best-played of the Series. It was also a very hard loss for Hoyt, who gave up only an unearned run. For the Series, he pitched 27 innings without giving up an earned run, the equivalent of Christy Mathewson's great performance in the 1905 Series. But an unearned run in his second outing robbed him of what should have been his second shutout, and the unearned run in the final game took away his chance at both another shutout and a third win.

The Giants' run came in the first inning, when Hoyt walked bancroft and Youngs, and Peckinpaugh couldn't handle Kelly's grounder.

The great Giants' infield saved the game and the Series in the bottom of the ninth. With Ward on first and one out, Frank (Home Run) Baker smashed a ball at the right side that seemed to be going through for a base hit. But second baseman Rawlings knocked it down and threw out Baker. Ward, running as the ball was hit, tried for third, but Kelly threw a strike to Frisch for the final out of the Series.

It was a frustrating Series for Ruth, who had hit .313 but with only one extra-base hit, his third-game homer, among his five hits, before being forced out of action by his injured arm.

During the Series, New York sportswriter Joe Vila had implied that Ruth was faking the seriousness of his injury, citing other instances in the 1920 and 1921 seasons in which the Babe had been reported hurt but had returned quickly to the lineup and played well. Ruth, he noted, had played well this time even when his arm was bandaged.

Angered by Vila's comments, Ruth shouted at him before the sixth game, gesturing at his wounded arm. That only served to focus attention on what Vila had written.

Ruth and Bob Meusel were suspended for the first month of the 1922 season because they had defied Commissioner Landis and gone on a postseason barnstorming tour. Nevertheless, the Yankees won their second straight pennant, though just by a game over the St. Louis Browns.

The Giants, too, won again in 1922, and with a slightly stronger lineup because McGraw had traded for Cincinnati third baseman Heinie Groh. Ironically, Groh had started his career with the Giants and been a member of the 1912 pennant winner before being traded the following year to Cincinnati.

Groh's acquisition allowed McGraw to move Frisch to second, where he was even better than he had been at third. Frisch was probably the ultimate extension of McGraw on the playing field, an all-out competitor who was a natural leader (and, later, manager), excellent hitter, strong fielder, and effective base stealer.

Groh was a fine all-around player who was best known for his "bottle bat." When he had come to the Giants the first time, McGraw had told him to get a bat with a bigger barrel. But Groh, a compact man at 5–7 and 160 pounds, had small hands and could not grip the larger bats, which in those days had large handles to go with their large barrels.

So, he took a large-barrelled bat and whittled down the handle so it was fat at one end, skinny at the other. The bat weighed 46 ounces, and almost all of it was in one end. Groh choked up on the bat, his hands almost to the barrel; he wanted to be able to hit inside pitches with authority.

The Yankees, too, were an improved team, once again because of Boston owner Frazee, who had turned the Red Sox into a farm club for the Yankees. This time, Frazee had sold the Yankees third baseman Joe Dugan, shortstop Everett Scott, and pitcher Joe Bush.

Bush was the Yankee pitcher in the opening game against Nehf but got the loss when the Giants won, 3–2. Rosy Ryan got the win in relief of Nehf.

In the second game, Bob Shawkey and Jesse Barnes were locked in a duel that was 3–3 after ten innings when the game was stopped by umpire George Hildebrand because of "darkness."

It was a curious decision, to say the least. Apparently, it was Bill Klem who had advised Hildebrand to call the game, though it was only 4:46, about 45 minutes before sunset.

Fans thought the game had been called so that clubs could get another game's receipts, and that it had been called by orders of the commissioner.

Actually, Judge Landis had nothing to do with the decision, and he was as surprised and angered by it as anybody else. He ordered the clubs to turn over the entire receipts for the game to hospitals for wounded soldiers.

The third game produced an unexpected hero in Jack Scott, who represented an outstanding reclamation project by McGraw.

Scott had won 15 games for the Boston Braves in 1921 and had then been traded to Cincinnati, but his arm went dead in the 1922 season and he was cut by the Reds. He returned to his tobacco farm in Ridgeway, North Carolina, his career apparently finished.

In mid-July, though, his arm seemed to have recovered and he traveled to New York to plead with McGraw. "I'm sure I can pitch," he told McGraw. "I've been resting the arm for a couple of months now and it feels mighty good."

McGraw agreed to give Scott a trial, after the Giants returned from their road trip. He told the pitcher to work out in New York while the Giants were gone and he'd take a look when the Giants were back at the Polo Grounds.

When the Giants returned, McGraw did as he'd said he would, and he liked what he saw. He signed Scott to a contract, and Scott surprised everybody by winning eight games for the Giants in the rest of the season.

His 8–2 record was deceptive, however; he had only a 4.46 earned run average, and he had given up 85 hits in 80 innings. He seemed no match for Yankee ace Hoyt in the third game, but he surprised everybody—possibly including McGraw—by throwing a four-hit shutout as the Giants won, 3–0.

That gave the Giants a 2–0 edge, a big one in a Series that had again been reduced to best-of-seven (it would stay that length from that point on).

The next day's game started in a drizzle, and the field was even darker than it had been when the second game had been stopped. The Yankees got off to a quick lead in the first inning, scoring twice off Giants starter Hugh McQuillan. But the Giants bounced back to score four times off Mays in the fifth inning, en route to a 4–3 win. McQuillan got a big hit for himself in the inning, a double, but the biggest hit was a single by Bancroft that drove in two runs.

Still, the Yankees battled back and took a 3–2 lead into the bottom of the eighth inning of the next game. Then the roof fell in.

With one out, Groh singled and Frisch doubled him to third. Shortstop Scott threw out Groh on a grounder by Bob Meusel, and then Youngs was intentionally walked by Bush to load the bases. Kelly singled to center to score the tying and go-ahead runs, and Lee King followed with another single to score Youngs for the final 5–3 margin. The Giants had swept their crosstown rivals, discounting the tie game.

The hitting star of the Series was Groh, who hit .474. Although Groh played on six World Series teams (1912 Giants, 1919 Reds, 1922–24 Giants and 1927 Pirates) that was the highlight of his career. To the day he died, his car's license plate carried the number "474."

The big story, though, was the way Ruth had been stopped. The Babe had only a single and double in 17 at-bats, a miserable .118 batting average.

What had happened? It couldn't have been the "pressure" of the Series because Ruth had played, and starred, in two World Series before he even came to the Yankees. As a pitcher for the Red Sox in the 1916 and 1918 Series, he had pitched three games and won all three, with an ERA of 0.87 and two complete games, including a 14-inning game that is the longest in Series history. He had also set a record with 29 consecutive scoreless innings that lasted until Whitey Ford broke it in 1961.

Some thought it was McGraw's strategy: He had told his pitchers to throw mostly low curve balls to Ruth and make him chase the pitches.

The Babe's sportswriting nemesis, Joe Vila, agreed. Vila had been writing baseball since before the turn of the century, and he had a natural bias toward the game of strategy that McGraw played and against the power game of Ruth. He was pleased to see his judgment vindicated.

Wrote Vila: "The exploded phenomenon didn't surprise the smart fans who long ago realized that he couldn't hit brainy pitching. Ruth, therefore, is no longer a wonder. The baseball public is onto his real worth as a batsman and in the future, let us hope, he will attract just ordinary attention."

Nobody, least of all Vila, realized it at the time, but the 1922 Series was essentially the last gasp for McGraw and his style of baseball. It would be the last Series one of his teams would win.

It was perhaps an omen when the 1923 Series opened in Yankee Stadium. Angered by the Yankees' popularity, the Giants had told them they could no longer play in the Polo Grounds after the 1922 season, so the Yankees had built their own stadium. It would become a showplace for baseball, perhaps the most famous stadium since the Colosseum had been built in Rome.

It was also fitting that the star of the first game was Casey Stengel. Later generations knew Stengel chiefly as a great Yankee manager, but long before that he had been a player, 14 years with five National League clubs.

How good a player was Stengel? His contemporaries thought highly of him, particularly as a hitter. "Casey was a real good hitter," said Charlie Grimm. "He would punch the ball anywhere it was pitched."

"He always stood with his right foot closer than his left to the plate, sort of looking over his right shoulder at the pitcher," said pitcher Burleigh Grimes, who later succeeded Stengel as manager of the Brooklyn Dodgers in 1937.

"He would move his feet around in the box a lot. If he moved that front right foot up he was trying to get you to pitch inside so he could pull the ball. If he moved back, he was looking for an outside pitch he could slap to left field. A real smart fellow, that Stengel."

But Stengel was best known by fans for his unpredictable antics. His most famous stunt was an unplanned one during a game while he was with Brooklyn. Standing in right field, he had seen a bird fly against the bull pen wall and knock himself out. For no reason, Stengel stuck the bird under his cap. By the time he came to bat, the bird had revived and was moving around, so Stengel knew he had to do something with it. He promply bowed to the crowd, lifted his hat—and the bird flew out, to the immense enjoyment of the fans.

By 1921, Stengel was 31 and on the way downhill as a player. McGraw picked him up and used him as a reserve outfielder and pinch hitter. The two sat side-by-side on the bench, discussing strategy. Despite his reputation as a clown, Stengel had a sharp mind and a great interest in baseball strategy.

Stengel played in only 75 regular season games in 1923; he was platooned—a word which he would make famous in his later years as Yankee manager—with Bill Cunningham, a right-handed hitter. Used in that way, he hit .339 in 218 at-bats.

With a right-hander, Hoyt, the Yankee starter, McGraw started Casey in the first game of the '23 Series and kept him in there when another right-hander, Joe Bush, relieved Hoyt.

With the score tied, 4–4, in the ninth inning, Stengel hit a Bush change-up into left-center. The ball didn't appear to be particularly hard-hit—Fred Lieb said he thought at first it would only be a single—but the outfielders were well spaced. Because of Stengel's ability to slice the ball down the left field line, Yankee left fielder Bob Meusel was playing close to the line. Meanwhile, center fielder Whitey Witt, thinking Stengel might be trying to pull the ball, was in right-center.

The ball sailed between the two outfielders and went all the way to the wall, 450 feet from home plate. Witt finally ran it down and threw it to Meusel, who had the strongest arm on the club. Meusel rifled it to the cutoff man, shortstop Scott.

Meanwhile, Stengel was running as hard as he could. "You could hear him yelling to himself, 'Go, Casey, go, go, Casey, go' above the noise of the crowd," said Dugan, the Yankee third baseman that day. "It was the damndest thing."

Casey had had a sponge in the heel of one shoe because of a bruise, and the sponge popped out as he rounded third. He thought he had lost the shoe and was limping, though still running as hard as he could, as he came in with the winning run. He stumbled the last 20 feet and dove for the plate just ahead of Scott's throw.

The home run caught the fancy of the public, partly because it was written up in unique fashion by Damon Runyon, then a New York sportswriter. This was Runyon's account:

> This is the way old Casey Stengel ran yesterday afternoon running his home run to a Giant victory by the score of 5 to 4 in the first game of the World Series of 1923. This is the way old Casey Stengel ran running his home run home when two were out in the ninth inning and the score was tied, and the ball still bounding inside the Yankee yard.
>
> This is the way—
>
> His mouth wide open.
>
> His warped old legs bending beneath him at every stride. His arms flying back and forth like those of a man swimming with a crawl stroke.

His flanks heaving, his breath whistling, his head far back, Yankee infielders, passed by old Casey Stengel as he was running his home run home, say Casey was muttering to himself, adjuring himself to greater speed as a jockey mutters to his horse in a race, saying, "Go on, Casey, go on."

The warped old legs, twisted and bent by many a year of baseball campaigning, just barely held out under Casey until he reached the plate, running his home run home.

Then they collapsed.

Runyon's account made Stengel a hero, but it had one backlash effect: When he was trying to persuade Edna Lawson to marry him (which she did), Edna's father wondered if she should marry such an "old man." Edna quickly pointed out that Stengel was 33, old by baseball standards but not by society's.

In the second game, Ruth finally showed the kind of hitting for which he had become famous, rapping back-to-back home runs in the fourth and fifth innings as the Yankees won, 4–2, behind Herb Pennock to square the Series.

It was Stengel's turn again in the third game. The Yankee bench had been riding him unmercifully—about his floppy ears, his advanced age. With the game a scoreless tie in the seventh inning, Sad Sam Jones threw another change-up to Stengel. That was supposed to be the pitch Casey couldn't hit, but not in this Series. He drove this one over the right field wall for what turned out to be the game's only run, before a stunned Yankee Stadium crowd of 62,430, the largest crowd ever to watch a game to that point.

As he rounded the bases, Casey pretended to be flicking a fly off the end of his nose, the gesture obviously aimed at the Yankees. He was later fined $50 by Judge Landis. Yankee owner Jake Ruppert had demanded a stiffer fine but, said Landis, who could always appreciate another actor, "Casey Stengel can't help being Casey Stengel."

That gave the Giants a 2–1 lead in the Series, but the momentum changed overnight. In the fourth game, the Yankees knocked out Scott in a six-run second and won easily, 8–4. The next game was even easier, an 8–1 win behind Bush.

The final game was closer. The Giants actually carried a 4–1 lead into the top of the eighth. But then the Yankees knocked out the tiring Nehf in a five-run explosion to win the game, 6–4, and win their first World Series.

Probably no Yankee savored the victory more than Ruth, who had a dramatic reversal from his 1922 fiasco. In six games, Ruth hit .368, with three home runs, a triple, and a double among his seven hits. He scored eight runs and knocked in three.

That was just the start for Ruth, who went on to set two dozen World Series records (some since broken) before his Yankee career ended.

So much for Joe Vila.

8. Score One for the Immortals

The seventh game of the World Series is always a moment of high drama, and never more so than in the Series of 1924 and 1926. The games themselves were so unusual that they stick out in memory above most of the hundreds of Series games that have been played; equally important, they were won by great pitchers Walter Johnson and Grover Cleveland Alexander, both in the twilight of their careers, and in such a manner as to suggest divine intervention.

Johnson is the measure by which all fastball pitchers are compared, though his career strikeout total of 3508 was surpassed by both Steve Carlton and Nolan Ryan in 1983. Garry Schumacher, who saw all the power pitchers of the 20th century through Carlton and Ryan as a baseball writer and then publicist for the Giants, always claimed that Johnson was "a yard faster" than any of them—a baseball expression meaning that Johnson's fast ball traveled a yard farther than anybody else's in the same time.

Johnson's nicknames were related to speed—"The Big Train" and "Barney" for Barney Oldfield, though that nickname came equally from the way Johnson drove his car. He threw with a deceptively smooth motion, and the pitch came hurtling at the batter as if it were thrown from a slingshot.

Eddie Ainsmith, who caught Johnson for part of his career, sympathized with those who tried to hit him. "If you tried to hit against him on a dark day," said Ainsmith, "you were out of luck. I had all I could do to see the ball when he let fly. Sometimes, I got my mitt up just in time."

His fastball was really Johnson's only pitch. He never had more than a fair curve, but right to the end of his career, the fastball was enough. With it, he won 416 games, an American League record that will almost certainly never be matched. Only Cy Young, who won 511 games pitching in first the National and then the American League, ever won more.

Johnson was a gentle, kindly man and a folk hero, much as Christy Mathewson was for the Giants. Legends grew up around him. It was said, for instance, that he would not pitch inside because he was afraid his fastball would seriously hurt a batter if it hit him. Yet, if you look in the baseball record book, Johnson is the all-time leader in hit batsman, 206, far ahead of everybody else. Since he had good control—he averaged only slightly more than two walks per nine innings—that doesn't quite square with his reputation.

The remarkable aspect of Johnson's record is that he accomplished what he did while pitching for clubs that were often mediocre or worse. The crack in the first part of the century was, "Washington, first in war, first in peace, and last in the American League." That wasn't quite true, but it was close enough. In Johnson's first 13 years, the prime years of his 21-year career, the Senators finished last twice and seventh five times. Six times, Johnson's wins were more than a third of the club's total; another six times, he had more than one-quarter of the club's wins.

By 1924, Johnson was almost 37 and nearing the end of his career, but the Senators had finally put together a team worthy of him, winning their first pennant and one of only three they would ever win before being moved to Minnesota prior to the 1961 season.

Johnson had responded with his best year since 1919, leading the league in six pitching categories, including most wins; his 23 were exactly one-fourth of the Senators' total. His strikeout total, 158, led the league and was his highest since 1918.

(A word of explanation about strikeout totals: Although the lively ball was in use during this period, hitters still were using bigger bats than they do now and making contact much more frequently. Pitchers' strikeout totals were considerably lower than they are today, and so were batters'; Babe Ruth led the league in strikeouts with 81.)

John McGraw's Giants had won the National League pennant in 1924, the first team ever to win four straight pennants. That should have been the big story, but McGraw and his Giants were overshadowed by the fact that Johnson had finally made it to the World Series. Johnson and the Senators were the sentimental favorite outside of New York—and perhaps among some fans in New York, too.

There was even more than the usual ceremony before the first game of the Series, which was played in Washington. A group of fans gave Johnson a new car, the Automobile Association of America threw in a lifetime membership, and Mutual Life insured the car for its lifetime. President Calvin Coolidge threw out the first ball, a wild pitch. Those watching thought Coolidge was bored, but it may only have been his normal expression.

Johnson's fastball was as good as it had been during the season as he struck out 12, but in between strikeouts, the Giants hit the ball hard, getting 14 hits. Two of them were home runs, solos by George Kelly in the second and Bill Terry in the fourth.

After that, Johnson got tougher and the Senators came back to score single runs in the sixth and ninth off Giants' ace Art Nehf to tie the score.

It stayed that way until the top of the 12th inning, starters Johnson and Nehf both still in the game. Then, Hank Gowdy led off for the Giants with a walk. Nehf singled, and he and Gowdy both took an extra base when Washington center fielder Earl McNeely threw wildly to second. Pinch hitter Jack Bentley walked to load the bases, and Billy Southworth ran for him.

Johnson then got the first out of the inning, as Frankie Frisch bounced to player-manager Bucky Harris at second and Harris threw to the plate to force Gowdy. But Ross Youngs followed with a single to score Nehf and Kelly's fly scored Southworth.

The Senators could score only one run in the bottom of the inning as they, and Johnson, lost the game, 4–3.

The Series seesawed back and forth, Washington winning the second game, 4–3, New York the third game, 6–4, and the Senators taking the fourth game, 7–4, to even the Series again. It was Johnson's turn in the fifth game.

This time, it seemed his aging arm had finally given out. He had no zip on his fastball, striking out only three in eight innings as the Giants pounded out 13 hits.

Nonetheless, he still had a chance to win the game as it went into the bottom of the eighth, the Giants leading only by a single run, 3–2.

Kelly led off the inning with a single and Terry walked. Hack Wilson (later to gain fame with the Chicago Cubs when he set National League season records with 56 home runs and 190 RBIs in 1930) was safe when Johnson fumbled his bunt, loading the bases.

Harris came out to the mound to talk to Johnson. Perhaps he thought of taking Walter out at that point, but it was a very difficult situation for Harris, nine years younger than Johnson and in his first year as manager.

As did everybody on the team, Harris idolized Johnson. In one of the first games Harris had played for the Senators, his error had caused Johnson to lose a game, and he had delayed going into the dressing room until Johnson had come up to him, put his arm around Harris's shoulders and said, "Don't worry about it, son. It happens to everybody."

Harris remembered this, and he also thought this might be Johnson's last chance to win a World Series game. He left Walter in, a decision for which he would later be sharply criticized.

Travis Jackson followed with a fly to left that scored Kelly. Gowdy forced Wilson at second with a grounder to Harris, but then Hugh McQuillan, who was pitching in relief of starter Bentley, blooped a single that scored Terry with the second run of the inning. Still, Harris stayed with Johnson and Fred Lindstrom followed with his fourth hit of the game to knock in the third run, and that was the final score: New York 6, Washington 2.

It was a disheartening time for Johnson and the Senators; it seemed now that, not only had Johnson lost his chance for a Series win but that the Senators, because of Harris's sentimental decision, might lose the Series.

But it was a heady time for Lindstrom, who had not even reached his 19th birthday. Lindstrom was playing third base because Heinie Groh had been injured in late season, and he wound up hitting .333 for the Series.

Lindstrom later told Donald Honig that he hadn't even been nervous, because he was too young to be aware of the significance of what was happening. "Sometimes a person's innocence can work to his advantage," he said. ". . . I was just dumb enough not to be aware of his [Johnson's] greatness. To me he was just another pitcher."

As it happened, Lindstrom's time in the spotlight was just beginning. He would inadvertently play a key role later in this Series and, though he had a fine career which eventually won him a spot in the Hall of Fame, he will always be remembered chiefly for what happened to him in this Series.

The Senators came back to beat the Giants behind Tom Zachary, 2–1, over Nehf, and the stage was set for the dramatic final game.

A strange thing happened even before the start of this game: Harris, the rookie manager, outsmarted the legendary McGraw. That year, McGraw platooned Bill Terry, who was a virtual rookie (he had played three games with the Giants in 1923). Terry would go on to become one of the most feared hitters in the league against all pitching—.341 lifetime average and the last National Leaguer to hit .400 with a .401 mark in 1930—but McGraw used him only against right-handers in 1924. George Kelly played center when Terry was in the lineup, moving to first when Terry was benched against left-handers.

Harris started the little-used Curley Ogden, a right-hander who had won nine games and lost eight during the regular season, and Terry started for the Giants. After Ogden had pitched to only two batters, Harris relieved him with left-hander George Mogridge.

Terry grounded out and struck out against Mogridge, and McGraw used Irish Meusel as a pinch hitter for him in the sixth. Harris then brought in right-hander Firpo Marberry.

As a result of all this maneuvering, Terry (the leading hitter in the Series with a .429 average) was no longer available to the Giants. It was an indication that McGraw was beginning to lose his touch, a trend that would accelerate in the years to come; this would be his last World Series though he didn't resign as Giants manager until 40 games into the 1932 season.

Despite all this, it seemed McGraw might go out a winner when the Giants took a 3–1 lead into the bottom of the eighth. Then, with one out, pinch hitter Nemo Leibold started a Washington rally with a double. Muddy Ruel singled off Kelly's glove at first base, Leibold holding at third, and pinch hitter Bennie Tate walked to load the bases.

McNeely flied short to left field, and the runners all held, but then Harris's grounder, which should have ended the inning, took a bad bounce over Lindstrom's head at third and two runs scored. The Senators had tied the game.

Walter Johnson won a dramatic World Series game in 1924, his first Series. *(Washington Senators)*

Harris brought Johnson into the game in the ninth, and the fastball that had deserted him two games before had returned. Whenever he got into trouble, he reached back for the smoke.

In the ninth, for instance, Frisch tripled with one out, but Johnson blew three fastballs by Kelly and got Meusel to ground out to end the threat. In the 11th, with two men on and only one out, he struck out Frisch and Kelly in succession.

It didn't hurt Johnson, of course, as the October shadows lengthened and it became even harder for the Giants hitters to pick up his fastball, and he struck out five Giants as he held them scoreless over four innings.

But the Senators couldn't do anything with Giant relievers McQuillan and Bentley, either—until they got three big breaks in the bottom of the 12th.

The first break came with one out. Ruel popped a pitch up behind the plate that should have been caught, but Gowdy got his foot caught in his catcher's mask and couldn't reach the ball. Given that reprieve, Ruel then doubled to left.

Johnson hit a ground ball to shortstop and Jackson, momentarily distracted by Ruel, bobbled it. Ruel returned to second. Instead of two outs, there were two men on with nobody out.

McNeely then hit a grounder to Lindstrom and, like Harris's ball in the eighth, the ball took a bad bounce over Lindstrom's head. Accounts differ over whether it was just a bad bounce or whether the ball hit something. Lindstrom said it hit a pebble, and he was the closest to the ball.

Ruel, who was not a fast runner, came in to score on the hit to win the game and Series for Washington. It's possible he could have been thrown out by Meusel, the left fielder, but Meusel had anticipated that the play would be made in the infield and got a late start. By the time he reached the ball, he saw he had no chance to get Ruel and just stuffed the ball in his pocket.

The Giants seemed resigned to their loss. "Walter Johnson is such a lovable character," said Bentley, "that the good Lord didn't want to see him beat again."

McGraw was concerned that his young third baseman would be forever scarred by his experience; he had seen Fred Merkle and Fred Snodgrass suffer because of mistakes that hung over them for their careers. On the train back to New York, he called Lindstrom into his drawing room and gave him a couple of shots of bourbon.

Unfortunately for Lindstrom, he was drinking on an empty stomach, and the liquor knocked him out. He was still unconscious when the train got to New York, and he was carried off by Kelly. "I guess a lot of people who saw us must have wondered what had happened," said Lindstrom, "but it was just a kid coming home from his first World Series."

Unlike Johnson, Alexander was not a lovable soul. He was, in fact, a man beset by problems, physical and emotional. He had been deafened by artillery shells exploding around him in World War I, and he suffered from epilepsy, an illness which also developed during his service time. He had an on-and-off marriage—twice married, twice divorced by the same woman—and he was an alcoholic, spending time in a sanitarium after the 1925 season.

But how the man could pitch! He won 373 games, tying him with Mathewson as the most prolific winner in National League history. (He actually was one game up on Mathewson for a while, but a search through old box scores showed that Christy had one more win than the 372 he had been credited with at retirement.)

Alexander had a variety of pitches and superb control. He won 28 games as a rookie in 1911 and won 30 or more games three seasons in a row, 1915–17. In 1915, he won a World Series game for the Philadelphia Phillies that was the Phillies' only Series win until 1980; the following season, he pitched an astounding 16 shutouts.

As late as 1920, Alexander led the National League in seven pitching departments, including most wins (27) and ERA (1.91). After that, though he was still an effective pitcher and even had two more 20-win seasons, he was no longer the great pitcher he had been. His alcoholism was taking its toll, and he was becoming increasingly difficult for managers.

He had been traded to the Chicago Cubs in 1918. By 1926, Joe McCarthy was the Cubs' manager, and he tired of Alexander's erratic behavior, especially since it seemed

Rogers Hornsby batted and managed the St. Louis Cardinals to a triumph in the 1926 World Series. *(George Brace)*

the once-great pitcher was virtually through. In mid-season, the Cubs traded Alexander to the St. Louis Cardinals.

With the Cardinals, Alexander won nine games as the Cards surprised the baseball world by winning a pennant, the first since 1888. Some baseball people had thought a St. Louis team would never again win a pennant because the summer heat and humidity took so much out of their players.

The Cardinals were facing a New York Yankees team that was on the verge of becoming perhaps the best team in baseball history, with a wrecking crew led by Babe Ruth and Lou Gehrig.

The great Yankee hitters got only six hits off Bill Sherdel in the first game, but that was enough as Herb Pennock threw a three-hitter for a 2–1 Yankee win.

St. Louis playing-manager Rogers Hornsby gave Alexander the ball for the second game. Hornsby got along with Alexander, perhaps because Rogers was a difficult man to deal with, too, though he lacked the extenuating excuse of drinking.

Alexander was shaky early and the Yankees scored twice off him in the bottom of the second, one of the runs being unearned. But the Cardinals struck back for two runs to tie the game in the top of the third and then added three runs in the seventh and another in the ninth.

Given that kind of support, Alexander coasted home, retiring 21 consecutive batters in one stretch in a four-hit, 6–2 win that evened the Series.

Jesse Haines pitched a 4–0 shutout in the third game to give St. Louis the lead, but then Ruth shocked the St. Louis fans by hitting three homers in the fourth game, the first time that had ever been done. The Yankees won the game, 10–5.

Pennock again topped Sherdel in the fifth game, but it took ten innings this time before the Yankees triumphed, 3–2, to take a 3–2 lead in the Series.

Once again it was Alexander's turn, and once again, the Cardinals gave him great hitting support. This one was broken open by a five-run Cardinal rally in the seventh, en route to a 10–2 win.

The seventh game started in a drizzle, and the first two innings were scoreless as Waite Hoyt and Haines each tried for a second win in the Series.

Ruth opened the scoring in the third with his fourth home run of the Series, and the Cardinals struck for three runs in the fourth, through no fault of Hoyt's.

With one out in the fourth, Jim Bottomley singled and Les Bell followed with a grounder to short that should have been the start of a double play. But Yankee shortstop Mark Koenig bobbled the ball, his fourth error of the Series, and both runners were safe.

Chick Hafey dumped a pop fly into short left that seemed catchable by either Koenig or outfielder Bob Meusel, but neither handled it and the ball dropped in for a single, loading the bases. Meusel then dropped a fly ball hit by Bob O'Farrell and a run scored. The Yankees were obviously having a bad case of Series nerves.

Tommy Thevenow then singled in two more runs before Hoyt registered the final two outs of the inning.

The Yankees got one run back in the sixth on a single by Joe Dugan and a double by Hank Severeid. Haines, though he still had the lead, was having problems. A blister had formed on his index finger from throwing the knuckleball.

Earle Combs walked to open the seventh and was sacrificed to second by Koenig. Ruth was intentionally walked. Meusel forced Ruth with a grounder, Combs going to third, and then Gehrig was intentionally walked to load the bases.

Haines' blister made it impossible for him to pitch any longer. Hornsby brought in Alexander, even though "Old Pete" had pitched the game before and even though Alexander was nearing his 40th birthday. Hornsby wanted somebody who wouldn't be bothered by World Series pressure.

Legend has it that Alexander had gotten royally drunk the night before, celebrating his sixth game win and thinking he wouldn't be pitching again in this Series. Possibly. Such behavior would be neither a first nor a last for baseball.

Legend also has it that Hornsby looked into Alexander's eyes to make sure the pitcher was capable of facing the Yankees. Doubtful. Alexander had been warming up in the bull pen already. If he were unable to pitch, Hornsby would have been told by the bull pen coach.

The first batter was Yankee second baseman Tony Lazzeri. A rookie that season, Lazzeri had come up from the Pacific Coast League where he had had an incredible season in 1925, hitting 60 home runs (in 197 games; the PCL played a very long schedule) and knocking in 222 runs. For that, he had acquired the nickname of "Poosh 'Em Up."

During the regular season, Lazzeri had knocked in 114 runs, second only to Ruth in the powerful Yankee lineup. He had also struck out a league-leading 96 times. Which characteristic would be the more important this time?

Alexander's first pitch was a ball, the second a called strike. Then Lazzeri came around on a fastball inside and lashed it deep to left field. At the last moment, the ball curved foul, a few feet from a grand-slam home run. On the next pitch, he swung and missed. In the space of two pitches, Lazzeri had gone from possible hero to goat, and Alexander from possible goat to hero.

That moment is one of the most famous in baseball history, and it was so dramatic that many people think it was the final out of the game. Not at all. Alexander still had to get through the dangerous Yankee lineup for two more pressure innings.

He breezed. The Yankees couldn't get the ball out of the infield. In the eighth, Dugan grounded out, Pat Collins fouled out, and Pennock, who had relieved Hoyt in the seventh, popped out. In the ninth, Combs and Koenig grounded out to put the Cardinals one out away from victory.

There was one anxious moment left. Alexander worked very carefully to the

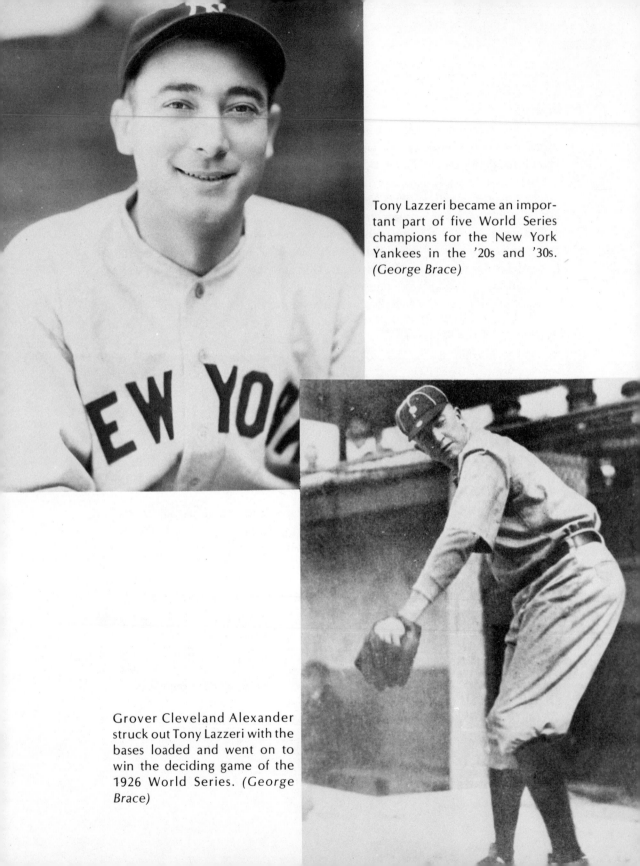

Tony Lazzeri became an important part of five World Series champions for the New York Yankees in the '20s and '30s. *(George Brace)*

Grover Cleveland Alexander struck out Tony Lazzeri with the bases loaded and went on to win the deciding game of the 1926 World Series. *(George Brace)* awesome Ruth, knowing how easily one Ruthian swing could tie it up. Finally, on a full count, he walked Ruth, the 11th time Babe had walked in the Series.

Meusel was the next hitter and, though he had not had a good Series, batting just .238, he was a feared hitter, .315 in the regular season. The Yankee Stadium crowd stirred. Something might happen yet.

Something did indeed, but not at all what the crowd—or anybody else—had anticipated. Acting strictly on his own and for reasons he himself couldn't even explain later, Ruth tried to steal second and was thrown out by catcher O'Farrell. On that strange note, the Series ended.

9. The Window Breakers

There had been four-game sweeps before and there would be more after, but the 1927 World Series was unique: It was over before it actually began.

It ended when the Pittsburgh Pirates came out to watch the Yankees take batting practice. Babe Ruth was swinging as they came out, and the Babe put ball after ball into the right field stands. As he strutted away from the batting cage, he saw the Pirate players. "If you chase down any of those balls," he said, "I'll autograph them for you."

Lou Gehrig followed him into the cage and was almost as awesome. From the right-handed side, Bob Meusel and Tony Lazzeri pumped their share into the left field stands.

The Pirates were mesmerized. They had a good team, and the Waner brothers, Paul (Big Poison) and Lloyd (Little Poison), were excellent hitters; Paul had led the National League with .380 that year and Lloyd had hit .355. But the Pirates were still playing the game one base at a time (Lloyd Waner had 198 singles among his 223 hits), and the sun had set on that baseball era.

The Yankees, with Ruth always the leader, had ushered in the era of the big inning. Manager Miller Huggins had first stated it: that in most games, the winning team will score more runs in one inning than the losing team scores in the game.

The Yankees didn't sacrifice runners along to get one run. Stolen bases weren't a big thing, either; four teams had more than the 90 stolen bases they totaled, and another team had as many.

No, the Yankees waited for that inning when the big bats swung and the ball went over the fence on the fly, and they scored the runs that won the game. That strategy worked often enough for them to win 110 games that season, and to earn the nickname "Window Breakers" for their home run power.

No team wins 110 games just on home runs, of course. The Yankees were a beautifully balanced club that year, the team many baseball historians rank as the best of all time.

Lloyd and Paul Waner (Little and Big Poison) were great hitters for the Pirates, but they were awed by the Yankees' power in 1927. *(George Brace)*

Miller Huggins managed the 1927–28 New York Yankees who swept
Pittsburgh and St. Louis in eight games in consecutive World Series.
(George Brace)

Waite Hoyt was the staff leader for the great 19[...] Yankees team that swept the World Seri[...] *(George Brace)*

The pitching was outstanding. Starting pitchers Waite Hoyt, Herb Pennock, and Urban Shocker won 23, 19, and 18 games, respectively. Thirty-year-old rookie Wilcy Moore, pitching mainly in relief, won 19 games. Hoyt and Shocker had the two best earned run averages, 2.63 and 2.84, in the league.

Defensively, the club was strong. Outfielders Earle Combs and the strong-armed Meusel were excellent and Ruth, though slowing down, was still a reliable fielder; some said he never made a wrong throw. Lazzeri and Mark Koenig were a good double-play combination.

The Yankees hit for average, too, with a team mark of .307. Gehrig hit .373, Ruth and Combs each .356 and Meusel .337. They led the league both in batting average and in team ERA, 3.20.

But it was their power that set them apart. This was the year Ruth hit 60 home runs, a record that lasted until Roger Maris hit 61 in an expanded season in 1961.

Ruth and Gehrig had conducted an unprecedented home run race for most of the season. Nobody else was even close; Lazzeri's 18 was the third highest total in the league.

On August 15, Gehrig was actually ahead of Ruth, 38 to 36, but then Lou slowed down and Ruth accelerated. The Babe hit seven in the last half of the month to open September with 43.

Babe Ruth was as dominating a figure in World Series play for the New York Yankees as he was during the regular season. *(New York Yankees)*

Nobody expected him to make a run at his record of 59, but when Ruth was hot, he was like no other hitter before or since. He was almost literally unstoppable. He hit 24 homers in his last 42 games, 17 in September (still a record for that month), and, possibly most incredible of all, seven in his last nine games to reach 60. Gehrig ended with 47, and only Ruth had ever hit that many before.

This is what the Pirates were watching in batting practice that day. They had never seen anything like it; indeed, they had hit only 54 homers as a team that year, less than Ruth himself. They knew they were in the path of a runaway truck. "If they had played a hundred games," said Joe Devine, then with Pittsburgh but later a Yankee scout, "I honestly believe the Yankees would have won them all. That's how scared the Pittsburgh club was."

But, though it was the Yankees' power that scared the Pirates, it was their pitching which was at least equally responsible for their sweep of the Pirates, especially the pitching of Pennock and Moore.

Moore was a fantastic story, the kind that Hollywood scriptwriters would never dare touch. He had pitched in obscurity in the minor leagues for years before being brought up by the Yankees' general manager, Ed Barrow, who thought he saw something. That something was a sinker ball which worked like magic in 1927, but did little before or after that year.

On the strength of his one great year, Moore lasted five more mediocre seasons in the majors, winning 32 and losing 37 in that span. Most telling, in all five seasons, he gave up more hits than innings pitched.

But in 1927, he was the Yankees' stopper out of the bull pen. Thirteen of his 19 victories came in relief (and only three of his seven losses) and he was also credited with 13 saves, at a time when relief pitching statistics were not so generous as they are now. He had an earned run average of 2.28.

Wilcy Moore was a one-year relief flash for the 1927 New York Yankees, who swept the World Series that year. *(George Brace)*

Moore showed his stuff to the Pirates in the first game of the '27 Series. Hoyt, the only Yankee pitcher the Pirates had any success against in the Series, was trying to hold on to a 5–3 lead when, with one out, in the eighth, Glenn Wright and Pie Traynor hit successive singles. Huggins brought in Moore.

Moore got George Grantham to ground into a force out for the second out of the inning. Joe Harris singled in a run, but then Earl Smith grounded out to end the inning and the last Pittsburgh threat of the game, and almost of the Series. In the ninth, Moore got the Pirates 1–2–3 to save the 5–4 win.

The Yankees won easily in the second game, 6–2, behind George Pipgras, and then showed both power and pitching in the third game. Pennock had a perfect game going until, with one out in the eighth, Traynor broke it up with a single to left. Disappointed at losing his shot at immortality, Pennock then yielded a run-scoring double to Clyde Barnhart before settling down again.

In the first inning, Gehrig had hit a two-run triple that would have been enough for the Yankees to win, but the New Yorkers made it a lopsided game with a six-run rally in the seventh. The big blow in the inning was a three-run homer by, who else, Ruth, as the Yankees rolled to an 8–1 victory.

To their credit, the Pirates didn't give up, though the outcome of the Series was a foregone conclusion. They battled the Yankees all the way in the fourth game, tying the score at 3–3 with two unearned runs in the seventh inning off Moore, who went all the way as a starter.

In the ninth, though, the Yankees showed they could win games even when their power was momentarily shut down. Combs led off the inning with a walk off Johnny Miljus and advanced to second when Koenig beat out a bunt.

A wild pitch moved both runners up, so Ruth was intentionally walked, to set up a force at home. Miljus still had to face Gehrig, Meusel, and Lazzeri. Surprisingly, he struck out both Gehrig and Meusel, but then the pressure told and he uncorked another wild pitch which scored Combs with the winning run.

Although the final game was won in a style that looked more like John McGraw than Babe Ruth, the Series showed what a difference power could make.

The Waner brothers actually had one more hit (11) than Ruth and Gehrig combined, but their hits included only two doubles and a triple and no home runs, and their only RBIs were Paul's three.

In contrast, Gehrig's four hits were all for extra bases—two doubles, two triples—and Ruth had two home runs among his six hits. Together, they knocked in 11 runs, with Ruth having seven of the RBIs.

That hitting, though, was as nothing compared to what the Yankees did to the St. Louis Cardinals in 1928. The Yankees not only won four straight again, but all four were lopsided wins; the closest the Cardinals came was their 4–1 loss in the opener.

In the regular season, the Yankees were not as overpowering as they'd been in 1927, and they had a battle to beat the Philadelphia Athletics by 2½ games; their margin over the same A's had been 19 games in 1927. The A's actually were in first place in early September, but the Yankees swept them in a three-game series later in the month that decided the pennant.

Although they had beaten back the A's challenge, the Yankees had serious problems. Lazzeri had hurt his shoulder and had missed 40 games, and even when he could play, he had throwing problems. Koenig wasn't quite the shortstop he'd been. At third base, Joe Dugan's bad knee kept him out of 60 games.

Meusel, though he'd had another productive year (.297 with 113 RBIs), was hurting going into the Series. Combs was out with an injured wrist. So was Pennock, and Moore was now just another arm. Ben Paschal and Cedric Durst, neither close to Combs as a player, split time in center field during the Series; Gene Robertson, another journeyman, played third. Leo Durocher, later to become a famous manager, filled in well defensively at short or second but was a weak hitter.

The Cardinal team that played the Yankees that year was a much different one from the 1926 National League champion (and World Series winner), with five new regulars. The most notable was second baseman Frankie Frisch, who had come to the Cardinals in a blockbuster trade for Rogers Hornsby. The trade had been made because Cardinal owner Sam Breadon couldn't get along with Hornsby (which hardly made Breadon unique) and John McGraw, who was not aging well, could not get along with Frisch, even though (or, perhaps, because) Frisch was McGraw's mirror image on the field.

The Cardinal team was a good one and, because of the many Yankee injuries, was actually favored to win the Series. But the oddsmakers forgot that Ruth's and Gehrig's bats were not injured.

The great Yankee power hitters put on an awesome show. Gehrig hit .545 with four home runs and nine RBIs. His slugging percentage (at-bats divided by total bases) was an incredible 1.727.

Ruth hit .625, still a Series record, and had three homers and three doubles among his ten hits. He drove in four runs and scored nine.

They had key hits in every game. In the first game, for instance, Ruth and Gehrig hit back-to-back doubles in the first inning. In the fourth, Ruth doubled again in front of a two-run homer by Meusel. In the eighth, Koenig singled, Ruth singled (his third hit of the game), and Gehrig singled in Koenig. Hoyt pitched a three-hitter, yielding only a seventh-inning run, as the Yankees won, 4–1.

Between them, Ruth and Gehrig had five of the Yankees' seven hits in the game. Ruth scored two runs, Gehrig knocked in two.

In the first inning of the second game, Gehrig boomed a three-run homer deep into the right field seats off Grover Cleveland Alexander. There would be no Series heroics for the veteran Alexander, now 41, this time around.

The Cardinals bounced back with three of their own in the second off Pipgras, but the Yankees scored a single run in the second and four more in the third, en route to a 9–3 victory. Again, Ruth and Gehrig were involved, with an inning-opening single and walk, respectively.

Gehrig continued his assault in the third game. The Cardinals actually got off to a 2–0 lead in the first inning of this game, but then Gehrig hit a solo homer in the second and a two-run job (this one inside the park) in the fourth, and the Yankees went on to a 7–3 win. The final run came on a seventh inning single by Ruth.

Gehrig wasn't through. In the fourth game, another 7–3 Yankee win, he hit his fourth homer, which tied Ruth's record, set in six games in 1926, and got his ninth RBI, breaking Meusel's record of eight set in the 1923 Series.

But as long as Ruth was with the Yankees, it was Gehrig's fate to be overshadowed, and that happened once again in that fourth game.

In the fourth inning, Ruth hit a solo homer to tie the score at 1–1. In the seventh, he came up again with the bases empty and the Cardinals back in the lead at 2–1.

Bill Sherdel, a left-hander who had won 21 games for the Cardinals in the regular season, got two strikes on Ruth and then tried to "quick pitch" Ruth, throwing a pitch before Ruth was ready.

The pitch was apparently a strike, but this maneuver had been declared illegal before the Series started, so the umpire ruled it "no pitch." The Cardinals protested bitterly, their bench emptying, with the usual result.

Ruth had watched the protest with amusement, and when Sherdel finally returned to the mound, he said something which angered Sherdel, who then made an insulting remark of his own.

"Put one in here again," Ruth said, "and I'll knock it out of the park for you."

That was in keeping with Ruth's personality. He had a habit of "predicting" home runs, though the only one most people remember is the one in the 1932 World Series when he waved vaguely at center field while hitting against Charlie Root and then put a ball in that spot with one mighty swing.

He didn't get a chance with Sherdel on the next two pitches as the Cardinal left-hander threw two balls to even the count at 2–2. Then Sherdel tried to get a fastball past Ruth, always a fatal mistake. Ruth hit it out of the park to tie the score, Gehrig followed with his home run, and the Yankees never trailed again.

Ruth had one more time at-bat in the eighth. With one out, he hit his third and longest homer of the game, on top of the pavilion in right field. That marked the second time Ruth had hit three home runs in a World Series game, a feat no other hitter managed even once until Reggie Jackson bombed three in the 1977 Series. Truly, the World Series had become Ruth's forum.

His heroics didn't stop with his hitting in this game, either. With two outs in the bottom half of the ninth and the Cardinals making a mild rally—one run scored, two runners on base—Frankie Frisch hit a pop fly in foul territory down the left field line.

Ruth, playing left field, raced over and reached into the temporary box seats that had been erected in front of the Sportsman's Park bleachers to make the catch. Still running, he held the ball aloft to show to the St. Louis crowd as he went into the Yankee dugout.

That was the last moment of glory for this great Yankee team. Age and injuries slowed the team and it didn't win another pennant until 1932. By that time, it was a vastly different team, though Ruth and Gehrig remained.

The Cardinals actually fared better in the immediate future, winning National League pennants in 1930 and 1931. And they really had nothing to be ashamed of in 1928, either. They had just run into a great team, and two superb players, in a hot spell.

Owner Breadon thought overwise. In the traditional owner's answer to all problems, he fired the manager, Bill McKechnie.

10. Pepper Stops the A's

George Earnshaw had won 24 games, Lefty Grove 20 and Rube Walberg 18 for the 1929 Philadelphia Athletics, but when the A's took the field against the Chicago Cubs in the Series opener at Wrigley Field, it was Howard Ehmke on the mound.

Howard Ehmke? Although he would be forgotten now but for the '29 Series, Ehmke had been a solid pitcher. Pitching mainly for bad clubs, Ehmke still managed to win 167 games in a 15-year career, and had one 20-win season.

But by 1929, Ehmke was 35 and obviously on the way out. He had pitched only 54⅓ innings for the A's that year, winning seven, losing two. He hadn't even pitched the last month.

Sportswriters wondered if A's manager Connie Mack was trying some bizarre strategy, remembering back to how Bucky Harris had started Curly Ogden in the last game of the 1924 Series and then yanked him after Ogden had pitched to two batters.

Mack's own players wondered what was going on. Left fielder Al Simmons rushed up to Mack when Ehmke started warming up and blurted out, "Mr. Mack! You're not going to pitch him, are you?"

"Why, yes I am, Mr. Simmons, if it's all right with you," replied Mack, with laughter in his eyes.

One of the great stories in World Series history was about to unfold, a story that had had its beginning more than a month earlier.

In late August, Mack had called Ehmke into his office and told the veteran pitcher he was going to be released. Ehmke begged for one more chance. "I've been in this game since 1914," he told Mack, "and I've never been on a winning team. Now I'm on one, and I'd like to have the honor of pitching in a World Series."

Mack thought for a time and then told Ehmke to stay behind and scout the Cubs, who were winning the National League pennant easily, and keep in shape. "Be ready to start the first game of the World Series," he said.

True to his word, then, Mack started Ehmke in the first game of that Series. Mack's decision has usually been regarded as a sentimental one, but Connie Mack was never a man to let sentiment get in the way of sound business or baseball strategy. He had his reasons for starting Ehmke, and they were all based on baseball principles.

First, the Cubs were almost entirely a right-handed hitting lineup, from Rogers Hornsby to Hack Wilson, and Mack wanted to use a right-hander, which Ehmke was. Second, they were fastball hitters, and both Earnshaw and Grove were fastball pitchers. Ehmke threw off-speed pitches, tantalizing curves and sinkers which the Cubs would have trouble timing. Third, Wrigley Field in those days had bleachers in center field, and men wore white shirts to baseball games. Pitches came right out of those white shirts and were hard to pick up; Ehmke's low sidearm, almost underhand, delivery would be especially difficult to follow, Mack reasoned.

Ehmke had his shaky moments in the first five innings. He gave up four hits in the first three innings, including a single by Norm McMillan and a double by Woody English in the third. He needed help from his defense and got it—a fantastic diving catch by third baseman Jimmy Dykes of Rigg Stephenson's liner in the fourth and a great one-handed catch by Al Simmons of Zach Taylor's drive to the left field corner in the fifth.

But in the clutch, Ehmke was tough. In the third, when English doubled, McMillan stopped at third and was left there when Ehmke struck out Hornsby and Wilson to end the inning.

In the fifth and sixth, Ehmke struck out five consecutive hitters, giving him 11 after six innings, only one less than the World Series record of the time.

Cubs' starter Charlie Root matched Ehmke zero for zero on the scoreboard for six innings, but with one out in the seventh, Jimmie Foxx homered to give the A's a 1–0 lead.

In the ninth, the A's picked up two more runs and Ehmke came out for the bottom of the ninth with a 3–0 lead and the chance to make World Series history. He had 12 strikeouts now and needed just one more for the record.

Wilson led off with a line drive that hit Ehmke in the side, but the pitcher recovered and threw him out. Dykes threw wildly trying to get Kiki Cuyler on a grounder to third, Cuyler going to second on the error, and then Stephenson singled in Cuyler for the Cubs' first run. Charlie Grimm followed with another single.

The A's infielders all shouted encouragement to Ehmke, and Mack made no indication that he would take the old pitcher out of the game. His confidence bolstered, Ehmke got Footside Blair, a pinch hitter, to hit into a force out and then struck out another pinch hitter, Chick Tolson, to end the game and set a Series record simultaneously.

The dramatic Ehmke story overshadowed Mack's general Series strategy, which was to use right-handed pitchers exclusively as starters. Left-handers Grove and

A surprise choice as a starter in the 1929 World Series, Howard Emhke set a Series record with 13 strikeouts. *(George Brace)*

Walberg would be held back for relief duties only, though Grove was starting a run of seven straight 20-win seasons and was probably the best pitcher in baseball at the time. But Mack knew what many have forgotten since: Grove was a very effective pitcher in relief; as a reliever he won 33 games and saved another 55 during his career.

And, as a matter of fact, he saved the very next game for the A's, in relief of right-handed starter Earnshaw. Coming in with two outs in the fifth, Grove struck out pinch hitter Gabby Hartnett and went on to pitch 4⅓ scoreless innings in the 9–3 A's victory.

That win made it ten straight for the American League champions in Series play. The National League had not won since Grover Cleveland Alexander had struck out Tony Lazzeri in the final game of the 1926 Series, and it was beginning to look as if they'd never win again.

The Cubs ended all that speculation in the next game with a 3–1 win. Mack started Earnshaw again, but he could not match the Cubs' Guy Bush. That game, however, was quickly overshadowed by the dramatics of the fourth game, one of the most unusual in Series history.

Still sticking with his right-handed pitching policy, Mack started Jack Quinn in this game. This was even more of a gamble than his choice of Ehmke in the first game, Quinn was 45 (!), in his 19th big league season. He had won 11 games that year, but mostly because of the hitting behind him; his ERA was a quite ordinary 3.97, and he had allowed 182 hits in 161 innings.

Quinn was not the mystery to the Cubs that Ehmke had been, giving up seven runs (five earned) in five innings, before being relieved by Walberg.

With two runs in the fourth, five in the sixth, and a single run in the seventh, the Cubs were breezing with an 8–0 lead, on their way to tying up the Series.

Al Simmons was a big hitter for the Philadelphia Athletics in the 1929–31 World Series. *(George Brace)*

Lefty Grove starred both as a starter and as a reliever in three consecutive World Series, 1929–31. *(George Brace)*

Simmons led off the bottom of the seventh with a home run, which spoiled Root's bid for a shutout but otherwise didn't seem to matter. Then, Foxx, Bing Miller, Dykes, and Joe Boley singled in succession, two more runs scoring. It was beginning to get interesting.

Pinch hitter George Burns popped up, but then Max Bishop singled in the fourth run of the inning, and Chicago manager Joe McCarthy—who would go on to greater fame as a Yankee manager—relieved Root with left-hander Art Nehf.

Mule Haas lined a ball to center that should have been caught by Wilson, but Hack lost the ball in the sun and it went over his head, Haas came all the way around for a three-run, inside-the-park home run, and the A's were now within a run of the Cubs.

Nehf then walked Cochrane, and McCarthy made another pitching change, bringing in Sheriff Blake. Simmons, who had started the fireworks with his home run, singled and so did Foxx, and the second hit tied the score.

The beleaguered McCarthy, who was certainly getting his exercise walking from the dugout to the mound, brought in the fourth pitcher of the inning, Pat Malone. He hit Miller with a pitch, which loaded the bases, and then gave up a two-run double to Dykes, and the A's led, 10–8. Finally, Malone struck out Boley and Burns to end the inning.

It was, of course, the biggest inning in World Series history and, most remarkably, had all been accomplished before the second out was even recorded. How do you explain an inning like that? You don't. Baseball is a game of percentages, but only in the long run. In a short period—a game, an inning—it is the most unpredictable of games.

Grove came in to shut out the Cubs for the final two innings, striking out four as he retired the shocked Chicagoans 1–2–3 in each inning.

Few expected the Cubs to come back after that, but they made a battle of it in the fifth game. Mack brought Ehmke back, but this time, the Cubs knocked him out with two runs in the fourth, forcing Mack to bring in Walberg.

Malone had a two-hitter going for eight innings and the Cubs took a 2–0 lead into the ninth, but it wasn't enough.

Very quickly, the A's tied the score as Bishop singled and Haas homered. Simmons doubled and Malone walked Foxx intentionally, hoping to set up a double play. But Miller singled to score Simmons, and it was all over.

Memory can play tricks. What everybody remembers most about the 1929 Series is that Mack got away with a daring bit of strategy in pitching Ehmke. The real lesson of that Series is that the A's won *despite* Mack's pitching strategy.

Mack started all right-handers in the five games, but after the first game, the Cubs had little trouble with any of them. Earnshaw was knocked out of one game and, though he pitched a complete game in his second start, lost the game; Ehmke was knocked out in his second start; and Quinn was blasted.

In contrast, left-handers Grove and Walberg each pitched 6⅓ scoreless innings, and each gave up only three hits. Grove struck out ten and got two saves; Walberg had eight strikeouts and one win.

If Grove and Walberg had started, the A's probably would have done just as well. But Ehmke made a better story.

That was a great Athletics team, some think as good as the more famous Yankee dynasty that went just before them. Grove and Earnshaw were overpowering pitchers, Grove the best left-hander in American League history. Mickey Cochrane gets some votes as the best catcher of all time. Foxx was second only to Ruth as a power hitter, sometimes flattening baseballs because he hit them so hard. Simmons was a devastating hitter, particularly with men on base; he had 157 and 165 RBIs in 1929 and 1930.

Like the Yankees, they won three straight pennants. On either side of those pennants, they finished second—to the Yankees both times—and averaged 101 victories a season for that five-year span.

In their championship years, they were even more dominant than the Yankees had been, winning by margins of 18, 8, and 13½. They weren't quite so overpowering in Series play as the Yankees had been in 1927 and 1928, but when they won another World Series in 1930 and their third straight pennant in 1931, they had a chance to do what nobody else, not even the Yankees, had yet done: win three straight World Series.

Their 1931 opponents were the St. Louis Cardinals, the same team they had beaten in 1930, but there was one significant difference in the Cardinal lineup: Pepper Martin.

Martin played 13 years with the Cardinals and was a solid player for most of that time, with a lifetime batting average of .298. But his name is remembered by baseball fans because of what he did in the 1931 Series, when he was a hitting, running, and fielding marvel.

Pepper was a typical Cardinal player of that era—young, enthusiastic, and under-paid. One of the reasons he was even in the lineup, in center field, was because Branch Rickey preferred to play him (with a $4,500 salary) rather than Taylor Douthit, who was getting $14,000 before Rickey traded him early in the 1931 season.

Martin's background was colorful. His first year with St. Louis, he had hitchhiked to the Cardinals' spring training camp in Florida from Oklahoma, spending a night in jail during the trip. He reported looking as if he should go back there immediately.

On the field, he was awkward and aggressive, traits which led him to be nicknamed "The Wild Horse of the Osage." He had good speed which helped him both as a base runner (he led the league in stolen bases three times) and as an outfielder. When he was brought in to play third base later in his career, he disdained finesse, sometimes knocking balls down with his chest to make the play.

He had come up to the Cardinals briefly as early as 1928, but it was not until Rickey

Mickey Cochrane played for Philadelphia and Detroit in the World Series and even managed the 1935 Tigers to a championship. *(Detroit Tigers)*

Jimmie Foxx was one of the best hitters in World Series history for the 1929–31 Philadelphia Athletics. *(George Brace)*

traded Douthit in 1931 that Martin became a regular, and he responded with a .300 season. Still, few thought he would be a big factor in the Series—although J. Roy Stockton of the *St. Louis Post-Dispatch* suggested he might be a World Series hero.

Pepper himself wasn't so optimistic. Before the start of the Series, he prayed, "Please God, let me do well." He started well, but the Cardinals didn't. He had a first-inning double and two singles, and he stole a base, but Grove kept the rest of the St. Louis team under control in a 6–2 A's win.

The second game was all Martin and Bill Hallahan, who pitched a three-hitter to top Earnshaw, 2–0.

Martin was responsible for both runs. In the second inning, he stretched a single into a double with a belly slide, stole third, and scored on Jimmie Wilson's fly ball.

In the seventh, he singled, stole second, went to third on an infield out, and dived home on a squeeze bunt by Charlie Gelbert. He was 5-for-7 in the first two games, with three stolen bases.

There was a final bit of drama before the Cards could put the game away, though. With two on and two out in the A's half of the ninth, pinch hitter Jimmy Moore swung and missed the third strike, but catcher Wilson dropped the ball.

Wilson could have either tagged Moore for the third out or thrown to first. Instead, he threw to third baseman Jake Flowers. "I just made a dumb play," he said later in the clubhouse.

But, so did Flowers. Not realizing that Wilson had not caught the third strike, he made no attempt to tag third for the force out but stood holding the ball as the runners advanced and Moore finally ran to first. The reason: Flowers was looking for a nephew in the stands. Thinking the game was over, he was going to throw the ball to his nephew. Fortunately, he couldn't find his nephew because such a throw would have given the A's two runs and tied the game.

Hallahan then got Bishop to hit a foul pop-up down the first base line that first baseman Jim Bottomley grabbed as he slammed into the seats.

Rain delayed the third game for a day, which enabled Mack to come back with his ace, Grove, who had won 31 games and lost only four that year.

Martin had been so spectacular in the first two games that even the Philadelphia fans cheered him before the start of this game, and he responded by going 2-for-4 against the great Grove, a single and a double. He scored twice and spit baller Burleigh Grimes beat Grove, 5–2.

Pepper was the only man between Earnshaw and a no-hitter in the next game, as he got the only two hits, one of them a double, that Earnshaw yielded in a 3–0 win that tied the Series. Oh, yes, Martin stole another base.

In game five, Hallahan won again, 5–1. This time, Martin scored a run, had three hits—one of them a home run—and knocked in four of his team's five runs.

Pepper Martin staged a virtual one-man show in 1931 as his St. Louis Cardinals upset Philadelphia. *(George Brace)*

Had it not been for Martin's great play, the A's might well have beaten the Cardinals in five games. Instead, they were trailing in the Series as they went into the sixth game. This time, Grove held Martin hitless in an 8–1 win. That was perhaps the reason Mack announced after the game that he felt Grove was superior to both of his other great left-handers, Rube Waddell and Eddie Plank.

In the seventh game, as Grimes beat Earnshaw, 4–2, Martin was again hitless, but he still made a contribution, stealing a base.

And, fittingly, it was Martin who ended the game and the Series. With the tying runs on base for the A's in the ninth, Cardinal manager Gabby Street brought in his ace, Hallahan, to nail down the win. Bishop hit a ball sharply to left-center, but Martin raced over to make the catch, juggling it for one heart-stopping moment.

For the Series, Martin had hit .500 with 12 hits in 24 at-bats, including four doubles and one home run. He had stolen five bases. Most important, he had unsettled the Athletics, who were really the better team, and made it possible for his team to pull off a big upset.

In the clubhouse, Commissioner Landis told him, "Young man, I'd rather trade places with you than with any man in the country."

Replied Martin: "Why, that'll be fine, Judge, if we can trade salaries, too."

11. "Me 'n' Paul" Beat the Tigers

It was the day before the 1934 World Series was to start and the Detroit Tigers were taking batting practice at Navin Field. Hank Greenberg, a slugger who would go on to hit 58 home runs in 1938, was in the batting cage.

St. Louis Cardinal pitcher Dizzy Dean, in street clothes, walked into the cage and took the bat out of the hands of the startled Greenberg. "Here, Moe, let me show you how to do it," said Dean, and he drove a pitch into the left field bleachers.

That was typical of the 1934 Series, one of the most bitterly fought Series ever and the only one in which a player was ejected because spectators got out of control. The Cardinals continually upstaged the Tigers and, not incidentally, won the Series.

The Tigers were an outstanding team, Detroit's first pennant winner since 1909, when Ty Cobb was in the early years of his career.

The infield was particularly good, starting with catcher and playing manager Mickey Cochrane, who had been traded to the Tigers by Connie Mack before the 1934 season. Cochrane had hit .320, coincidentally his lifetime major league average, and provided the leadership a championship club needs.

At first base, Greenberg had hit a league-leading 63 doubles while knocking in 139 runs and batting .339. At second base, the smooth-fielding Charley Gehringer had led the league with 214 hits and 134 runs while batting .356 and knocking in 127 runs.

Third baseman Marv Owen had hit .317. Shortstop Billy Rogell, playing a position where defensive ability usually makes up for weak hitting, hit .296 and knocked in 100 runs.

In the outfield, Jo-Jo White hit .313 and Goose Goslin .305. Goslin had 100 RBIs, the fourth Tiger to have at least that many. Not surprisingly, Detroit had led the league with 958 runs.

The pitching, too, was good. Schoolboy Rowe had won 24 and curve ball specialist Tommy Bridges 22. Rookie submariner Eldon Auker and Firpo Marberry had each won 15 games.

But the Tigers were merely another good team. The Cardinals were unique, the most colorful team in baseball history, the famed "Gas House Gang."

There have been better teams—this was not even the best team in Cardinal history—but the 1934 Cards will always have a spot in baseball history. The Great Depression was in full swing (one reason the Cardinals drew only 334,000 that season) and the nation needed entertainment. The Gas House Gang provided it in a big way.

One club has never had such a collection of characters. Chief among them were:

• Dizzy Dean. An arm injury curtailed Dean's brilliant career, but for a short period, he was a great pitcher; his 30 wins in 1934 is a record for National League pitchers in the lively ball era.

Dean's nickname was a natural. He once gave out three different birthdates and birthplaces to interviewers because, he explained, he wanted each writer to have his own special story. He was named Jay Hanna at birth but adopted the names of Jerome Herman when a neighbor's son with that name died.

Dizzy had a tendency to make outrageous claims for himself, but as he said, "It ain't braggin' if you do it."

• Pepper Martin. The hero of the 1931 Series, Martin was an irrepressible character who wore no underwear (on or off the field) and not even a jockstrap to protect himself against the hard smashes at third, where he'd been moved from center field. He slid head first into bases—sometimes, even first base—and played third with reckless abandon. He hated it when hitters bunted on him, and he'd sometimes pick up a bunt and throw the ball at the runner, not to first base.

• Left fielder Joe Medwick. A tremendous hitter who ran the bases aggressively, a trait which got him into trouble in the final game of this Series, Medwick did not defer to anybody. One time he was embroiled in a contract dispute with tightfisted St. Louis owner Sam Breadon. The difference was $2,000, and Breadon claimed it was the principle that concerned him, not the money. "I'd throw the $2,000 out my window," he claimed, dramatically. Medwick countered, "If you threw $2,000 out the window, your hand would still be on it."

• Shortstop Leo Durocher, who owed everybody in town and wasn't nicknamed "The Lip" for nothing. Shortly after the Cards got him in a trade, Durocher walked into general manager Branch Rickey's office and told Rickey he'd win the pennant for him—but only after he got a raise.

• Pitcher Dazzy Vance. The one-time fireballer was near the end of the line—he won only four games in the 1934 season—but he showed he belonged by drinking a concoction which he called the "Dazz-Marie." He poured rye, bourbon, Scotch, gin, sloe gin, vermouth, brandy, and Benedictine into an oversized, ice-laden glass. Then he added powdered sugar and topped it with a cherry.

• Center fielder Ernie Orsatti, who acted in a movie, *Death on the Diamond,* during the 1934 season, in a scene shot at Sportsman's Park before a game. The handsome

Orsatti liked to go out on the town, and he bribed the hotel operator to have calls transferred from his room to the hotel's supper club. When manager Frankie Frisch made a curfew call, Orsatti feigned a yawn to persuade the skeptical Frisch that he'd been in bed already.

- Rookie catcher Bill DeLancey, who would not let even the great Dean relax. One time, Dizzy was loafing along with a big lead when DeLancey zinged the ball back faster than Dean had pitched it, and then ran out to the mound. "If you ever throw any of that crap again when I'm catching," DeLancey said, "I'll knock you right on your seat."

Dean and Martin were the zaniest of the bunch. Dean once walked into the Brooklyn clubhouse as Dodger manager Casey Stengel was going over the Cardinal hitters. "When you're through," he told Stengel, "I'll tell you how I'm going to pitch to your fellas." He did—and still beat the Dodgers.

Another time, he told the Boston Braves he would use only a fastball, which he did. He won that game, too.

Martin raced cars in the off-season. Once he showed up for a game with his clothes even dirtier than usual and announced that he'd been in a foot race, fallen, and still won. His prize for winning: two quarts of strawberry ice cream.

Together, Dean and Martin would do anything. Once, at the instigation of first baseman Rip Collins, they pretended to fight in a hotel lobby. Before they did, they stuffed their mouths with popcorn. When they swung at each other, the popcorn flew out of their mouths, looking like teeth to horrified onlookers.

Another time, they dressed up as painters and disrupted a convention meeting in the hotel in which they were staying. At other times, they'd drop sacks of water from their hotel windows on people passing by. If one of the people happened to be manager Frisch, so much the better.

Frisch was not a bland character himself. He had been known from the start of his career for his hot temper, and he was a fierce competitor. Those two characteristics had gotten him traded after the 1926 season from the New York Giants, and he had a running feud with John McGraw that ended only two years before McGraw's death in 1934.

The relationship between Frisch and McGraw was always a volatile one. The friction had started between the two in 1924, shortly after Frisch had been named captain of the Giants. In a guest column in a newspaper, McGraw criticized Frisch. Among other things, he "wrote" that "Frisch, by being given free rein, developed an individuality that proved to be a detriment to the teamwork of my other players."

The final blow came in 1926, in a game against St. Louis. The Cardinals had runners on first and third and McGraw suspected they would try a double steal. He signalled for his catcher to fake a throw to second and throw instead to the pitcher, hoping to trap the runner off third.

A Hall of Fame player, Frankie Frisch was the playing-manager as the St. Louis Cardinals won the 1934 World Series. *(George Brace)*

Because the throw would not go through to second, neither the second baseman nor the shortstop needed to cover the base. Apparently, Frisch missed the sign, however, and when the Cardinal runner on first broke for second, he moved to cover the base.

The Cardinal hitter, Tommy Thevenow, hit a slow grounder to the right side. Frisch could normally have gotten the ball, but he couldn't recover in time and the ball went through for a hit.

When the Giants came back to the dugout, McGraw started in on Frisch, "You dumb Dutchman . . . you cement head."

After the game, Frisch jumped the club. He eventually returned, but he knew his days as a Giant were numbered. McGraw would never allow such insubordination. After the season, Frisch was traded for Rogers Hornsby—a trade McGraw had earlier insisted he would never make.

Frisch was a great player who had come directly to the majors from Fordham; thus, his nickname of "The Fordham Flash." By 1934, he was nearing 37 (though his official age was a year younger; like many athletes, Frisch had fudged on his age), and his great skills were eroding. In spring training, Branch Rickey told an aide that he should have traded Frisch, and Frank himself had amended his nickname to "The Old Flash."

But he was a natural leader, and it was that quality that Breadon and Rickey had recognized in naming Frisch manager of the Cardinals in July of 1933, replacing Gabby Street.

It took all of Frisch's leadership qualities to manage the 1934 Cardinals, who spent almost as much time fighting among themselves as against their opponents.

Most of the trouble came between Medwick and Dean. One time, Dean and Medwick were shouting at each other from opposite ends of the dugout. Dizzy and his brother, Paul, started walking toward Medwick, who picked up his bat and told them he'd use it to separate them.

Later in the same game, Medwick hit a grand-slam homer. In the dugout, he took a mouthful of water from the water cooler and spat it out on Dean's shoes. "All right, you big meathead," he told Dean, "there's your three runs back and one extra. Let's see you hold the damned lead."

But the Cardinals were too good a team to let their inner squabbling stop them. Trailing most of the season, they passed the Giants in September and won by two games.

The most memorable games were a doubleheader with Brooklyn. Dizzy pitched a three-hit shutout to win the first game, and Paul pitched a no-hitter in the second game.

"Shucks, if I'd known Paul was going to throw a no-hitter, I'd have thrown one, too," Dizzy announced.

Stengel, coaching third base that day, moaned, "Eighteen innings and I didn't have any company at all."

Before the season, Dean had announced that "Me 'n' Paul" would win 45 games.

Everybody had laughed, because Paul was a rookie in 1934. In fact, the Dean brothers won 49, Paul contributing 19. For perhaps the only time in his life, Dizzy had been too modest.

The morning of the World Series opener, Dizzy and Paul were invited to have breakfast with Henry Ford. Dizzy was his usual unabashed self. Shaking Ford's hand vigorously, he said, "Put 'er there, Henry. I'm sure glad to be here 'cause I heard so much about you, but I'm sorry, I'm gonna have to make pussycats out of your Tigers."

Arriving late at the park, Dean draped a tiger skin around his baseball uniform and momentarily joined a band playing on the field, grabbing a tuba.

He then won the Series opener, 8–3.

For reasons which were never adequately explained, Detroit manager Cochrane had passed over his top pitchers and started Alvin "General" Crowder, a late-season pickup, in the opener.

It was not an inspired decision. The Cardinals knocked Crowder out in the sixth inning with their final four runs; Dean had an 8–1 lead at that point and breezed home.

He even had time to do some clowning, when he was pitching to Greenberg in the eighth inning with a six-run lead and nobody on base. Frisch came in from second base and threatened to take him out.

Dizzy just laughed. "Oh, Frankie," he said, "you ain't gonna take out Ol' Diz. All these good folks would think you was crazy. I'm just figurin' that Moe can't hit my high hard one."

Dizzy was wrong. Greenberg hit the next pitch deep into the left field seats. Dean assured Frisch it wouldn't happen again and admitted, "You're right, Moe can hit the dog-shit out of a high fast one."

The term "Moe" was, of course, a derogatory name for a Jewish ball player. It was not an enlightened era, and ball players often used such epithets to taunt opponents.

The bench jockeying in this Series was particularly vicious. The Cardinals had heard an interview that Schoolboy Rowe had given on the radio in which he had said at one point, "How am I doin', Edna?" to his listening fiancee, and Rowe heard that phrase over and over from the St. Louis dugout when he was pitching.

On the field, too, competition was fierce, even by World Series standards. Dean was never reluctant to throw his fastball at a hitter who tried to crowd the plate, and he did that frequently in the Series. Martin dove headlong into Tigers covering bases and even put Cochrane into the hospital overnight with one collision. In retaliation, Tiger runners banged so hard and so frequently into Frisch at second base that the Cardinal manager looked like a bowling ball.

Frisch tried some strategy for the second game, starting Bill Hallahan instead of Paul Dean. He had his reasons. He felt it would be better for rookie Paul to pitch his first game before a hometown crowd and though Hallahan had won only eight games that season, he was a veteran of World Series play.

In fact, Hallahan pitched well enough to win and he was leading, 2–1, going into the ninth, against Rowe, whose ears were red from the roasting he was getting from the Cardinal dugout for his ill-advised radio ad-lib.

Then Pete Fox led off with a single and was sacrificed to second by Rowe. Gerald "Gee" Walker hit a pop foul that should have been caught but dropped between catcher DeLancey and first baseman Collins. Walker then singled in Fox to tie the score. Frisch brought in Bill Walker who picked Gee Walker off first and struck out Cochrane to end the inning and send the game into extra innings.

The game stayed at 2–2 until the 12th when, with one out, Gehringer and Greenberg walked and Goslin singled in Gehringer to win the game.

The angry Frisch stormed into the clubhouse and told his players, "You chowder-heads blew the damned ball game for Hallahan."

McGraw would have been proud of him.

Abusive oratory wasn't all that Frisch had learned from McGraw, as he showed the next day. In the fifth inning, with the Cardinals already leading, 2–0, Pepper Martin opened with a double and Jack Rothrock tripled. The Tiger infield drew in to cut off a fourth run that could put the game out of reach.

In McGraw's playing days, the Orioles had perfected a maneuver called the "Baltimore chop," hitting down on the ball and bouncing it so high in the air that a hitter would be to first base before an infielder could make the play. Frisch did the same thing with a Bridges' curve, bouncing it high off the infield and over the head of second baseman Gehringer for a run-producing single.

Given that cushion, Paul Dean pitched shutout ball for eight innings and won, 4–1.

On and off the field, the Series was heating up. DeLancey was fined $50 for a profane outburst to umpire Brick Owens. Bill Klem, the most famous umpire in baseball history, got into an argument in a hotel elevator with Detroit's Goslin. Judge Landis fined them both.

The Cardinal bench jockeys got more ammunition when a Detroit newspaper ran a picture of Cochrane in the hospital and labeled it, "Our Stricken Leader."

Frisch and Durocher were so angered by what they regarded as overly aggressive base running by White, Detroit's lead-off hitter, that they gave him the one-two when White next slid into second: Leo sat on White's head, Frisch on his back.

The Cardinals lost the next game, 10–4, and seemed for a time to have lost their pitching ace. Pinch-running for Spud Davis in the fourth inning, during which the Cards tied the score at 4–4, Dizzy Dean was hit in the forehead on a throw to first by Detroit shortstop Rogell. That broke up the double play, but Dean collapsed and was carried off the field.

It looked serious, but brother Paul was convinced Dizzy was all right. Why? "Because he was talking," said Paul. "He wasn't saying nuthin', just talkin'."

In the hospital later, Dizzy told reporters, "They x-rayed my head and found nothing. I saw stars, moons, and all sorts of animals, but no Tigers."

Why did Frisch put Dean in as a pinch runner. "For one thing," he told reporters, "we do have only a 21-man roster, and Spud is slow. For another, Dean is a helluva good athlete, and fast. For a third . . ." Frisch paused and admitted, "For a third, the hard-playing S.O.B. was down there running himself for Davis."

That's what it was like managing the Gas House Gang.

The next day, though, Dean was pitching again. Before the game, Rogell kidded him by giving him a World War I helmet. Dizzy pitched like a healthy man—six hits and three runs (only two earned) in eight innings—but Bridges pitched even better for Detroit, and the Tigers won, 3–1.

So the Tigers had a 3–2 lead in the Series, and they were going back to Detroit for the final two games, if both were needed. Their ace, Rowe, was well rested.

Before the Series had started, the Tigers had had trouble taking the Cardinals seriously. The Cards' reputation for bizarre behavior had overshadowed their playing ability in the minds of the Detroit players. Only Cochrane, who was still smarting from the way Martin had run wild on the bases, stealing five times, in the 1931 Series, respected the Cardinals. In vain, he cautioned his players against overconfidence.

Now it seemed the Tiger players had been right and Cochrane wrong. The Series seemed in the bag for Detroit.

But momentum in a short Series can swing back and forth quickly, and events were turning in the Cardinals' favor. The first sign came when Rowe showed up for the game with an injured pitching hand for reasons which were never adequately explained—especially by Rowe, who later gave four different accounts of his injury.

St. Louis scored in the first on a double by Rothrock and a single by Medwick. Detroit tied it in the third when White walked with two outs, stole second and went to third on an error by Frisch, and scored on Cochrane's infield single.

In the St. Louis half of the fifth, Durocher led off with a single. It was one of three hits in the game for Leo, who had been taunted as "No Hit" by the Tiger bench jockeys earlier in the Series.

Paul Dean sacrificed Durocher to second. Martin singled to score Durocher, went to second on the throw to the plate by Goslin, and moved to third when the poor throw got by Cochrane. He scored on Rothrock's groundout to shortstop.

The Tigers tied it in the bottom of the sixth. White led off with a walk and went to third on Cochrane's single. Gehringer grounded back to the mound, but the ball went through Paul Dean's legs for an error, White scoring. Goslin's attempted sacrifice was turned into a force out at third, and Rogell flied to center, Gehringer going to third after the catch. Greenberg, always at his most deadly with men on base, singled in Gehringer with the tying run.

But Paul Dean got his lead back in the top of the seventh when he singled after a double by Durocher, and he held that 4–3 lead for the final three innings. It got a little hairy at times: Durocher threw out Fox at the plate to prevent a tying run from scoring in the seventh, and the Tigers slammed three hits in the seventh and eighth.

In the ninth, though, Paul set down the Tigers 1–2–3, and the Series was tied again.

The final game, though it became a lopsided one, had some moments of high drama. One of them came in the selection of the Cardinals' starting pitcher, as Frisch tried a little child psychology on Dizzy Dean, who was certainly a natural for it.

Frisch, asked by reporters after the sixth game who his starter would be the next day, replied, "Hallahan." He was lying.

"I knew it had to be Dizzy," Frisch said later. "I had great respect for Hallahan in a clutch, but Dean had got us that far. He deserved to win or lose it. But, I wanted him to want it badly enough so that he wouldn't sit up and swap stories with Will Rogers or show off with his friends."

Frisch's strategy worked. When Dean heard his manager say, "Hallahan," to reporters, he followed Frisch into the showers, begging and pleading to have the chance to win the Series the next day. Frisch listened to him and then extracted a promise: that Dizzy would get a good night's sleep. "You win this damned game," he told Dean, "and, Depression or not, you'll be able to write your own ticket for $50,000 or more in extras."

Dizzy's natural cockiness was back the next day. When he saw Auker warming up for Detroit, he went over and pretended to watch the submariner for a time. Then he turned to Cochrane and said, "He won't do, Mickey."

He was right, as the Tigers found out quickly, in the third inning.

Dean himself started the excitement when, with one out, he stretched what should have been a single to left into a double, sliding in just ahead of Goslin's throw.

Martin beat out a slow roller—Dizzy going to third on the play—and then stole second. Cochrane then ordered Auker to walk Rothrock intentionally to load the bases and bring up Frisch. It seemed the right move. Rothrock had been tough in the clutch, winding up with six RBIs in the Series, tops among the Cards. Frisch batted a weak .194.

This was the 50th World Series game for Frisch, but it had never become routine for him. He had, in fact, been so nervous before this game that he couldn't eat any breakfast; a little tomato juice was all he could trust to stay on his stomach.

He was tired, beat up from all the hard slides into second; his 37-year-old legs had taken a pounding playing through the hot summer on the concrete-like infield at Sportsman's Park in St. Louis.

Frisch had long been known as a "money player," the kind of player who got the clutch hit or made the big play in the field when it counted most. Plays didn't come any bigger than this: bases loaded in the seventh game of a World Series.

All hitters have a ritual they go through before they hit, partly superstition and partly preparation. Frisch went through his. First, he rubbed the toe of his left shoe on the back of his right stocking. He took a choked grip on his bat, spread his legs and worked the bat up and down, loose-wristed. Then he brought it up and waggled it back and forth, facing Auker. He was ready.

Auker ran the count to 3–and–2, and then Frisch fouled off four consecutive pitches. Finally, Auker came in with a sweeping curve and Frisch lined it just over Greenberg's glove and into the right field corner. Three runs scored, and Frisch went into second with a double.

That finished Auker. Cochrane brought in Rowe, who had pitched the day before; Rowe would have the whole winter to rest, after all. But the Detroit ace didn't have it. Although he got Medwick to ground out for the second out, Collins then singled and DeLancey doubled for two more runs. Cochrane brought in reliever Chief Hogsett.

And still, the Cardinals weren't finished. Orsatti walked and Durocher singled to load the bases. Dean beat out an infield hit to score one run and Martin walked on four pitches, forcing in the seventh run of the inning.

Dizzy Dean lived up to his bragging statement in the 1934 World Series. *(George Brace)*

Joe Medwick, pictured in a quieter moment, had to be removed from the last game of the '34 World Series when angry Detroit fans threw garbage on the field. *(St. Louis Cardinals)*

Bridges was brought in by the dazed Cochrane, and he finally got the Tigers out of the inning by getting Rothrock to hit into a force-out.

But the Series was over. Dean was bearing down, and he was pitching as if he were protecting a one-run lead. The Tigers, the best-hitting team in baseball, got just six hits, and Dizzy didn't walk a man, striking out five. He didn't yield a hit until the fourth, and the Tigers got a man as far as second only three times in the game. The only Tiger who bothered Dean at all was Fox, who doubled twice, the sole extra-base hits for Detroit.

Meanwhile, the Cardinals were taking batting practice. All ten Cardinals who played got at least one hit; Collins garnered four; and as a team, the Cardinals had 17.

They scored twice more in the sixth as well as in the seventh, and the most exciting moment of the game after the deciding third inning came in the sixth.

In the top of the inning, Medwick had hit a long drive that bounced off the right-center field wall, scoring Martin, who had singled. Going successfully for a triple, his 11th hit in the Series (one short of the existing record), he slid hard into Detroit third baseman Owen. The two became entangled and kicked back at each other as they shook loose, Owen from frustration and Medwick as an expression of his normal temperament. The fans booed and booed, and they didn't forget when Medwick scored on Collins' fourth hit, a single.

When the Cardinals ran out to the field in the bottom of the sixth, the Detroit fans showered a barrage of garbage down on Medwick. He retreated to the dugout, came out, and retreated again—three times in all. The fans showed no signs of stopping their barrage.

"They can't do that to you, Joey," Durocher told him. "Don't back off."

"If you're so damned brave," snapped back Medwick, "why don't you play left field and let me play shortstop?"

Commissioner Landis sat with chin on railing as the fans' barrage continued for a full 20 minutes. If he had truly been as courageous as his admirers claimed, he would have forfeited the game to the Cardinals.

But Landis didn't want to forfeit a Series game. He considered that the Cardinals had a 9–0 lead and, behind Dean, weren't likely to lose it (although the Chicago Cubs had blown an 8–0 lead in a ten-run inning in the 1929 Series). He told Frisch to put in a replacement for Medwick.

Chick Fullis went in for Medwick and later got a hit. The Cardinals went on to an 11–0 lead and Medwick was given a police escort until the Cardinals caught a midnight sleeper train back to St. Louis.

Before that, Dizzy lectured the press.

"Imagine, back there in the spring when I said me 'n' Paul would win 45 games and none of you people would believe me. For pity sake, I didn't even know myself then how good we were."

12. McCarthy Pushes the Buttons

For four years, 1936–39, it was the New York Yankees against the world. The world lost.

The Yankees in that period didn't just win, they annihilated their opponents. They won four straight pennants by margins of 19½, 13, 9½, and 17, an average of nearly 15 games. They won four straight World Series, losing only three games in that stretch. They scored a record 18 runs in one Series game.

Because the Yankees have dominated baseball since they traded for Babe Ruth, the standard for measuring Yankee champions is always other Yankee teams, but even matched against the other great Yankee dynasties, the 1936–39 champions look good.

The most popular choice as the best team of all time has been the 1927 Yankees, at least partially because that club had the charismatic Ruth in the year in which he hit 60 home runs. But that Yankee team didn't have the consistency of the 1936–39 Yanks, winning but three straight pennants and only two World Series.

The 1949–53 Yankees surpassed the record of four straight and even won five straight World Series, a mark which probably will never be equalled. But that team had to scramble to win pennants. Their largest winning margin was seven games, three pennants were won by three games or less and once, in '49, they had to go to the last game of the season to win.

The 1960–64 Yankees also won five straight pennants, but that team lost three of the five World Series in which it played—and got two managers fired. Moreover, it collapsed and fell out of contention after 1964, while the 1936–39 Yankees came back to win three more pennants, 1941–43, making it seven pennants in eight years.

The 1936 Yankees were the first Yankee team to win a pennant without Babe Ruth, who had been traded to the Boston Braves in 1934 for a pitiful end to a great career. But the 1936 team had Lou Gehrig as a holdover from 1927, catcher Bill Dickey, and

Lou Gehrig played in Babe Ruth's shadow, but he was still the all-time first baseman in World Series history. *(New York Yankees)*

rookie center fielder Joe DiMaggio; all three were probably as good as anybody who ever played their positions.

The era of buying players from less prosperous major league teams was coming to a close, so the Yankees were spending more money on developing a minor league system that ranked with the best, and they also bought minor league players from other organizations. DiMaggio had been bought from the San Francisco Seals, an independent team in the Pacific Coast League. Second baseman Joe Gordon came up from the Yankee system in 1938, outfielder Charley Keller in 1939. When Tommy Henrich was cut loose from the Cleveland farm system by Commissioner Landis because of rule-breaking by the Indians, the Yankees signed him.

The Yankees didn't have to make a lot of changes in that four-year stretch. Five of their eight (nonpitching) regulars remained the same, and the top three starters were Red Ruffing, Lefty Gomez, and Monte Pearson throughout the streak.

Gordon replaced Tony Lazzeri at second, and Keller and Henrich broke into the outfield lineup, Henrich becoming the starter in 1938 and Keller replacing him in 1939.

But there was one sad change: The great Gehrig, the victim of a version of polio so rare it is still known today as the "Lou Gehrig disease," ended his consecutive game record in 1939 and died two years later.

The 1936 Series was another "Subway Series," the first time the Yankees and Giants had met since 1923 and the most competitive of the four Series the Yankees won in this stretch.

The Giants were not a great club but they had two great players. One was Mel Ott, who hit 33 home runs and would go on to hit 511 to set a National League record, since broken.

The other was Carl Hubbell, the left-handed, screwball-throwing pitcher was aptly nicknamed "The Meal Ticket." Hubbell had had a great season, winning 26 and losing only six, and winning his last 16 games. His earned run average, best in the league, was 2.31. Because pitchers can be so dominant in a short Series, fans believe that Hubbell would give the Giants a chance, though a slim one.

Hubbell, in fact, got the Giants off winging in the first game, played in a steady drizzle, the worst weather conditions since the final game of the 1925 Series.

George Selkirk homered off Hubbell in the third to give the Yankees a momentary lead at 1–0, but Giants shortstop Dick Bartell evened it in the fifth with a solo homer.

The Giants went ahead in the sixth when Ott doubled and scored on a single by Gus Mancuso and then broke it open with a four-run rally in the eighth, during which the Yankees uncharacteristically made four errors.

Manager Bill Terry, who had played in only 79 regular season games, opened the inning with a single, and Hubbell contributed a single himself during the rally.

Carl Hubbell was the "Meal Ticket" for the New York Giants, but even Hubbell couldn't stop the awesome Yankees in the World Series. *(George Brace)*

Hubbell probably didn't even need those last four runs. He gave up only two hits over the last five innings and set the Yankees down 1–2–3 in the ninth to win, 6–1.

The dam burst in the second game, though, as the Yankees embarrassed the Giants with an 18–4 shellacking. Every Yankee starter, including pitcher Lefty Gomez (notorious as a weak hitter), got at least one hit, and DiMaggio and Frank Crosetti each banged out three hits. Altogether, the Yankees totaled 17 safeties.

The carnage started early with two Yankee runs in the top of the first and seven in the third, and it never abated; the Yankees even scored six times in the top of the ninth!

Starter Hal Schumacher, one of five Giants pitchers, got the loss. Gomez was shaky—he gave up only six hits but walked seven—but was able to last nine innings for an easy win.

The next game was a startling contrast, a pitcher's duel between the Yankees Bump Hadley and Fred Fitzsimmons of the Giants. For the first seven innings, the only runs were scored on solo homers by Gehrig in the second and the Giants' Jimmy Ripple in the fifth.

In the eighth, with two outs and runners on second and third, Crosetti hit a squibber back to the mound that Fitzsimmons couldn't handle, and the Yankees scored the run they needed for a 2–1 victory. The grounder was charitably called a hit, though many thought that Fitzsimmons, a good fielding pitcher, should have handled it.

Gehrig's two-run homer capped a three-run rally in the third as the Yankees beat

Hubbell the next day, 5–2, and the Giants were ready to concede. If their ace couldn't beat the Yankees, who could?

As it happened, the answer was Schumacher, the same pitcher who had been shelled in the second game. It took ten innings, but the Giants finally won it, 5–4, when manager Terry's long fly scored Joe Moore.

But the Yankees were just toying with their crosstown rivals. In the sixth game, they nailed down the Series with another lopsided win, 13–5. Jake Powell got three hits (he led everybody with a .455 average in the Series) and tied Ruth's record for a six-game series with his eighth run.

Both teams were back for the 1937 Series, but the Giants might have wished they had stayed home. This one went five games, but it wasn't even that close. Only a Hubbell victory in game four, by 7–3, kept it from being a complete rout.

Even Hubbell wasn't his usual sharp self in this Series, despite the one win. He started against Gomez in the opener and had a 1–0 lead going into the sixth, but then the Yankees knocked him out with a seven-run inning, en route to an 8–1 lead.

As an indication of how rattled the Giants were at this stage, the weak-hitting Gomez was walked twice in the inning, first by Hubbell and then by reliever Dick Coffman.

The second game was another 8–1 Yankee win, Ruffing beating Cliff Melton, and then the Yankees made it three straight by beating Schumacher, 5–1. The winner was Pearson, a hypochondriac who always seemed to be able to forget his various aches and pains to win the big games.

After that game, Giants' manager Terry got a telegram from Satchel Paige, the great pitcher who was to be kept out of the majors until 1948 because of the color line. "Giants Seem to Be Having Trouble," wrote Paige. "Try Ethiopian Pitchers."

Even Paige probably wouldn't have been enough against the rampaging Yankees. After Hubbell delayed the inevitable for one game, the Yankees came back behind Gomez in game five, 4–2, to wrap it up.

It had been a Series without any drama, unless you enjoy rooting for bulldozers.

Gehrig did not join in the clubhouse celebration after the final win. He had hit his tenth World Series home run off Hubbell in the fourth game but he had not felt good during the last month of the season.

For the veteran second baseman, Lazzeri, it was a bittersweet moment, too. He had hit .400 in the Series, but he knew he was on the way out. He would be traded before the next season to the Chicago Cubs, replaced by Gordon.

It was the Cubs who were led to the chopping block for the 1938 Series and, not for the last time, the cry was going up, "Break up the Yankees." Nobody had any illusions that the Cubs were any match for the pinstriped monsters from the Bronx.

"Why should we break up the Yankees?" asked New York owner Colonel Jake Ruppert. "Let the other teams build up to our level."

The Cubs had provided the only drama in baseball that year with one of the most dramatic finishes in history. They trailed Pittsburgh by a game and a half going into a three-game series at Wrigley Field that would close out the season.

A win in the first game brought them to within a half-game of the fading Pirates, and they battled to a 5–5 tie after eight innings of the second game.

Night games were being played in baseball by then, but Wrigley Field, of course, did not have lights. It was getting darker and darker, and the umpires decided that if the game were not decided in the ninth, it would have to be replayed as part of a doubleheader the next day. That would increase the pressure on the Cubs, who would have to win both games.

Pittsburgh went down in the top of the inning, and Pirate right-hander Mace Brown got the first two outs in the Cubs' half. Playing-manager/catcher Gabby Hartnett came to the plate and took two strikes. Then, Brown came in with a fastball, hoping to whip it by Hartnett in the fading light.

"I swung with every ounce of strength I possessed," remembered Hartnett years later, and the ball went into the left field stands. Though Cubs fans held their breath as the ball went sailing through the air, Hartnett himself claimed he had no doubts. "I felt it was gone the very second I hit it."

Joe McCarthy managed the New York Yankees to a near-perfect seven of eight World Series championships in the 1936–43 period. (New York Yankees)

But one miracle was all the Cubs had in them this year. Reality set in when they came up against the Yankees in the World Series, and they were swept in four straight.

Yankee manager Joe McCarthy often said that he regarded the 1938 team as the best of his Yankee career, though it was the only one in that four-year stretch which did not win 100 games, stopping at 99. Certainly, they were invincible in the Series.

The Yankees got help they probably didn't need in the first game as first base coach Earle Combs, the center fielder on the great 1927 team, was able to steal the Chicago pitching signs. When Chicago starter Bill Lee, a 22-game winner in the regular season, was going to throw a fastball, Combs would yell to the batter, "Get hold of it!" When he saw the sign for a curve, he'd cry out, "There it is!"

With this help, the Yankee beat Lee, 3–1, behind Ruffing.

The second game was the highlight of the Series, providing one of those unique moments of courage that become highlighted in a Series.

The Cubs had bought Dizzy Dean from St. Louis before the 1938 season, but this was not the same Dean who had thrown a buzzing fastball by hitters in the 1934 Series. Pitching in the 1937 All-Star Game, Dean had had his right toe fractured by a line drive off the bat of Earl Averill. Changing his motion to favor the injured toe, Dizzy had strained his arm and his fastball had disappeared forever.

Cubs' owner Phil Wrigley knew Dean had a bad arm, but he felt Dizzy would be worth the money for his box office value alone. As it happened, Dean helped the Cubs, though he had to be used very sparingly. He won seven games in eight decisions that year and had an ERA of just 1.80—but in only 75 innings.

Dizzy started the second game, against the Yankees' Gomez. Getting by on his cunning and a variety of soft stuff he would have scorned earlier in his career, Dean carried a 3–2 lead into the eighth.

Selkirk singled to lead off the inning but was out when Gordon hit into a force-out. Myril Hoag, batting for Gomez, also hit into a force-out. Crosetti was the next batter.

The Yankee shortstop was in the lineup for his fielding, not his hitting. In a 17-year major league career, he averaged .245 and with little power. But he had flied out three times to deep left against Dean in this game.

This time he smashed another pitch to left field, and this one carried into the seats to put the Yankees into the lead. Two more anticlimactic runs in the ninth made the final margin 6–3.

As Crosetti rounded the bases, Dizzy shouted at him, "I wish I could call back one year, Frank. You wouldn't get a loud foul off me."

"You're so right, Diz!" Crosetti answered back.

Almost lost in the drama was the fact that Gomez had won his sixth World Series game without defeat.

The next day, home runs by Gordon and Dickey enabled Pearson to win, 5–2, and the Yankees clinched the Series with an 8–3 rout in the fourth game. Once again,

Known for his humor, Lefty Gomez was a perfect 6–0 in World Series competition for the New York Yankees. *(George Brace)*

Crosetti got a big hit, a triple in the second. It was a big Series for the shortstop who, though he hit only .250, knocked in six runs.

But manager McCarthy was sad in victory. Gehrig had had what amounted to an off season for him, hitting 29 home runs and batting just .295, and he had followed that with a Series in which he got only four singles in 14 at-bats and didn't knock in a run. Lou was 35, but this was obviously more than just a great athlete slowing down.

The Yankees won again in 1939, of course, but their triumph was clouded by personal tragedy.

Owner Ruppert, who had been too sick to see his team win the '38 Series, died in January of 1939 of phlebitis.

Gehrig, whose disintegration was becoming painfully obvious, took himself out of the lineup after eight games, having set a consecutive games record of 2130 that will probably never be approached, let alone matched.

Ironically, it was his teammates' encouragement that led Gehrig to make his decision. Making a routine play at first base, he had been cheered by his teammates and he realized how far his game had fallen if they would cheer that.

He went to Mayo Hospital in Rochester, Minnesota, and was told that he had a fatal disease. He would die in June of 1941, but not before telling a Yankee Stadium crowd on July 4, 1939, that he considered himself the "luckiest man on earth."

Babe Dahlgren replaced Gehrig in the lineup and, though he was only a shadow of the player Gehrig had been, the Yankees didn't miss a step as they rolled to another pennant.

Facing them in the Series this time were the Cincinnati Reds, winning their first pennant since the Black Sox year of 1919. The Reds had a great one-two pitching punch in Bucky Walters (27–11 with a 2.29 ERA) and Paul Derringer (25–7, 2.93 ERA). Walters was a converted third baseman, and Derringer had come to the Reds years before from St. Louis in the trade which sent Leo Durocher to the Cards.

Derringer dueled Ruffing through eight innings of a 1–1 battle in the Series opener, but he got into trouble immediately in the ninth when he gave up an inning-opening triple to Keller. DiMaggio, Dickey, and Selkirk were the next hitters. Shudder.

Cincinnati manager Bill McKechnie ordered DiMaggio walked and many thought he should have done the same to Dickey, a great clutch hitter throughout his Yankee career. But he chose to have Derringer pitch to Dickey.

"If I had walked Dickey and pitched to Selkirk," McKechnie explained later, "the infield would have been drawn in to make the force at the plate, and I would have had to pitch low to Selkirk to make him hit the ball on the ground. But Selkirk is a low-ball hitter.

"Now, Dickey, though a wonderful hitter, is a slow runner. With the infield halfway, I could get him to hit the ball on the ground, and the infielder would have the option of throwing to the plate or trying for the double play."

Unfortunately for McKechnie's strategy, Dickey punched the ball past second baseman Lonnie Frey, and the game was over.

Pearson pitched the second game (primarily because Gomez was still suffering from the arm trouble that had plagued him during the season) and pitched a no-hitter for seven innings. He finally yielded singles to Ernie Lombardi in the eighth and Billy Werber in the ninth and won, 4–0.

Gomez tried to pitch the next day but had to give up after just one inning, in which he yielded three hits and a run. No matter. The Yankee hitters were back for this game.

Keller started the Yankees going with a two-run homer in the first, DiMaggio hit a two-run homer in the third, and Keller blasted still another two-run home run in the fifth. Dickey varied the routine with a solo homer, also in the fifth, and the Yankees breezed, 7–3.

Keller and Dickey again homered in the next game, each hit with nobody on, but the Reds battled to a 4–4 tie after nine innings. Actually, they could have won it in nine but second baseman Frey threw high to shortstop Billy Myers in the ninth and the Yankees went on to score twice to tie the game.

In the tenth, Crosetti walked and Red Rolfe sacrificed. Myers fumbled Keller's ground ball, and then DiMaggio singled to right, scoring Crosetti with what would be the winning run.

The play wasn't over, though. When right fielder Ival Goodman booted the ball, Keller also came around third and, on the play at the plate, kicked catcher Lombardi in the groin. As Lombardi lay there in pain, DiMaggio raced around third to add the final run in the 7–4 win.

Sportswriters later made much of Lombardi's plight, calling it the Act of the Dying Swan and labeling him a "goat." But in fact, his plight only made possible a totally unnecessary run. There were certainly more logical Cincinnati goats than Lombardi.

Nobody had had a bigger Series than Keller, nicknamed "King Kong" because of his brutish appearance. "He's the only player Frank Buck ever brought back," quipped Gomez. Keller, a left-handed hitter whose power was primarily to left-center, hit .438 for the Series with three home runs, six RBIs, and eight runs scored.

When the cry of "Break up the Yankees" once again arose, one Cincinnati fan said, "Hell, I'd be satisfied if they'd just break up Keller!"

Joe DiMaggio was the key figure on New York Yankee teams that played in ten World Series during his 13-year career, which began in 1936. *(New York Yankees)*

Stan Musial was just a rookie when his St. Louis Cardinals upset the Yankees in the 1942 World Series. *(George Brace)*

13. Speed Kills

The atmosphere coming into the World Series in 1942 was decidedly different, with the country at war for nearly a year.

Commissioner Landis had ruled that the USO, an organization that provided recreational facilities for servicemen, be given part of the gate receipts. Two squads of Marines led the traditional march to the flagpole. And, as one more indication of what was happening, Giants' manager Mel Ott, en route to the Series, was bumped off his plane at Dayton, Ohio, to make room for a serviceman, and Ott could not even get train transportation from there to St. Louis.

Otherwise, the Series looked distressingly familiar. The New York Yankees were once again the American League champions. This time, it was the St. Louis Cardinals who were being led to the chopping block as National League pennant winners.

"The Yankees were a little bit cocky," noted Cardinal pitcher Max Lanier later, "though any ball club that had won as many pennants as they had had a right to be cocky."

Yes, indeed. The Yankees, in beating second-place Boston by nine games, had just won their sixth pennant in seven years and 13th since Babe Ruth had first joined the club.

Their recent record in World Series play had been equally spectacular. Since losing the dramatic final game of the 1926 Series to Grover Cleveland Alexander and the Cardinals, the Yankees had won eight straight Series and had dropped only four games; five of those Series had been sweeps.

The first game of that '42 Series seemed to be more of the same. The Yankees had breezed to a 7–0 lead in the first eight innings, knocking out Cardinal ace Mort Cooper. The Cardinals seemed in awe of the American League champions, committing four errors and getting only one hit, a single by Terry Moore with two outs in the eighth inning, off Yankee ace Red Ruffing.

Then the Cards came to life in the bottom of the ninth, scoring four times on six hits and knocking out Ruffing. With two outs and the bases loaded, Stan Musial came to the plate for the second time in the inning. Also for the second time in the inning, he made an out, grounding to first baseman Buddy Hassett, to end the inning and the game.

Few of the experts thought the Cardinal rally had done anything more than make the final score respectable. The Yankees had, after all, won the game.

Dizzy Dean, interviewed on the radio that night, thought otherwise. "That was just the shot in the arm our boys needed. We'll never stop now."

It had been eight years since the Cardinals had last been in the World Series, and the turnover in players had been complete since the "Gas House Gang" had beaten Detroit.

Gone were the stars of the '34 Series—the Dean brothers, Pepper Martin, Joe Medwick. In their places were new stars. The Cooper brothers formed a great battery; Mort won 22 games on a 1.77 earned run average (good enough to win the Most Valuable Player award) and Walker was a good defensive catcher who hit a solid .281.

Movie star handsome Johnny Beazley was just a step behind Mort Cooper with 21 wins and a 2.14 ERA. Defensively, the Cardinals were outstanding, especially at shortstop with Marty Marion and in the outfield with Enos Slaughter, Terry Moore, and Stan Musial, just warming up for a spectacular career with a .315 batting average as a rookie.

But, although the players got the attention, it was Branch Rickey, working behind the scenes, who had made the Cardinals into a dynasty team, one that would win four pennants and three World Series in a five-year span in the '40s.

Rickey was an organizational genius, gifted at recognizing and evaluating talent. He realized that the Cardinals, who did not draw as many as a million fans in St. Louis until after World War II, could not compete in buying talent against teams like the Yankees. His solution was to build an organization of minor league teams, the "farm system," to supply talent at the major league level.

In the '40s, that worked perfectly for the Cardinals, who had so many fine young prospects that Rickey continually traded away many of them to other clubs—though almost never a truly outstanding prospect.

There never seemed to be a clog in the Cardinals' pipeline. When a major leaguer faltered, or was traded because his contract demands got too high, there always seemed to be a player waiting to step in.

And when Rickey left the Cardinals to go to Brooklyn after the 1942 season, he did the same thing for the Dodgers, who succeeded the Cardinals as a dynasty team.

Rickey's influence was felt throughout the National League. One example: the 1941 Dodgers, who had won the National League pennant. Club owner Larry MacPhail had started in baseball by running Rickey's American Association team at Columbus, Ohio. Manager Leo Durocher had played shortstop for the Cardinals' "Gas House

Gang." Center fielder Pete Reiser had been in the Cardinal minor league system until Judge Landis had declared him a free agent because the Cardinals had violated a rule. Left fielder Joe Medwick, catcher Mickey Owen, and pitcher Curt Davis had all been traded from St. Louis.

The players Rickey kept all seemed cut from the same mold. They were generally young, fast, and underpaid. Before they became old, slow, or, most important, well-paid, they were sent to other teams.

The key to the Cardinal game was that speed. It didn't show up much in stolen bases—in that era, the stolen base had fallen into disfavor, and the Cardinals' total of 71 was second in the National League—but the Cards' speed put constant pressure on the other team. Time after time, the young Cards took an extra base and "stole" runs. Against the Chicago Cubs late in the 1942 season, for instance, Musial was on second when Coaker Triplett hit a little dribbler out in front of the plate. Catcher Clyde McCullough came out for the ball but his throw was a split-second too late to get the fleet Triplett at first. With McCullough out from the plate and first baseman Babe Dahlgren arguing the call, Musial came whipping around third to score.

Thus, although the Cards had little power (only 60 home runs in 1942) and a relatively low team batting average (.268), they parlayed their speed and ability to seize opportunities into a league-leading 755 runs.

Defensively, too, the Cardinal speed made a big difference. In the outfield, and especially in center field, what should have been hits were often turned into outs.

That 1942 team was Rickey's—and the Cardinals—finest. It had to be to even win the National League pennant. At one point, in early August, the Cards were ten games behind the defending champion Dodgers, but they won 43 of their final 52 games, even better than the 34 of 44 by the 1914 Braves and 38 of 47 by the 1951 Giants. The Dodgers won 104 games that season, but the Cardinals won 106.

That stretch run had made believers out of the rest of the National League. Now, their first game jitters behind them, the Cardinals were ready to make believers out of the Yankees.

Beazley, only a rookie, was the second-game starter for the Cardinals, and he had plenty of supporters in the stands at Sportsman's Park, where he had not lost a game since May 24.

Six years before, as a high school student in Nashville, he had promised his friends that if he ever appeared in a World Series, they would be there as his guests. Typical bravado from a 15-year-old, of course, but Beazley had made it, and he had fulfilled his promise.

This time, the Cards got out in front early. Walker Cooper doubled to knock in two runs in the first, and Whitey Kurowski's triple scored another in the seventh.

In the eighth, the Yankees' home run asserted itself as Charlie "King King" Keller capped a game-tying three-run rally with a two-run homer.

When Keller had first come up to the Yankees in 1939, he had not been a pull hitter because in the International League's small parks he was able to hit home runs to all fields. As a rookie with the Yankees, Keller had hit only 11 home runs, despite the obvious power emanating from his muscular frame—although he did belt three home runs in the World Series.

Manager Joe McCarthy took him aside the next year and said, "Why do you think they built such a short right field in this [Yankee Stadium] ballpark?"

"For Babe Ruth," said Keller.

"That's right," said McCarthy. "So, why aren't you taking advantage of it? You're a left-handed power hitter."

In batting practice, McCarthy had his pitchers throw nothing but inside pitches to Keller, so he'd become accustomed to pulling the ball. It worked. Keller hit 21 home runs in 1940, 33 in 1941, and 26 in 1942.

The Cardinals weren't discouraged by Keller's tying blast. In the bottom half of the eighth, they went ahead again when Slaughter doubled and Musial singled him home, and in the top of the ninth, their speed again asserted itself.

Bill Dickey had singled to lead off the inning, and McCarthy sent in Tuck Stainback to run for him. Buddy Hassett singled into the right field corner and Stainback hustled around second on the way to third, but Slaughter dashed into the corner to cut off Hassett's drive, whirled and threw a perfect strike to Kurowski at third base to nip Stainback.

Pinch hitter Ruffing followed with a fly ball which would have scored Stainback if he'd been at third. Instead, it was only the second out of the inning. Beazley soon got the third out, and the Cards had evened the Series at 1–1.

The Cardinal fielding was even better in the third game, as Ernie White shut out the Yankees, 2–0, the first time the Yankees had been blanked in the Series since Jesse Haines had done it for the Cardinals in 1926.

Musial turned in a good running catch, Slaughter leaped to cut off a potential extra-base hit, and Moore completed a play that made those seem routine. Jumping over Musial, who had slipped and fallen in left-center, Moore made a backhanded grab of Joe DiMaggio's drive, averting what would probably have become an inside-the-park home run for the Yankee Clipper.

Although he needed that kind of fielding help, White, who had been held to seven regular season wins because of a sore arm, yielded only five hits. Spud Chandler was nearly as effective for the Yankees, giving up just six hits. Kurowski scored the first Cardinal run on an infield out and Slaughter singled in Jimmy Brown with the clincher in the ninth—after Chandler was gone.

The fourth game was a wild one. The Yankees took a 1–0 lead with a run in the first, but the Cardinals scored six times in the fourth to knock out Yankee starter Hank Borowy. The rout seemed on in reverse—but the Yankees came back with a five-run rally in the sixth, knocking out Cooper and tying the score.

But the Cardinals bounced back again, scoring two runs in the seventh and adding another in the ninth for a 9–6 win. Max Lanier got the win in relief.

The Yankees were in shock. Even their haughtiness had deserted them. They had started complaining about calls—something they'd never had to bother with before—and before the fifth game, McCarthy complained because Morris "Butch" Yatkeman, the Cards batboy for eight years and then the clubhouse attendant since 1932, was in the dugout.

McCarthy's complaint was made through coach Art Fletcher, presenting the starting lineup to umpire Bill Summers. Moore, the Cardinals' captain, was incredulous when he heard that. "Okay," he said to Fletcher, "you can go back and tell McCarthy that there won't be any 'tomorrow' in this Series."

Moore's confidence was justified. The Cardinals were on a roll, though they made four errors in this game.

McCarthy had gone back to Ruffing in this game, and Cardinal manager Billy Southworth had countered with his star rookie right-hander, Beazley. An injury in the service during World War II would take the zip out of Beazley's right arm, but he was brilliant at this time. He battled Ruffing on even terms, 2–2, going into the ninth, and then Kurowski hit a two-run homer to put the Cards ahead.

In the bottom of the ninth, the Yankees got two runners on base with no outs. But shortstop Marion sneaked in behind Joe Gordon, the runner at second, and took a throw from catcher Walker Cooper to put out Gordon and the Yankee rally simultaneously. The Cards had won four straight after that opening game loss, and McCarthy had suffered his first (and what would be his only) Series loss as a Yankee manager.

In many ways, 1942 was the high water mark for the Cardinal organization. Not only had they won at the highest level of play, but Cardinal farm teams had won pennants at Sacramento (Pacific Coast League), Rochester (International League), Columbus (American Association), and Houston (Texas League).

The organization was so strong, said Buddy Blattner, who had just graduated to the major league club that season, "you probably could have taken the top players of our farm system and finished only behind the Cardinals and Dodgers in the National League and the Yankees in the American."

When Rickey left a month after the 1942 season for Brooklyn, the Cardinal system lost its impetus, but there were so many good players left that the Cards were able to go on to win pennants in 1943 (losing to the Yankees in the Series) and 1944 (beating the Browns), despite the inroads caused by players going to war.

By 1946, the war was over and most of the stars were back. The Cardinals had to win a playoff with the Dodgers for the National League pennant, and they met the Boston Red Sox in the Series.

This was a much different team, though, from the 1942 champions. Age, injuries, and the tightfisted policies of owner Sam Breadon had caused many changes. The Cardinals were still a very good team, but this was their last gasp. The Dodgers, with Rickey's genius working for them, would now be the team coming up with good young players. The Cardinals were trying to hold back time with veteran players.

Some 1942 stars were still around: Slaughter, Marion, Musial (though shifted to first base), and Moore, held by injury to just 66 games.

The pitching staff had had almost a complete turnover. The leader now was Howie Pollet, who had come up late in the 1942 season, with 21 wins and a 2.10 ERA.

But the potential staff leader, Max Lanier, was gone. Unhappy because of a salary of just $10,500, Lanier jumped to the Mexican League after winning his first six starts, all complete games, with an ERA of 1.93. With him went second baseman Lou Klein (ably replaced by Red Schoendienst) and another pitcher, Fred Martin.

The Cardinals also got a 15–6 season out of right-hander Murray Dickson, but it was Harry Brecheen, only 15–15 after war year seasons of 16–5 and 14–4, who would be the key to the Series. In an unusually prophetic statement, a Philadelphia gambler told St. Louis writer Bob Broeg before the Series, "I'm betting on St. Louis because you got a skinny little guy [Brecheen] who is a big-game pitcher."

The "smart money," though, was on the Red Sox, and not just because the American League was still considered the stronger league at the time.

Since he had bought the Red Sox in 1934, Tom Yawkey had poured money into it, trying to buy a winner. By 1946, his dream came true. The Red Sox, much the same team that had finished second to the Yankees in 1942, before everybody went to war, surpassed even Yawkey's dreams. Winning 40 of their first 50 games, Boston romped home by 12 games over Detroit; the Yankees slipped to third.

The Red Sox were a solid team, one that, with 104 wins, had fallen just one win short of the Boston team record set in 1912. Defensively, they were sound, with a double-play combination of shortstop Johnny Pesky and second baseman Bobby Doerr, backed up by Joe DiMaggio's younger brother, Dom, in center field; Dom couldn't hit with his bigger brother, but Boston fans argued that he was an even better fielder.

They had four solid starters—Dave (Boo) Ferriss, 25–6; Tex Hughson, 20–11; Mickey Harris, the only lefthander, 17–9; and Joe Dobson, 13–7. Ferriss had an incredible year, the best for a Boston pitcher since Smokey Joe Wood had gone 34–5 in 1912. He started the season with ten straight wins and later had a streak of 12 straight.

(Sadly, both Ferriss and Hughson had arm trouble after 1946 and never pitched back to their form of that year. Had they remained effective, the Red Sox—who lost pennants in '48 and '49 on the last day of the season and finished just four games back in '50—might well have been a dynasty team.)

But the big story on the Red Sox was Ted Williams, who had hit .406 in 1941, the last major league hitter to hit .400 or better. His batting average was considerably lower in 1946, at .342, but he hit 38 home runs, drove in 123 runs, and scored 142 to become the AL's Most Valuable Player.

Williams was such a deadly hitter that Cleveland manager Lou Boudreau devised a radical defense to use against him. Boudreau had his first baseman playing almost on the line and his second baseman in short right field. Boudreau himself came over from shortstop to play a normal second base position and third baseman Ken Keltner played directly behind second base. Boudreau had his right and center fielders pulled to the right and his left fielder stationed just behind where the shortstop would normally play.

Had Williams bunted down the third base line, he would have had an easy base hit. Any medium-deep fly to left would have gotten him a double. Boudreau was willing to concede that for two reasons: (1) Williams wouldn't hit a home run to right that way; and (2) The shift might get Williams to change his swing.

In the Series, Cardinal manager Eddie Dyer used a less drastic version. He stationed third baseman Whitey Kurowski about where a second baseman would normally play and had second baseman Schoendienst directly between Kurowski and Musial at first. Marion remained in a normal shortstop alignment and left fielder Harry Walker played straightaway and in normal depth, while Moore and Slaughter were pulled around to right.

But Dyer's defense didn't bother Williams nearly so much as what should have been a meaningless pitch thrown against him after the regular season had ended but before the World Series started.

Baseball fans have long argued—without coming to a definite conclusion—whether a team is better off winning easily, which means it can be rested coming into the Series, or staying sharp through a long battle for the pennant.

This year was a classic study. The Red Sox had never been pressed while the Cardinals had not only had a tough race but had to go into a playoff to beat the Dodgers.

Boston manager Joe Cronin feared that his team would get rusty and have to face a hot team in the Series, so he arranged a three-game exhibition between the Red Sox and a team of American League players. In the first game, pitcher Mickey Haefner threw a curve on the inside to Williams that hit the Boston slugger on his elbow.

Williams was sent to the hospital, where X rays showed there was no break. But the elbow had swollen to three times its size, and, though the swelling came down, it remained tender throughout the Series, in which Williams hit only .200—five singles in 25 at-bats.

To his credit, Williams never used his sore elbow as an excuse for his performance, but it was certainly an important factor.

Despite the injury to Williams, the Red Sox were 20–7 favorites. They had never

Ted Williams's elbow injury limited him to a disappointing .200 average in his only World Series, in 1946. *(Boston Red Sox)*

lost a Series in five previous attempts, so they had history on their side. Of course, they had not been in a Series since 1918, so it's questionable how much importance that history had.

One other bit of history held true, however: The Cards had won only one opening game in their previous seven Series, and they lost this one, too. It took ten innings, though, as Rudy York's solo homer into a refreshment stand on top of the left field bleachers gave the Sox a 3–2 win. "York was one of the smartest hitters I ever saw," commented Williams years later. Ted himself hit a ball against the screen in right field—but it was foul. It would be the best drive he hit in the Series, and it didn't count.

In the second game, Brecheen, nicknamed "The Cat" because of the sure-footed way he moved on the mound, shut out the Red Sox, 3–0. Williams couldn't get the ball out of the infield. "Brecheen had the ball doing just what he wanted," said Williams. "I hate to admit it, but he was beautiful to watch."

The teams took a day off to travel back to Boston, and Red Sox manager Cronin was still confident, despite Williams' ineffectiveness. "We'll handle this thing back at Fenway," he said. "The boys are not going to want to come back to St. Louis."

It seemed that way in the third game, as Ferriss blanked the Cards, 4–0. "I had everything breaking right," he said. York's three-run homer in the first inning was all Ferriss needed. But there was that disquieting note: Williams still wasn't hitting. Ted was so desperate, in fact, that he laid down a bunt—and beat it out. The Cards were willing to give him all of those he would take.

But in the fourth game, the Cardinals buried the Red Sox, 12–3, getting 20 hits off starter Hughson and five pitchers who followed him. Slaughter, Kurowski, and Joe Garagiola, a young catcher who became more famous later telling Yogi Berra stories, all got four hits.

This had been a back-and-forth Series, and in the fifth game, it was the Red Sox' turn, as they won 6–3 behind Dobson, who could have had a shutout but for two uncharacteristic errors by Pesky at shortstop. To make it worse for the Cardinals, Slaughter had been hit by a pitch on the right elbow. Trainer Harrison "Doc" Weaver spent the train trip back to St. Louis packing the elbow in ice and advised Slaughter not to play in the sixth game.

But Slaughter was not the type of player who could be kept out of a big game with anything short of two broken legs. He played in the sixth game and contributed a good catch and a hit to Brecheen's second victory, 4–1, over Harris.

The Series was tied again, and the final game would be played in St. Louis. But the Red Sox still had reason to be confident. Ferriss was well rested for what would be his second start of the Series, matched against Dickson, a good pitcher but not in Ferriss's class. Everybody else on both teams would be in the bull pen, of course. "We'll have all winter to rest," said Brecheen.

Williams still was not hitting, but a great hitter can break out of a slump in a hurry, and for a time, it seemed Williams would do that in this game.

In the first inning, Wally Moses led off with a single, Pesky sent him to third with another single, and DiMaggio scored Moses with a long fly to right.

Up came Williams, and he smashed a towering drive to left center, too far back for left fielder Walker. But Moore, one of the great outfielders of all time, came all the way from right center to make an outstanding running catch which affected the entire game. Had he not made the catch, the Red Sox would have had a second run and still been in the middle of a rally, and Dickson would probably have been taken out. But, given that help, Dickson got York to pop out to end the inning and then settled down to pitch seven good innings.

Williams saved a run for the Red Sox in the bottom of the inning when he threw out Schoendienst trying to stretch a single into a double, just ahead of a double by Musial.

In the third, Kurowski doubled, moved to third on a ground out by Garagiola, and scored on Walker's fly to Williams.

The score remained tied at 1–1 until the Cards knocked out Ferriss with two runs in the fifth. Ironically, the big hit was a double by Dickson, the pitcher they had almost knocked out in the first. Ferriss was desolated. "I can't understand it," he said after the game. "I had my stuff today. Those were good pitches they hit."

Two pinch hitters triggered an eighth inning rally for the Red Sox, Rip Russell singling and Catfish Metkovich doubling, with Russell going to third.

Dyer brought in Brecheen, though he'd had only one day of rest. "I figured I could still get two good innings from him," said Dyer.

Brecheen struck out Moses and got Pesky on a short liner to Slaughter, Russell having to hold at third, but then DiMaggio doubled to right center, tying the score. Sliding into second, DiMaggio twisted his ankle and was replaced by Leon Culberson. That would be critical later.

Williams was up next, and he was due. He had been robbed twice, by Moore in the first and by Walker on another drive in the fourth. But this time, he could only hit a pop fly to Schoendienst for the final out of the inning.

Cronin brought in right-hander Bob Klinger in the top of the ninth, a decision for which he was second-guessed later. Although Klinger had pitched well in relief during the year, he hadn't thrown a ball in the Series.

Slaughter led off with a single to center. Kurowski, trying to sacrifice, popped to Klinger, and Del Rice flied deep to Williams. With two outs, Slaughter would be running on the pitch. Earlier in the Series, he had been held up by coach Mike Gonzalez on a play on which Slaughter thought he could have scored. He complained so much about it that Dyer told him, "All right, all right, if it happens again and you think you can score, go ahead. I'll take the rap."

Walker got a low sinker from Klinger, a tough pitch, but lined it to left-center. Culberson ran it down and threw back into the infield, to shortstop Pesky.

But Slaughter knew that Culberson had a weak arm, nothing like DiMaggio's, and that he would not get to the ball as fast as DiMaggio would have. He just kept running. Gonzalez started to put up his hands in a stop signal at third base, but saw that Slaughter was going to run right through it, so he didn't bother.

Pesky got Culberson's throw in short left field. Accounts of the day say he hesitated before turning around and throwing; Pesky says there was no hesitation. At any rate, his throw was just up the line and Slaughter scored to put the Cards ahead.

The Red Sox mounted a rally in the ninth when York and Doerr both singled, but Brecheen got the dangerous Pinky Higgins to bunt into a force-out, then induced Roy Partee to foul out and pinch hitter Tom McBride to ground out. Harry the Cat had won his third game of the Series, and the Cardinals were again World Champions.

Much later, Williams would say that the Series was his biggest disappointment. "I only had one chance," he said. "Ty Cobb played in three Series and really only played well in one."

After that game, though, Williams had nothing to say. He sat on the stool in front of his locker with his head in his hands. Finally, he got up and gave his Series check to clubhouse boy Johnny Orlando, and then went into the shower, where he stood and cried for many minutes.

14. The Ultimate Subway Series

Any World Series between the Brooklyn Dodgers and the New York Yankees—and there were six of them in one ten-year span, 1947–56—was special, not just because the two teams were so close geographically but for what they represented. The Dodgers were the street urchins, immortalized by cartoonist Willard Mullins as "The Bums." The Yankees were the aristocrats of baseball, accustomed to winning seemingly without breaking into a sweat. They were apt representatives of their communities, the Dodgers of Brooklyn, a city whose name alone got a laugh every time a comedian mentioned it, the Yankees of glamorous Manhattan, whose name symbolized success.

The first (1947) Series in this span, though, stood out more than the others, with memorable moments provided by the bit players, not just the stars.

There was extra interest in this Series because there were some unusual elements, including animosity between club owners. Yankee owner Larry MacPhail, a bombastic man, had been feuding with the Dodgers' Branch Rickey, and the Dodgers believed it was at MacPhail's insistence that baseball commissioner Happy Chandler had suspended Dodger manager Leo Durocher for a year for "conduct detrimental to baseball," which translated to being friendly to gamblers. Burt Shotton, who had worked for Rickey in different jobs over the years, replaced Durocher as manager.

More than that, this was the first World Series in which a black player participated. Rickey had integrated major league baseball that year with Jackie Robinson, the first of a series of black stars for the Dodgers.

Robinson had had to endure a season of racial taunts and epithets from other teams. One team, the St. Louis Cardinals, threatened not to play against the Dodgers, until National League president Ford Frick warned them they would be suspended if they carried out their threat. On Robinson's own club, there were players who didn't want to play with blacks; one, outfielder Dixie Walker, had put his feelings into a letter to Rickey and was traded to Pittsburgh after the 1947 season.

Through it all, Robinson had kept his mouth shut, though he was undoubtedly boiling inside; his behavior in later years, when he was free to express his emotions, showed how hard it must have been for him that year. Despite the provocations, and despite the fact that he was playing first base, an unfamiliar position, Robinson hit .296 for the Dodgers, led the league with 29 stolen bases, and won the Rookie of the Year award.

Finally, this was the first Series in which relief pitching played an important role for both teams, as it had during the season. Hugh Casey for the Dodgers and Joe Page for the Yankees, both of whom began in baseball as starting pitchers, pitched brilliantly in relief for their teams.

Casey had been a starter as late as 1939, winning 15 games, but his greatest success came as a reliever. In 1942, his last year before going into the service, he had won six games and saved 13 in relief. In 1948, he had his best year, winning ten games and saving another 18; the saves and total relief points (wins plus saves) were both National League records.

Yet, it was typical of Casey's luck that he was, and is, best remembered for one unhappy moment in the 1941 World Series. A pitch that was probably a spitball struck out Tommy Henrich for what should have been the last out of a 4–3 Dodger Series-tying win in the fourth game, but it got away from catcher Mickey Owen and Henrich reached base safely. In quick succession, Joe DiMaggio singled, Charlie Keller doubled, Bill Dickey walked, and Joe Gordon doubled off the shocked Casey to win the game for the Yanks 7–4. "I've lost games in a lot of ways," said Casey when he finally recovered, "but never by striking out a batter."

Page had been made a full-time reliever only in 1947—he'd had 17 starts among his 31 appearances the year before—and he'd had an even better year than Casey, winning 14 games in relief and saving another 17. He had allowed only 105 hits in 141⅓ innings.

Even by the standards of relief pitching, where today's hero is often tomorrow's bum, Page's success was very brief. He really had only two good years, '47 and '49, when he won 13 games and saved 27. But in those two years, he was as good as any relief pitcher had been to that date.

A record World Series crowd of 73,365 was present at Yankee Stadium for the first game, and the Yankees' MacPhail had arranged a special show, bringing on Guy Lombardo and his orchestra to play for the fans and Helen Jepson, a Metropolitan Opera soprano, to sing the National Anthem.

For the Yankees, though, it was business as usual, which meant winning. Frank "Spec" Shea for the home team and Ralph Branca for the Dodgers battled almost evenly for four innings (the Dodgers had scored one run in the first) but the Yankees got to Branca for five runs in the fourth.

Shea, a 14–game winner during the regular season despite on-and-off arm problems, pitched the five innings required to get the win. Page took over in the sixth and went the rest of the way in the 5–3 Yankee win.

Before the 1947 season, the Yankees and Cleveland Indians had swung a controversial deal which sent Yankee second baseman Joe Gordon to Cleveland. The Yankees were given their choice of Cleveland pitchers: Red Embree or Allie Reynolds. MacPhail asked DiMaggio's advice and he recommended getting Reynolds, who had always been tough against the Yankees.

The deal was unpopular with Yankee fans because Gordon had been a great player for the Yankees, and Reynolds' record with the Indians had been unspectacular; in 1946, for instance, he was just 11–15.

Gordon went on to play well for the Indians and, in 1948, played a key role in Cleveland's first pennant in 28 years. But Reynolds was an even bigger help to the Yankees, becoming the bellwether of the pitching staff for six years, 1947–52, in which he won 105 games.

In one year in that span, 1949, the Superchief was plagued by a bad back and could finish only four games; the Yankees, said the wise guys, had a great pitcher named Reynolds–Page.

But in the second game of the '47 Series, Reynolds needed no pitching help from Page or anybody else, going nine innings and winning easily, 10–3, as the Yankees exploded for 15 hits.

llie Reynolds was the staff leader for the New ork Yankees as they won an unprecedented ve straight World Series, 1949–53. *(George ace)*

It seemed that another Yankee runaway was in the making, but the Dodgers were not ready to quit. Back in friendly (to hitters) Ebbets Field, they faced the well-traveled Bobo Newsom and knocked him out with a six-run second inning.

It may seem strange that Yankee manager Bucky Harris even pitched Newsom, but Harris didn't have much choice. He had had to juggle his starters judiciously all season, and only the brilliance of Page had saved the Yankees. Reynolds, with 241.2 innings, was the only Yankee starter who had more than 200 innings, and the leading winner with 19. After Shea, no other Yankee starter had won in double figures. This was not the kind of pitching the Yankee fans had become accustomed to seeing.

The Yankees came back, chipping away for two runs in each of the third, fourth, and fifth innings, and single ones in the sixth and seventh.

DiMaggio hit a home run. So did a young man named Yogi Berra—the first pinch hit home run in Series history. But the Dodgers hung on for a 9–8 win, setting the stage for the fourth game, one of the most dramatic in Series history.

Shotton, who was hardly any deeper in starting pitchers than Harris, started Harry Taylor, a ten-game winner during the season. The rookie Taylor pitched to only four men. Snuffy Stirnweiss (who had replaced Gordon at second) and Tommy Henrich singled, and Berra's grounder was fumbled by Dodger shortstop Pee Wee Reese, loading the bases. Taylor walked DiMaggio, forcing in a run, and was relieved by Hal Gregg, who got out of the inning by getting George McQuinn to pop up and Billy Johnson to hit into a double play.

The Yankees scored another run in the fourth on a triple by Johnson and a double by Johnny Lindell, and threatened to score more in the top of the ninth when they loaded the bases with one out. But Casey came in against Henrich, his nemesis in 1941. This time, his first pitch was hit into an inning-ending double play.

Meanwhile, a strange drama was unfolding on the other side. Bill Bevens, only a seven-game winner in the regular season, was giving manager Harris a nervous stomach with his wildness, but he was also giving the Dodgers nothing but trouble.

Bevens started four of his nine innings with a walk, and he wound up walking ten batters, setting a Series record. He did not have a 1–2–3 inning until the eighth.

But he was also pitching a no-hitter.

There had been only three tough plays in the field. Left fielder Lindell had made a diving catch of a foul fly by Robinson in the third, and Gene Hermanski had twice driven Yankee outfielders to the wall for line drives, DiMaggio in center in the fourth and Henrich in right-center in the eighth.

Bevens opened the bottom of the ninth by getting Bruce Edwards on a fly to left, on which Lindell made a leaping catch. Then he walked Carl Furillo, and Shotton sent in Al Gionfriddo to run for Furillo and put Pete Reiser up as a pinch hitter for Casey.

The switch-hitting Reiser, who some National League observers thought could have had a career like Willie Mays, was the original hard luck kid. He had suffered concussions and a fractured skull from collisions with outfield fences, and he had twice been beaned by pitches. In 1947, injuries had limited him to 109 games, in which he had hit .309.

Continuing his string of bad luck, Reiser had chipped a bone in his ankle sliding into second the day before. But, afraid Rickey would make him sign a $1-a-year contract the next season (providing that he would get more only if he were able to play a reasonably full schedule), Reiser had called the injury only a sprain and taped it, so he could be used as a pinch hitter.

Bevens threw two balls and a strike to Reiser. On the next pitch, another ball, Gionfriddo stole second, running on his own. Harris, though he suspected Reiser had a broken ankle, ordered Bevens to throw a fourth ball to walk Reiser. The move violated basic baseball strategy, because it put the winning run on base, but Harris had great respect for Reiser's clutch-hitting ability.

Shotton sent Eddie Miksis in to run for Reiser and called up Harry "Cookie" Lavagetto as a pinch hitter for Eddie Stanky. Lavagetto had been a major leaguer since 1934. A good infielder and steady hitter in his prime, he was another player who had lost something in the war years, and he had played only 41 games for the Dodgers in 1947, 20 of them only as a pinch hitter.

On Bevens' first pitch, Lavagetto sent a line drive to right field. What followed, said right fielder Henrich later, was "the worst five seconds of my life."

Henrich had to make an instant decision: whether to try to go back and make the catch or to play the ball off the wall and try to keep the winning run from scoring. The fact that Bevens was throwing a no-hitter complicated his decision. "What if I played it off the wall and it only hit six feet up?" he asked, rhetorically, later. "I would have cost Bevens his no-hitter."

So, Henrich raced to the wall. At the last instant, he saw the ball was uncatchable, and he tried to stop himself and position himself for the carom off the wall. But when the ball came off the wall, it hit the heel of his glove and dropped. He wasted more time picking it up.

"If I catch the ball cleanly and throw it in," said Henrich, "Eddie Miksis will have to stop on third. But because I have to turn around and go back for the ball, that's one more base for him. It was no contest for him; he scored easily."

With one swing, Lavagetto had broken up Bevens' no-hitter (tne longest a pitcher would go with a no-hitter in World Series play until Don Larsen's perfect game in 1956) and won the game for the Dodgers. An elated Shotton told Lavagetto he could call his wife, who had just given birth three weeks before to Harry Jr., in Oakland and talk as long as he wanted; the club would pay for it.

The next day, the Yankees went ahead again, as Shea beat the Dodgers again, 2–1. This time it was the Dodger pitcher who was wild: Rex Barney, who could have had a great career if he had ever learned where the plate was, walked nine and threw a wild pitch in just 4⅔ innings. DiMaggio's home run in the fifth was the decider, but the Yankees had some anxious moments in the last of the ninth when, with two outs and a runner on first, Lavagetto came up again as a pinch hitter.

In the outfield, DiMaggio told Henrich to pray. In the dressing room later, Henrich asked DiMag why he wasn't praying. "I was praying," said DiMaggio. "I wasn't sure I was getting through."

But there were no more miracles for Lavagetto in this game. Shea struck him out to end the inning and game.

The Series went back to Yankee Stadium for the sixth game, and Gionfriddo played an important role for the Dodgers once again, this time for a catch some observers think is the greatest in Series history.

Gionfriddo had come in to play left field as a defensive replacement for Hermanski in the sixth inning, with the Dodgers leading, 8–5. The Yankees put two runners on base, Stirnweiss with a walk and Berra with a single, with two outs. DiMaggio hit a tremendous fly to left center that appeared to be out of the park, a three-run homer that would tie the score. But Gionfriddo took off after it.

The left-handed Gionfriddo took a look over his right shoulder as he neared the fence—and saw that the ball was coming down over the other shoulder. Somehow, he twisted around to make a one-handed catch just before he slammed into the wall.

The ball had been in the air so long that DiMaggio had come around second base as it was caught. He stopped and kicked the dirt in frustration.

The Yankees did manage one run in the bottom of the ninth, but that was as close as they got, losing, 8–6.

Fittingly enough, in this year of the relief pitcher, it was Page who made the difference in the final game, going the last five innings and yielding only one hit and no runs to the Dodgers to nail down a 5–2 Yankee win. The Yankees had beaten the Dodgers again, a streak that would reach five before it was broken in 1955.

Page had pitched in four of the games, winning one (the last game) and saving one. Casey had been even better, winning two of the three Brooklyn wins and saving the other; he had finished all six games in which he had appeared.

Lindell had hit an even .500 for the Yankees, nine hits in 18 at-bats, while knocking in seven runs, high for the Series. Henrich, always a deadly clutch hitter, had hit .323 with a Series-leading ten hits. Furillo had led the Dodgers with .353.

And what of the players who had had the most memorable moments in the Series—Gionfriddo, Lavagetto, and Bevens? None of them played again in the major leagues.

15. Who Is This Clown?

In 1948, the New York Yankees finished third in the American League. Yankee managers do not often survive a third-place finish. On a couple of occasions, they haven't even survived when they've won the pennant. Although the Yankees had set a franchise attendance record of 2,373,901 that year, Bucky Harris was fired.

It was a time of change for the Yankees. Owners Dan Topping and Del Webb had bought out Larry MacPhail, who had acted as the club's general manager, and had hired George Weiss as general manager.

At a press conference following Cleveland's win in the 1948 World Series, Topping and Webb presented their new manager: Casey Stengel.

The reaction among fans, writers, and players was one of amused skepticism. Some of the New York writers had known Stengel since he was a player with the New York Giants; others had known him as the Brooklyn Dodger manager in the '30s. They all liked him, because he was always good for a laugh and a story, but few took him seriously as a manager.

The players felt the same way. "I think a lot of guys looked at him as an interim manager," recalled pitcher Ed Lopat many years later. "We all knew about him. When you thought about Casey Stengel taking over, all you could do was smile."

Lopat noted that the Yankee coaches at the time were men like Bill Dickey, Jim Turner, and Frank Crosetti, all capable of managing. "Weiss was ready with a successor if Casey failed."

Within the organization, the reaction was stronger. "The general consensus," said Lee MacPhail, then in the Yankee farm system and later president of the American League, "was that Stengel simply didn't fit in with the Yankees, that image of dignity, class, refinement. There were a lot of people around the Yankees who said, 'My God, we've hired a clown.'"

There was nothing in Stengel's major league managing career to suggest that he was the man for the Yankees. In nine years of managing the Dodgers and Boston Braves, he had never had a team that finished higher than fifth. In 1943, his last year with the Braves, Stengel suffered a broken leg when he was hit by a car while crossing the street. *Boston Record* columnist Dave Egan nominated the driver as Boston's "Man of the Year."

Stengel's hiring had, indeed, been a subject of fierce controversy between Weiss and Webb. Weiss had hired Stengel as manager of the Kansas City club in the American Association, a Yankee farm club, in 1945, and he admired Stengel. But Webb at first wanted no part of Casey. "He's a clown," shouted Webb. "I don't want a clown managing the New York Yankees."

Weiss insisted that Stengel was a great baseball man, despite his reputation for clowning. "I never knew a man who could talk baseball all night the way Casey can," he told Webb. "You can ask him anything about any move he makes in a game and he'll always have an answer. Casey never makes a move without knowing why he does it."

Impressed by Weiss's argument, Webb said he'd agree if Topping did. Topping had turned over the running of the club to Weiss, and he couldn't interfere with this major decision. So, Stengel was given a two-year contract.

Weiss knew what he was doing. He had two major reasons for wanting Stengel. One was Stengel's ability to deal with the press. Weiss, a humorless man who preferred not to talk to writers at all, knew Stengel would be a buffer for him.

More important, Weiss knew that Stengel had learned a lot in his long apprenticeship, not just about strategy but about personalities and psychology. He knew that, given the right players—a luxury Stengel had never had in Brooklyn and Boston—he could be a winner.

Much was made later of Stengel's platooning, a strategy that Casey learned firsthand when John McGraw used him only against right-handers with the Giants. He got the most out of players like Gene Woodling, Hank Bauer, Johnny Lindell, and Bobby Brown by platooning them.

Weiss supplied him with the players, and Stengel had a gift for getting the most out of them, juggling players, getting the hot bat in the lineup, pinch-hitting at the right moment. He was not afraid to go against the book: In the 1952 Series, he used left-hander Bob Kuzava against the Dodgers' right-handed hitters because Kuzava's fastball tailed away from right-handers.

Most of all, though, Stengel's success was due to his total dedication to the game. No detail was too small to be overlooked.

"I had this player in Brooklyn," Stengel said once, "and you could ask him for a match and find out what bar he was in the night before. After we traded him to another club I always went up to him before the game with a cigarette and asked for a match. If he pulled out a match from some bar, I knew he had been out late and I could pitch him fastballs."

Casey Stengel was all baseball. "One day we lost a game to Washington," remembered Tommy Henrich. "We were playing 'Twenty Questions' on the train to Cleveland later. Casey walked by and listened for a second and then said, 'I got a question. Which of you guys ain't gonna be here next year?'"

During a 14–1 rout of the Philadelphia A's, Stengel started bawling out his players for blowing a cutoff play the week before. Henrich thought he was going crazy, and he asked Stengel about it in the dressing room. "I learned that from McGraw," said Stengel, winking. "If you bawl them out while they're losing, they may punch you in the nose. Do it while they're winning and they'll listen."

And so, at age 58, fresh from a pennant with the Oakland Oaks of the Pacific Coast League, Charles Dillon "Casey" Stengel became the Yankee manager and set about making baseball history. For the first time, a team would win five consecutive pennants. For the first and probably last time, a team would also win five consecutive World Series.

You could look it up.

The best job of managing Stengel did was probably in his first season. The Yankees had been picked to finish third again, which didn't bother Casey. "Third place sounds pretty good," he said. "I've never been there before."

A rash of injuries hit the club, forcing Stengel to juggle his lineup daily. The worst was a bone spur on Joe DiMaggio's right heel that sidelined the great center fielder for the first 65 games.

When DiMaggio did come back, it was as if he had never been gone: In a three-game series in Boston with the Red Sox, he hit four homers as the Yankees swept.

The Red Sox, a great hitting club with Ted Williams (43 homers, 159 RBIs), Vern Stephens (39 homers, 159 RBIs), and Bobby Doerr (18 homers, 108 RBIs) knocking in Johnny Pesky (.306) and Dom DiMaggio (.307), battled back and actually led the Yankees by a game with two games left. But the Yankees won both games in Yankee Stadium to take the pennant.

Their World Series opponents were again the Brooklyn Dodgers, and this was a stronger Dodger team than had faced the Yankees in 1947.

The elements of the Dodger dynasty were in place now. Jackie Robinson had been moved to second base after the trade of Eddie Stanky to Boston, and Robinson had his best year, .342 with 37 stolen bases and 124 RBIs, good enough to be named Most Valuable Player.

Gil Hodges, originally a catcher, had settled in for a long run at first base. Pee Wee

Jackie Robinson was the catalyst for the Brooklyn Dodger dynasty team
that played in six World Series in ten years. (*George Brace*)

Roy Campanella was a great catcher and an important part of the Brooklyn Dodgers hitting lineup in five World Series. *(George Brace)*

Reese was still the shortstop; Spider Jorgensen, later to give way to Billy Cox, was the third baseman. Roy Campanella was behind the plate.

In the outfield, Duke Snider was in his first full season in center and Carl Furillo in right. Left field, a Dodger trouble spot until they finally traded for Andy Pafko in 1951, was shared by Luis Olmo and Gene Hermanski.

Fireballing Don Newcombe, the third black player to be brought up by the Dodgers (Robinson and Campanella were the first two) was the staff leader with 17 wins.

Over the next five years, the Dodgers would provide an interesting counterpoint to the Yankee success. Physical talent is the first and most important requirement for winning, of course, but a team that wins year after year must also have the psychological determination.

In that stretch, the Dodgers were as physically talented as the Yankees. The day-to-day lineup they put on the field was probably stronger; the pitching not quite as good.

But the Dodgers lost two pennants in that stretch, to inferior teams. And, of course, they could not win a World Series. Stengel was able to keep the Yankees driving year after year to that incredible accomplishment of five straight World Series triumphs.

The first game of the '49 Series was a brilliantly pitched one. Going into the bottom of the ninth at Yankee Stadium, Don Newcombe had been overpowering for the

Don Newcombe was the staff leader for the great Brooklyn teams of the late '40s and '50s, but the World Series jinxed him, and he never won a Series game. *(Los Angeles Dodgers)*

Dodgers, striking out 11 as he yielded only four hits. Allie Reynolds had been even stingier, allowing only two hits. The teams were locked in a scoreless duel.

Then, leading off the bottom of the ninth for the Yankees, Henrich lined a shot to right field. As soon as he saw the ball heading out, Newcombe put down his head and walked off the mound. He knew it was a home run. It was that kind of hitting that had earned Henrich the nickname "Old Reliable."

Tommy Henrich was known as "Old Reliable" for his consistent play in the World Series for the New York Yankees. *(George Brace)*

In the second game, the Yankees learned why Robinson had become known as the "black Ty Cobb" in the National League.

Leading off the second inning, Robinson doubled and advanced to third when Hermanski fouled out to Yankee second baseman Jerry Coleman down the right field line. Marv Rackley grounded to third, and Robinson had to hold his base. Hodges was up with two outs.

Although Robinson hadn't scored, his dashes up and down along the third base line had bothered Yankee pitcher Vic Raschi, the staff leader with a 21–10 record during the season.

"You never knew what he was going to do," noted Raschi years later, "and he was fully capable of doing almost anything he wanted. He was just about the best base runner I've ever seen. He could get away from a standing position in a flash."

Raschi decided to pitch from the stretch position, instead of a full windup, giving Robinson less chance to steal home. "But Robinson had broken my concentration," he said. "I was pitching more to Robinson than I was to Hodges, and as a result, I threw one up into Gil's power."

Hodges hit Raschi's high fastball for a single that scored Robinson, and that was the only run in the second straight 1–0 game. Preacher Roe, who scattered six hits for the Dodgers, was the winner.

The Series shifted to Ebbets Field for the next three games, but that was no advantage for the Dodgers, who lost all three and the Series.

The Dodgers didn't go down without a struggle, however, especially in the Series' third game. For eight innings, it was 1–1. Ralph Branca, later to achieve a fame he never wanted as the pitcher who gave up Bobby Thomson's home run in the 1951 National League playoffs, had given up only two hits for the Dodgers.

Tommy Byrne had started for the Yankees but was relieved in the fourth after giving up a solo homer to Reese and loading the bases on a single to Furillo and walks to Robinson and Hodges.

Page, who had bounced back from a mediocre season in 1948 for the second and last of his great years, ended that inning by getting Olmo to foul out to Henrich at first base and Snider to ground out to second. In the next four innings, he ran his streak to 15 consecutive batters retired before Reese walked in the eighth.

In the top of the ninth, the Yankees struck for three runs, the big blow Johnny Mize's two-run pinch single. Olmo and Campanella raised the hopes of Dodger fans in the bottom of the inning with home runs, but Page ended the threat by striking out Bruce Edwards.

The last two games were easier for the Yankees. They knocked out Newcombe with a three-run rally in the fourth inning of the fourth game and went up 6–0 with three more runs in the fifth inning off Joe Hatten.

Yankee starter Lopat faltered in the sixth, yielding four runs, so Stengel rushed in

Reynolds to stop the rally and save the game. It was the kind of unorthodox move that Casey loved: That was the year in which Reynolds had needed frequent relief help from Page, finishing only four of 31 starts. Maybe Casey thought he should learn how it was done at the end of a game.

The final game went to the Yankees, 10–6, and it wasn't even that close, the Yankees being up 10–1 before the Dodgers rallied to make it fairly respectable. Page finished up again; in this, his last World Series, he had won one game and saved another.

DiMaggio had played with a virus that had required pregame shots of penicillin, but if he was weak, the Dodgers didn't notice it; he hit a fourth-inning home run and had two RBIs.

There was a surprise in 1950: The Philadelphia Phillies, who had not won a pennant since 1915, were the National League champions.

The Phillies were called the "Whiz Kids" because of their youth, especially on the pitching mound, with Robin Roberts and Curt Simmons. But an old-timer, Jim Konstanty, was at least as responsible for their success as the youngsters, appearing in a then-record 74 games in relief and winning the Most Valuable Player award.

If the Series had been held in early September, it might have been a more interesting one. The Phillies were dying by October. Leading by seven games with nine to go, they

Joe Page was a key figure in relief for the New York Yankees in their 1949 World Series triumph. *(George Brace)*

had to beat Brooklyn in ten innings in the final game of the season, 4–1 on Dick Sisler's homer and behind Roberts' pitching, to win the pennant.

It wasn't quite the El Foldo it seemed. The Phillies had lost 17-game winner Simmons to the service in September, and two other starters, Bubba Church and Bob Miller, on injuries. Simmons and Church were unavailable for the Series; Miller pitched just one-third of an inning.

Meanwhile, the Yankees came into the Series in a hitting slump. The result was a Series in which all four games were close but the outcome was never really in doubt.

Because Roberts had pitched four games in the last eight days of the season, including the clincher, Philadelphia manager Eddie Sawyer surprised everybody by starting Konstanty in the opener, though he hadn't started a game all season.

Konstanty pitched well, allowing only four hits in eight innings. The only Yankee run came in the fourth on a double by Bobby Brown and long flies by Bauer and Coleman.

But Raschi was even better for the Yankees, going the distance and giving up just two hits for a 1–0 win.

The strong-armed Roberts was ready for the second game and he matched Reynolds pitch for pitch into the tenth inning, the score tied, 1–1. Up came DiMaggio, who had popped out four straight times.

"I think I might have been a little overconfident," recalled Roberts later. "The moment the pitch left my hand, I knew it didn't have the drive it should have had, and I saw DiMaggio's whole body moving into it."

DiMaggio hit the ball into the left field stands, and that was the ball game.

The Yankees waited almost as long to win the third game, two–out singles by Woodling, Phil Rizzuto, and Coleman breaking a 2–2 tie in the bottom of the ninth.

An eighth inning error by young Phillie shortstop Granny Hamner had allowed the Yankees to tie the score, and Hamner was disconsolate as he walked off the field after the game.

He felt an arm around his shoulder. It was DiMaggio. "Don't feel too bad, kid," said DiMaggio. "You're too good a ball player to let it get you down."

The final game was the closest to a lopsided one, the Yankees winning, 5–2. The winner was Whitey Ford, who had come up in late season to go 9–1 for the Yankees down the stretch. A home run by Yogi Berra and a triple by Brown were the key blows in a three-run sixth that nailed down the win.

And, oh yes, about that clown Stengel. Before the Series, Stengel had analyzed the Phillies for his pitchers, and he talked about that afterwards:

"A free-swinging club like the Phils . . . is usually a low-ball hitting team but can't hit the high ones too well. We had our pitchers throw high and keep going higher if they chased the high pitches. Sisler was an outstanding example. We pitched him chest-high. When he swung at that one, we went up a few inches. Finally, we had him swinging at pitches around his neck."

Sisler was one–for–17, a single, in the Series.

The Series was almost an anticlimax in 1951, because that was the year the Giants came from 13½ games back (between games of a doubleheader) in early August to catch the Dodgers and then beat them in an unforgettable playoff.

Still, there were some extraordinary elements to this Series. Willie Mays for the Giants and Mickey Mantle for the Yankees were both rookies, and the debate over which was the better player would rage for much of the next two decades.

It would be DiMaggio's final season and Series, and the Giants would be the first World Series team to field an all-black outfield, with Mays flanked by Monte Irvin in left and Hank Thompson, replacing the injured Don Mueller, in right.

The Giants had to come back the next day after beating the Dodgers, which required both a physical and an emotional adjustment. "I would have preferred a few days off to savor the victory," Irvin admitted later. "Also, I wanted some time to think about the Yankees, about their pitchers, about how to play certain hitters. But we didn't have that luxury."

Even worse, the Giants had exhausted their pitching staff. Sal Maglie and Larry Jansen, both 23-game winners, and 17-game winner Jim Hearn had all pitched in the final three days, so manager Leo Durocher had to use left-hander Dave Koslo, who had won just ten games, as his first game starter.

Amazingly, Koslo and the Giants won, 5–2.

Yankee starter Reynolds had had two no-hit games among his 17 victories during the season, but he was not sharp for this one. In six innings, he walked seven batters, gave up eight hits, and allowed all five Giant runs.

Irvin had a great day, belting four hits and stealing home in the first inning. That was not a novelty for him; he had stolen home five times during the regular season.

Irvin had singled with two outs and gone to third on a double by Whitey Lockman. "I noticed that Reynolds was taking a long time to deliver the ball," said Irvin later. "He was ducking his head and looking down as he went into his motion."

Irvin called time and told Durocher, in the coaching box, that he thought he could steal home. Durocher told him to go ahead.

Thomson was at the plate and, when he realized Irvin was coming, hung back for a moment to obscure Berra's vision. The pitch was high and Irvin swept across the plate a split-second before Berra tagged him.

When the umpire called Irvin safe, Berra jumped up and yelled, "No, no, no!"

"Yes, yes, yes," said Irvin. "That's what it's going to say in the papers tomorrow: Yes."

Berra got his revenge later in the game. Irvin came up in the eighth, having gone 4–for–4, and Yogi told him, "You're hitting everything today. I don't know what to throw you. I think I'll tell him [pitcher Tom Morgan] just to throw it down the middle."

Yogi Berra was a key player for the New York Yankees and later managed them in the World Series of 1964. *(George Brace)*

Irvin laughed because catchers—especially talkative ones like Berra—often say such things to hitters to throw them off balance. But Yogi was as good as his word: The next pitch was right down the middle.

"I was so surprised that I swung late and hit a line drive right into Joe Collins' glove at first," recalled Irvin. "Another few inches either way and I would have had that fifth hit."

It was Lopat against Jansen in the second game, the best-pitched game of the Series. Lopat was the kind of pitcher who looks easy to hit but was nothing but trouble. He seldom threw his fastball for strikes, preferring to nibble away at the corners with a variety of breaking stuff, most of it slow and slower. He was a steady pitcher for the Yanks for years, and 1951 was his best season, as he won 21 games.

He was at his best in this game, yielding only five hits—three of them by the hot Irvin. Jansen pitched well, too, giving up only four hits, two of them bunt singles, before leaving the game after six innings. But the Yankees got three of the hits, including the two bunts, for one run in the first and a home run with nobody on by Collins in the second, and went on to a 3–1 win.

The game ended Mantle's first Series. Chasing a fly ball in the sixth, he caught his foot in the wooden cover of a drainpipe outlet and twisted his knee—the first of many injuries that would plague him in an otherwise great career.

The Giants came back with a 6–2 win in the third game, knocking out Raschi with a five-run fifth. The tone for the inning was set when Eddie Stanky kicked the ball out of Rizzuto's glove for what should have been an out, and Lockman capped the rally with a three-run homer.

But then, the Giants ran out of steam and lost the next three games, 6–2, 13–1, and 4–3. "We just weren't psychologically ready for a World Series," said Irvin, "and I guess you could say that was understandable."

The Yankees also got a break because the fourth game was delayed a day because of rain. Morgan had been scheduled to pitch but, with that extra day of rest, Stengel was able to go back to his top three, Reynolds, Lopat, and Raschi.

The one high point for the Giants was Irvin's hot bat. Monte got 11 hits and just missed a 12th when he hit a line drive to left-center in the ninth inning of the fifth game. "Hardest ball I hit all Series," he said. "I figured it was going to be in for a triple or maybe even an inside-the-park homer." But Woodling dove for the ball in left-center and came up with it, and Irvin went hitless in the final game.

The Giants battled the Yankees on even terms for 5½ innings of the sixth game, 1–1. But then Bauer tripled with the bases loaded in the bottom of the sixth, and those runs stood up for the Yankee win.

After the Series, a scouting report that had been prepared for the Dodgers by Andy High (and passed on to the Giants) appeared in *Life* magazine with a devastating analysis of the declining DiMaggio:

"Fielding—he can't stop quickly and throw hard. You can take the extra base on him if he is in motion away from the line of throw. He won't throw on questionable plays. . . .

"Speed—he can't run and he won't bunt.

"Hitting vs. right-handed pitcher—his reflexes are very slow and he can't pull a good fastball at all. . . . Throw him nothing but good fastballs and fast curveballs. Don't slow up on him.

"Hitting vs. left-handed pitcher—will pull left-handed pitcher a little more than right-handed pitcher. Pitch him the same. Don't slow up on him. He will go for a bad pitch once in a while with two strikes."

The report didn't tell DiMaggio anything he didn't already know. The Yankees were willing to pay him $100,000 just to be a part-time player, but the proud DiMag couldn't accept that. He announced at a press conference in the Yankee offices early in December that he was retiring. When a reporter asked why, Joe answered, "I no longer have it."

Although Stengel always praised DiMaggio, Joe's retirement made it easier for Casey. There had been some friction between the two; Stengel had once benched DiMag, another time dropped him a spot in the batting order and played him one game at first base, and DiMaggio hadn't agreed with any of the actions. Now, the Yankees were definitely Stengel's team.

As always in those days, the Yankees had another star ready to step in. As Lou Gehrig had taken over the top role when Babe Ruth left, as DiMaggio had taken over for Gehrig, now Mantle would take over for DiMaggio—and go on to hit .311, knock in 111 runs, and belt 23 homers in 1952.

And the Yankees had another leader: feisty Billy Martin, a second baseman who had first caught Stengel's eye with Oakland of the Pacific Coast League and who would go on to become a manager much in Stengel's style.

The Dodgers were back as the Yankees' World Series opponent in 1952, and they waged a classic seven-game battle. In the end, it took one of the most famous of World Series plays for the Yankees to win—a play made by Martin.

Joe Black had had a great rookie season as a reliever for the Dodgers, winning 14 games (plus one as a starter) and saving 15. But Brooklyn manager Chuck Dressen, as smart a baseball man as Stengel, pulled a surprise and started Black in the Series opener. Dressen looked like a genius when Black beat Reynolds, 4–2, all of the Dodger runs coming on solo homers by Robinson and Reese and a two-run homer by Snider.

Raschi got the Yankees even in the next game with a 7–1 win over Carl Erskine. Raschi gave up only three hits, all of them in the third inning when Brooklyn scored its single run.

Preacher Roe, a confessed spitballer after his retirement, beat Lopat and the Yankees, 5–3, in the third game, despite homers by Berra and Mize.

Reynolds got revenge for his first game loss by beating Black, starting again, 2–0, in the fourth game, striking out ten, including Robinson three times, and giving up just four hits. Mize hit another home run in the Yankee win.

Mize hit his third home run of the Series the next day in a strange game won by the Dodgers, 6–5. Erskine gave up all five Yankee runs in the fifth as the Yankees took a 5–4 lead, but he settled down after that and retired 19 straight batters.

Meanwhile, the Dodgers tied it in the seventh when Snider singled in Reese and finally won it in the 11th when Snider's double knocked in Cox.

The Yankees came back for the third time to tie the Series in the sixth game, another strange one. Billy Loes had the Yankees shut out, 1–0, in the seventh when Berra homered to tie it. Woodling singled to center and Loes balked him to second, but he should have gotten out of the inning with no more damage when Raschi hit the ball back to the mound with two outs. However, the ball hit Loes on the knee and rolled into center, Woodling scoring.

After the game, the daffy Loes "explained" that he had lost the ground ball in the sun! This, remember, is a pitcher who once said he didn't ever want to win 20 games because people then expected too much of you.

Billy Martin was a surprisingly good hitter in World Series play and saved another title for the New York Yankees with a spectacular catch. *(George Brace)*

Gil Hodges once went 0–for–21 in World Series play, but, with the support of Dodger fans, he rebounded from this debacle during his playing career and had a happier time in 1969 when he managed the New York Mets to a surprising Series title. *(George Brace)*

"I never saw the ball at all," said Loes. "I lost it in the sun and threw my glove out, hoping to stop it."

Mantle hit a homer in the eighth for a third run, and then Reynolds preserved the win for the tiring Raschi.

The Yankees led the final game, 4–2, in the seventh inning when the Dodgers loaded the bases with one out. Stengel brought in Kuzava, the fourth Yankee pitcher. Kuzava got the dangerous Snider to pop up for the second out, but that brought up Robinson, the Dodgers' best clutch hitter.

Stengel, no lover of black players (Casey had grown up in an era when virtually the only blacks he saw were in menial positions, and he was quite content with the Yankees' all-white policy), had been needling Robinson throughout the game, calling him "Duck-ass" because of the way Robinson ran, his rear sticking out.

That made Robinson all the more determined, but his determination did him no good: He hit a little pop-up to the infield that looked like the third out. The Yankee infielders, however, seemed frozen by the play, with nobody moving for the ball.

"Mr. Collins, which was my first baseman, was counting his money so he never seen it," Stengel "explained" years later to Maury Allen, "and Mr. Berra, my catcher, is standing with his hands on his hips yelling for Mr. Collins, and Mr. Gazzara [Kuzava] did the pitchin' and he ain't about to do the catchin', so that leaves the second baseman. . . ."

The second baseman was Martin, who came dashing in to snatch the ball just above the grass and only a few feet from home plate. The play made Movietone News and made Martin quite famous. It also won the ball game for the Yanks, who held on to their 4–2 lead the rest of the way over the now demoralized Dodgers.

One factor that made the Dodgers vulnerable was the disastrous batting performance turned in by a bewildered Gil Hodges, one of their leading sluggers. Gil went 0–for–21 in the Series. The well-liked Hodges, coming off a season in which he belted 32 home runs, drove in 102 runs, and batted .254, remained in the grip of a slump throughout the Series. The Brooklyn faithful stayed behind him, however, and sent him all kinds of magical devices to break the collar. Many parishes in the Borough of Churches even offered prayers for a fine man mired in a nerve-wracking situation.

Perhaps because of the public's help, Hodges rebounded from this debacle and went on to become a slugger of note for the Dodgers in the next decade—finishing his career with a World Series mark of .267, a formidable figure when one takes into account the 0–for–21 year!

Martin was also a hero in the 1953 Series, getting a Series record 12 hits in six games against the Dodgers, and he even had fun in a game the Yankees lost.

It was the third game, at Ebbets Field, and Erskine was making history for the Dodgers, striking out batter after batter. Stengel was on his hitters for swinging at

Casey Stengel, once regarded as a clown, managed the New York Yankees to a record five straight World Series titles, 1949–53. *(New York Yankees)*

Erskine's big-breaking curve ball, which often ended in the dirt. "He's killin' worms, he's killin' worms. Lay off the pitch."

Mize echoed Stengel's words, second-guessing his teammates. "Make him get it up," said Mize, repeatedly.

In the ninth, Mize was sent up to pinch-hit for Raschi. Erskine had tied Howard Ehmke's Series record with 13 strikeouts, and he got two strikes on Mize. The next pitch broke into the dirt. Mize swung and missed for Erskine's 14th strikeout. "Make him get it up," needled Martin.

The Series had an unusual pattern, the Yankees winning the first two and last two, the Dodgers the two games in between.

Mantle had a big Series. His two-run homer in the second game was the difference as Lopat topped Roe, 4–2. In the fifth game, a wild one with six homers, he hit a grand-slam homer that was again the difference in the 11–7 game.

But it was again Martin who made the big play in the final game. With the score tied, 3–3, in the bottom of the ninth, Bauer walked and, after Berra lined out, Mantle beat out an infield hit.

Martin then lined his 12th hit of the Series to center field and Snider didn't even bother to make a throw as Bauer scored the winning run.

Stengel ran out of the dugout to hug Martin. When he had been asked the previous October how it felt to win his fourth straight world championship he had winked and said, "It's a short record. You gotta win eight or nine before they pay any attention."

But, five would do. Nobody had done it before and you can bet that nobody will do it again.

Willie Mays made an inforgettable catch in the 1954 World Series but his Series hitting wasn't as impressive as his fielding. *(Dennis Desprois)*

16. Say Hey and Dusty, Too!

It was the eighth inning of the first game of the 1954 World Series. Sal Maglie of the New York Giants and Bob Lemon of the Cleveland Indians were locked in a 2–2 pitching duel.

Larry Doby walked to lead off the inning for the Indians, and Al Rosen followed with a single off shortstop Alvin Dark's hands, bringing up Vic Wertz. Trouble. Wertz had already gotten three hits off Maglie, including a first-inning triple which had knocked in the first Cleveland run.

Giants' manager Leo Durocher, playing the percentages, brought in left-hander Don Liddle to pitch to Wertz, but percentages often mean little to a hitter with a hot bat. Wertz laced a Liddle pitch to the deepest part of the Polo Grounds, straightaway center field.

Giants' center fielder Willie Mays, his cap flying off as always, turned his back on the plate and ran for the fence, but it was obvious he had no chance for the ball. Left fielder Monte Irvin ran over to back up the play; he later confessed he was hoping he could get the rebound off the fence quickly enough to hold Wertz to a triple.

But, just before he ran into the fence, Mays stuck out his glove. The ball fell over his right shoulder and into Mays's glove, directly in front of the sign reading "460 feet." It was, some thought, the best catch in World Series history; only Al Gionfriddo's catch off Joe DiMaggio in 1947 could even be compared to it.

Mays not only made the catch but recovered in time to whirl around and throw the ball back to the infield. Doby, who had gone down only halfway between second and third, was able to tag up and go to third, but Rosen had to retreat to first.

The inning wasn't over yet. Both Durocher and his rival manager, Cleveland's Al Lopez, had much juggling to do yet. Lopez inserted right-handed hitting Hank Majeski for Dave Philley. Durocher took out Liddle (One wonders if the southpaw said to

• 173

himself, "Well, I did my job") and brought in right-handed Marv Grissom. Lopez then pinch-hit the left-handed hitting Dale Mitchell for Majeski.

Mitchell walked, but then pinch hitter Dave Pope struck out and Jim Hegan flied to left to end the inning.

As Irvin and Mays trotted in from the outfield, Irvin congratulated Willie on his catch. "That was the greatest catch I ever saw," said Irvin.

"Had it all the way," said Mays. "Had it all the way."

As it turned out, the Giants had the Indians all the way, too. Mays's catch should have been the tip-off, but it took a while for the reality to set in, not just for the Indians but baseball fans and writers.

That was a strange year, 1954, and an important one in baseball history. It was the first and last year that a Casey Stengel team would win more than 100 games—103, to be exact—but Stengel's Yankees couldn't win the pennant. The Indians did with an American League record 111 wins.

They did it primarily on pitching and power hitting. Doby led the American League with 32 homers and 126 RBIs. Rosen had 24 homers and 102 RBIs. Wertz, limited by injury to 94 games, hit 14 homers. Second baseman Bobby Avila led the league with a .341 batting average.

Bob Lemon and Early Wynn each won 23 games, Mike Garcia 19. Art Houtteman added 15. Bob Feller, pitching now with slow curves because his once-great fastball

Early Wynn was part of a great pitching staff as the '54 Indians won an American League record 111 games—but lost four straight to the Giants in the World Series. *(George Brace)*

was gone, was 13–3. In the bull pen, Lopez could call on right-hander Ray Narleski (three wins, 13 saves) or left hander Don Mossi (six wins, seven saves).

The Indians had spread-eagled the field, eight games ahead of the Yankees, 17 ahead of third place Chicago, a whopping 42 in front of the fourth place Red Sox.

The Giants, meanwhile, had finished five games ahead of the Dodgers with 97 wins. They had a great player in Mays, who had come out of the Army to lead the league in hitting with .345, along with 41 home runs, but Durocher's champions seemed only a good team, not a great one.

They had, for instance, one outstanding starter in Johnny Antonelli, who won 21 games, and a great reliever in Hoyt Wilhelm, who had pitched in 57 games.

But the other starters—Ruben Gomez and the aging (37) Maglie—didn't scare anybody.

Their defense was solid up the middle with Wes Westrum catching, shortstop Alvin Dark and second baseman Dave Williams making the double play and Mays playing center field as well as, and more spectacularly than, anybody ever had.

They also had a secret weapon in an obscure outfielder-pinch hitter named James Rhodes, nicknamed "Dusty" as has been every other player named Rhodes since the game began.

You won't find Rhodes' name in the Hall of Fame. He played only seven seasons, and only once got more than 200 at-bats. He was a throwback to an earlier era, a man who cared more about a good time than the ball game. Even with Mays around to catch some of his mistakes, people shuddered when balls were hit to him in the outfield; Durocher sent him out there for just 37 games in 1954.

But the man could hit. In only 164 at-bats in the '54 season, he had hammered 15 homers, one for every 11 at-bats, and hit .341. As a pinch hitter, he had 15 hits in 45 at-bats for a .333 average, exceptionally high for that most difficult of hitting roles.

None of this mattered to the writers covering the World Series. In wire service polls before the start of the Series, 37 of 54 writers contacted by the Associated Press thought Cleveland would win and 110 of 154 talking to United Press favored the Indians. After all, Cleveland had set a record in what was thought of as the stronger league.

They should have talked to the Giants first. "We were very confident, because we used to play them in the spring and beat them regularly," said Irvin, who had had a potentially great career reduced to an average one because of a broken ankle. "They had good power and outstanding pitching, but their defense wasn't too good and they didn't have much speed."

Irvin was right. Aside from their pitching, the Indians were little more than an average club. The power balance in baseball was shifting to the National League for two reasons: (1) The long dominance of the Yankees had discouraged many of the teams, and the overall quality of the league had declined. (2) The reluctance of

American League teams (the Yankees among them, but not the Indians) to sign black players had given the more aggressive National League teams first shot at a large pool of talent.

The Indians, in short, had won 111 games not because they were a great team but because they were playing in a declining league. In this Series, they would run into a hot team and all their deficiencies would become glaringly obvious.

But back to the first game.

The score remained at 2–2 until the bottom of the tenth. With one out, Mays walked and stole second. Lopez ordered Hank Thompson intentionally walked to set up the double play.

Irvin was the next hitter, but Durocher called him back and sent up Rhodes. "I knew he was going to use me," Rhodes said later. "Leo knew and I knew that that was my spot. The game meant something and that meant it was up to me."

Lemon's first pitch was a slow curve, just above the waist. Rhodes swung and sent a lazy fly right down the right field line. In any other park in the major leagues, it would have been a routine fly ball. But this was the Polo Grounds, where it was only 257 feet down the right field line. As Cleveland's Pope watched helplessly, the ball dropped just over the fence for a home run. The Giants had won the game, 5–2. Wertz had hit a ball 457 feet and it had been an out; Rhodes had hit one 257 feet for the winning home run.

Wynn and Antonelli were the second game pitchers, and Wynn was leading, 1–0,

Bob Lemon was a great pitcher for the 1954 Cleveland Indians, but he couldn't stop the New York Giants in the World Series. *(Cleveland Indians)*

going into the fifth inning. With one out, Mays walked and Thompson sent him to third with a single.

Durocher was a manager who knew how to use a hot bat. Instead of waiting for a spot later in the game, as most managers would have done, he hustled Rhodes up to the plate for Irvin once again, and Dusty blooped a ball into center. Mays scored, and Thompson went around to third. When the throw went to third to try to get Thompson, Rhodes went to second. Williams then struck out looking.

Lopez ordered Westrum walked to get at Antonelli with two outs, but the pitcher surprised everybody by beating out a hit to Avila, and the Giants had a 2–1 lead.

Durocher's managing became important now. As a manager, Leo had a good news, bad news reputation. The bad news was that, if his club was out of contention (admittedly seldom), he lost interest and did worse than another manager would do. The good news was that if his team had a chance, he had a way of driving it home like a good jockey.

Part of Durocher's success was psychology, part of it an ability to impart his desperate desire to win to the players, part of it was intuition. There has never been a hunch player like Leo the Lip.

He played one of his hunches here, leaving Rhodes in the ball game. It paid off. When Rhodes came to the plate again in the seventh, he hit a Wynn fastball over the roof in right field for the final run in the 3–1 Giants win.

When the Series moved to Cleveland, the Indians lost an important regular when an injury to his thigh forced Rosen out of the lineup, Majeski taking his place. At this point, though, it probably made no difference. The Giants were riding high.

For the first time, the Giants took the early lead, Mays singling in Don Mueller for a run in the first inning. In the third, Dark led off with a single and Mueller followed with another single, sending Dark to third.

On Mays' grounder, Dark was caught off third, but by the time he was run down, Mueller had advanced to third and Mays to second—a result of both heady base running by Dark and sloppy defense by the Indians.

Lopez, unable to believe that Durocher would use a pinch hitter as early as the third inning, had Thompson walked intentionally, loading the bases.

Durocher, of course, sent up Rhodes to pinch-hit for Irvin. Once again, Rhodes came through, singling in two runs. Williams followed with a bunt that scored the third run of the inning.

Rhodes stayed in the game again and, wonder of wonders, the Indians finally got him out, twice. It made no difference. The Giants had won their third straight game, 6–2, and Rhodes had gone 4–for–6, knocking in seven runs.

The Series was over, though they had to go through the motions of playing a fourth game. Once again, a manager's personality played an important role, this time Lopez's.

Cleveland's only chance was to try something totally unexpected, that would raise the players out of their torpor. Lopez had Feller in the bull pen. The once great right-hander had never won a World Series game, losing two in his only other appearances in 1948. He would have brought an emotion to that fourth game that might have inspired his teammates.

But Lopez, a very good manager over the course of a season, was not a man who could make that kind of daring move. Durocher could have made it—but he was in the other dugout. Lopez stuck with the pitching rotation that had done so well for him during the season, sending Lemon out again for the fourth game.

The Cleveland ace didn't have it, giving up seven hits and six runs, five of them earned, before departing after pitching to three batters in the fifth. He was so obviously ineffective, in fact, that Durocher passed up an opportunity to pinch-hit Rhodes again in the third. Leo had seen left-hander Hal Newhouser warming up in the bull pen and knew that Newhouser would come in if he sent Rhodes up to the plate, and he preferred to have Lemon stay in.

The Giants scored twice in the second inning. Thompson walked and Irvin doubled, moving Thompson to third. Williams lined to Wertz, who threw wildly to second trying to double up Irvin, Thompson scoring and Irvin going to third. Westrum flied to Wally Westlake in left field, but Westlake dropped the ball, Irvin scoring. (Westrum got credit for a sacrifice fly and RBI because Irvin would undoubtedly have scored anyway.)

Mays' third inning double scored another run, and the Giants turned it into a rout with a four-run fifth, knocking out Lemon in the process.

Dark and Mueller opened the inning with singles, and Mays walked to load the bases. Newhouser came in to pitch but walked in one run and gave up a two-run single to Irvin. Narleski relieved Newhouser and got out of the inning, but not before Westrum had hit another sacrifice fly for the fourth run.

The Indians came back to score three runs in the bottom of that inning and closed to 7–4 with a single run in the seventh. When they got two runners on with one out in the eighth, Durocher played his ace, Antonelli, the winner of the second game. Johnny struck out Wertz and Westlake to end the eighth and got the Indians 1–2–3 in the ninth to end the game.

It was the first time a National League team had swept the Series since the Miracle Braves had done it in 1914—and the Braves had been big underdogs, too.

Comedian Bob Hope, a stockholder in the Indians, moaned, "I spent plane fare and everything to see this. I could have gotten a bad stomach by just staying in Los Angeles."

But it was Lopez, years later, who had the most telling comment on the Series. "They say anything can happen in a short series," said Lopez. "Well, I knew that. I just never thought it was going to be *that* short."

17. A Miracle in Brooklyn

If 1954 was the Giants' year, 1955 was the year for the Brooklyn Dodgers, in every way.

The Dodgers had been nearly as dominant in the National League since the end of World War II as the Yankees had been in the American, winning pennants in 1947, 1949, 1952, and 1953 and losing on the last day of the season in 1950 and 1951, the latter in a playoff with the Giants.

But 1954 had been a vast disappointment. It had started in an unexpected way, as the Dodgers had acquired a new manager. The Dodgers had won two straight years under Charlie Dressen, and Dressen—prompted by his wife—had demanded a three-year contract, instead of the one-year contract owner Walter O'Malley believed in. When O'Malley wouldn't budge, Dressen quit (there were many who believed O'Malley pushed him a bit) and O'Malley hired Walter Alston.

There couldn't have been a more dramatic change, from the bombastic Dressen to the quiet Alston, who had managed many of the Dodgers in the minors; by his own count, 17 players who were on the 1954 roster at one time or another had played under him in the minors.

The Dodger team Alston inherited was virtually a National League All-Star team, with players like Roy Campanella, Gil Hodges, Jackie Robinson, Pee Wee Reese, Duke Snider, Carl Furillo, Don Newcombe, and Carl Erskine. Alston realized he was on the spot.

"The pressure was there, no question," he told Donald Honig years later. "The club had been winning, and I knew it was sort of expected of me to win. Nobody demanded it; there was no ultimatum from upstairs. But I knew what everybody was thinking."

There was only one problem: The Dodgers didn't win in 1954. Newcombe, back from two years in the service won only nine games. Campanella, playing with a hand injury, hit only .207. Preacher Roe, a 22-game winner as recently as 1951, won only three games and retired.

But that was 1954. In 1955, the Dodgers were a revitalized team. They stormed out of the gate, winning a then-record ten straight games at the start of the season and 22 of their first 24. They made a mockery of the pennant race, eventually finishing 13½ games ahead of a Milwaukee team, with Hank Aaron, Eddie Mathews, Warren Spahn, and Lew Burdette, that was still two years from its peak.

Healthy again, Campanella hit .318 with 32 homers and 107 RBIs to win the Most Valuable Player award. Snider had an even bigger offensive year, with 42 homers and a league-leading 136 RBIs to go with a .309 year. Hodges hit 27 homers, Furillo 26. It was an awesome lineup.

Back in stride, Newcombe won 20 games and lost only five, and he was equally effective as a hitter, with a .359 average and seven home runs (in only 117 at-bats), a league record for a pitcher. Newcombe was such a good hitter that year, in fact, that Alston used him as a pinch hitter in 23 games.

As they marched into the World Series for the eighth time, the opposing team was a familiar one: the Yankees, whom the Dodgers had played in their last five Series appearances.

This was a much different Yankee team from the one that had beaten the Dodgers in '53, however. Yogi Berra remained behind the plate, but the infield was almost totally changed. The only holdover was Gil McDougald, who had moved from third base to second because Billy Martin was in the service. Casey Stengel had platooned Joe Collins, a holdover from '53, and Bill Skowron at first base, as he would do in the Series. Billy Hunter was the shortstop, Andy Carey the third baseman.

In the outfield, Mickey Mantle was still the mainstay, with a 37-homer year, and Hank Bauer remained, but Irv Noren was now the left fielder.

The pitching staff had been almost totally overhauled. Whitey Ford had become the ace, winning 18 games in 1955; the old Big Three of Allie Reynolds, Vic Raschi, and Ed Lopat were all gone.

General manager George Weiss had traded for Bob Turley and Don Larsen, who had won 17 and nine games, respectively. Tommy Byrne, a left-hander whose success had been limited by wildness, had the best year of his career at age 35, winning 16 and losing only five.

For Brooklyn fans, watching the Dodgers play the Yankees in the World Series was like going to the dentist: They had to do it, but that didn't mean they had to like it. The Dodgers were 0–5 against the Yankees in the Series, 0–7 against everybody.

The Yankees seemed vulnerable. They had had much more trouble winning than the Dodgers, finally finishing three games ahead of Cleveland. Although Stengel had Martin, who had played 20 late-season games after being discharged from the Army, back at second base, a leg injury would limit Mantle to just three games. But, if the Yankees were vulnerable, it didn't show in the first two games.

The aces, Ford and Newcombe, were matched in the opener in Yankee Stadium, but this was no pitcher's duel.

The Dodgers got to Ford in the top of the second. Furillo opened the inning by hitting a home run into the right field stands, and a Jackie Robinson triple and Don Zimmer single got another.

The Yankees matched that in the bottom of the inning. Collins walked and then Elston Howard, the first black player to play for the Yankees, hit a two-run homer.

Snider hit a tremendous home run, into the third deck in right field, to lead off the third for the Dodgers and give them another lead. But the Yankees got that run back in the bottom of the inning on a walk to Ford and single by Bauer and successive groundouts by McDougald and Noren.

Collins put the Yankees ahead for the first time with a lead-off homer in the fourth, and then the Yankees knocked out Newcombe with two more runs in the sixth. Again, it was Collins—who had hit only 13 homers during the season, with a .234 average—who did the damage, following a single by Berra with his second homer of the game.

When Martin tripled with two outs, Alston decided that was enough for Newcombe and brought in Don Bessent. With Eddie Robinson at the plate as a pinch hitter, Martin tried to steal home but was tagged out to end the inning.

The Dodgers made it close with two runs in the eighth—the second coming as Jackie Robinson stole home—but it was still the Yankees' game, 6–5.

Byrne started the second game for the Yankees, and there is no better example of how Stengel's mind worked. The Dodgers were predominantly a right-handed hitting club; Snider was the only left-handed power hitter in the lineup. Casey did not want to pitch a left-hander against them in Ebbets Field, with its cozy dimensions. At Yankee Stadium, though, the left field fence sloped away sharply from the corner, making it a difficult home run park for a right-handed hitter (ask Joe DiMaggio about that!). So, Casey figured to start his left-handers, Ford and Byrne, in the first two games at Yankee Stadium, and he'd have them ready for the sixth and seventh games at the Stadium if it came down to that, as indeed it did.

It was quite a heady experience for Byrne, who had pitched in the minors the year before (winning 20 for Seattle in the Pacific Coast League). But if he felt the pressure, he didn't show it, pitching hitless ball for the first three innings.

In the top of the fourth, the Dodgers broke through as Reese doubled and Snider singled him home.

In the bottom of the inning, the Yankees rallied with two outs. Berra singled, Collins walked, and Howard singled to score one run. Martin singled to get another and pinch hitter Eddie Robinson was hit by a Billy Loes pitch, loading the bases and bringing up Byrne.

Byrne was no automatic out. At one time, in fact, the Yankees had talked to him about the possibility of becoming a first baseman because of his hitting ability. At Newark, he had hit .328 one year while pitching and playing first base and the outfield.

When he came out of the service in 1946, the Yankees asked him if he'd like to play first base at Newark. But Byrne had won 17 games for Newark in his last season before going into the service, and he felt his future was as a pitcher, not a first baseman.

Loes went to 2–0 on Byrne. "I sort of had to be looking for the hard one," Byrne said later. That's what he got, and he knocked it into center field, scoring two runs. From that point, Byrne and the Yankees coasted to a 4–2 win, Byrne yielding just five hits.

Amazingly, the Yankees had won both games without Mantle, whose leg had kept him out. No team had ever bounced back in a seven-game Series to win after losing the first two games, and with the Dodgers' lack of success in Series play, this seemed to be in the bag for the Yankees.

The Dodgers, though, were confident they'd do better in their home park, but an impartial observer had to wonder, especially when Alston picked a 23-year-old left-hander named Johnny Podres to start the third game.

Even Podres hadn't expected that he would start a Series game. It had been a bad luck year for Podres. He had won seven of his first ten, but had then injured his shoulder and gone on the disabled list.

When he got back into action, he had another mishap, this one a freak accident at Ebbets Field in September. Right after batting practice, Podres was preparing to hit fly balls to the outfielders as the groundskeepers were wheeling off the batting cage. The cage struck Podres in the right side, injuring his ribs and putting him out of action again.

Had the pennant race been close, Alston probably would have put Podres on the disabled list and brought up another pitcher from the minor leagues. As it was, he remained on the active list and, a week before the Series (the pennant long since clinched, of course), he pitched four strong innings against Pittsburgh, convincing Alston he was fit to pitch again.

Still, fit or not, Podres had finished the season only 9–10 and he seemed a strange choice to start a Series game. But Alston's choice turned out to be an inspired one when Podres breezed to an 8–3 victory, Brooklyn's first of the Series.

Podres's only bad inning was the second when he gave up two runs, the first on a home run by Mantle, playing with a heavily-taped thigh. For the rest of the game, Podres kept the Yankees off balance, particularly with a change-up he was willing to throw even when he had 2–0 or 3–1 counts on the batter, considered a "cripple" situation for hitters.

In the other dugout, second-game winner Byrne admired Podres's style, little thinking he would face Podres later in the Series. "If you can get that change-up over in a cripple situation," Byrne said later, "you're going to get a lot of guys out. Hitting is all timing, and if you can throw a guy's timing off, he's going to hit the ball where you want it to go."

The Dodgers never trailed in the game, getting two runs in each of the first, second, fourth, and seventh innings. The big hit of the day was Campanella's two-run homer in the first inning, but what turned out to be the winning run was scored in a much less spectacular fashion in the second, on a bases loaded walk to Reese. Both Dodger runs in the inning, in fact, came that way.

There was no question the Dodgers were more confident in their home park, as they showed again the next day in evening the Series with an 8–5 win.

The key to the victory lay in back-to-back three-run innings in the fourth and fifth, and the home run was the difference in both innings. In the fourth, Campanella led off the inning with a home run against starter and loser Larsen, and then Hodges hit another after an infield single by Furillo. In the fifth, Snider followed a walk to Jim Gilliam and an infield single by Reese with a blast into the right field screen, and that home run was the eventual difference.

Snider made Series history in the next game with two solo homers, giving him four for the Series, a feat he had also accomplished in 1952; he was the first man to have four homers in two separate Series.

Sandy Amoros, not usually a power hitter, had also popped a two-run homer into the right field screen in the second, and the homers were the key to a 5–3 Brooklyn win that put the Dodgers up, 3–2, in the Series.

Although the Series was moving back to Yankee Stadium, the Dodgers seemed to be in a position to win their first ever. They had the momentum, and they were

Duke Snider was a consistent World Series threat, twice smashing four homers in one Series. *(Los Angeles Dodgers)*

expected to win their fourth straight against the Yankees, especially since Mantle's leg was worse than ever and Mickey would not be able to do anything except pinch-hit. But Stengel wasn't conceding. Asked his pitching plans, he said, "Ford in the sixth game, Byrne in the seventh."

Ford's opponent would be Karl Spooner, a swift southpaw who had struck out 27 batters in his first (and only) two games in 1954, thus becoming the answer to a trivia question.

A sore arm knocked Spooner out of the majors after the 1955 season (he didn't pitch as much as an inning after that), but in 1955, he was still regarded as a potential star. He had won eight games as a spot pitcher for the Dodgers, and Alston felt confident in pitching him in this game.

But Spooner didn't have it, and he didn't even last out the first inning. Walks to Phil Rizzuto and McDougald, singles by Berra and Bauer and a three-run homer by Skowron brought in five Yankee runs and Dodger reliever Russ Meyer.

That was it. Given that commanding lead, Ford was in control all the way, pitching a four-hitter and striking out eight in a 5–1 Yankee win that evened the Series once more.

Now, it was down to the final game, and the improbable pairing of Byrne and Podres. Byrne had been Stengel's choice from the start of the Series, but Podres was a hunch call by Alston. The Dodgers' ace, Newcombe, was rested, but Alston knew that, for all his brilliance in the regular season, Newcombe had nothing but trouble in the World Series. He had pitched brilliantly at times (as in his 1–0 loss in the 1949 opener) and horribly. The one constant was that he always lost, 0–4 over three World Series. Alston decided to go with his hot pitcher, Podres.

You want to talk about pressure? Try the seventh game of the World Series, with 70,000 plus looking on in Yankee Stadium and baseball fans all over the country watching on that still new and strange invention, television.

Before the game, a representative from *Sport* magazine came into the Yankee clubhouse and told Byrne, "Tommy, if you win this ball game there's a good possibility you might be Most Valuable Player of the Series. We've got a Corvette sitting outside and we've got to give it to somebody."

Later, Byrne mused, "He probably went over to the Dodger clubhouse and told Podres the same thing."

No doubt. Although Snider had had a great Series with his four home runs, if either Byrne or Podres won a second game and it was the decider, it would be hard to vote against him.

Podres was confident. After the sixth game, when the Dodgers were depressed by their lopsided loss, Podres had gone by Reese, sitting with his head down in front of his locker, and said, "Don't worry, Pee Wee. I'll shut 'em out tomorrow."

He claimed later that he didn't even think about the game the night before. "I don't believe I ever thought about a game I was going to pitch the next day," he said. "Why worry today about what you've got to do tomorrow."

As superstitious as any other ball player, Podres ate the same breakfast he'd eaten the day he'd beaten the Yanks in the third game, and at the same time. He was buoyed up when he reached the park, especially when he learned that Mantle wouldn't be in the Yankees' lineup. He told third-string catcher Dixie Howell, who was warming him up, "Dixie, there's no way that lineup can beat me today."

He was right, but it took some luck and one big play for it all to come true.

The luck came in the third inning. With two outs, the Yanks threatened to break the scoreless tie when Rizzuto walked and Martin, always tough in the Series (he batted .320 in this one), singled.

Don Hoak, playing third for the Dodgers in place of the injured Jackie Robinson, was deep and protecting the line against McDougald, to prevent a ball from going down the line and scoring a couple of runs.

McDougald hit a soft grounder toward the third base bag. More than likely, Hoak would not have been able to make a play on the ball—but it struck Rizzuto on the leg as he slid into third. McDougald was given credit for a hit, but Rizzuto was out and the inning was over.

The Dodgers got on the board with a single run in the fourth, when Campanella doubled and Hodges singled. They made it 2–0 in the sixth when Hodges hit a sacrifice fly with the bases loaded.

There was another significant play in the sixth inning: Alston sent George Shuba up as a pinch hitter for Don Zimmer, who had been playing second base.

Alston had a double purpose in mind. He wanted a left-handed hitter in there against Bob Grim, a right-hander who had relieved Byrne just before the Hodges's fly; and he wanted to bolster his defense, by bringing Gilliam in from left field to play second base and putting Sandy Amoros in left field.

Shuba didn't produce, grounding out to strand three Dodger runners. But the defensive change would ultimately mean the ball game.

Meanwhile, Podres was pitching superbly, yielding four hits through the first five innings and blanking the Yankees. He had started the game using his change-up effectively, as he had in his winning third game, but he and Campanella had decided he should go more and more to his fastball as the game progressed. In October in Yankee Stadium, the shadows come early and deep, making it hard for hitters to pick up a fastball, and Podres's fast ball was as good as it ever was. He later remembered a third strike he threw to Bauer as the best fastball he ever threw—a pitch which was letter-high as Bauer started his swing but had risen up above his shoulders, well above his bat, by the time Bauer's bat came through.

In the bottom of the sixth, though, it appeared the Yankees were finally going to break through Podres. Martin led off with a walk and McDougald beat out a bunt for a base hit. Two on, nobody out and Berra at bat, the same Yogi who had won many a game with a home run in this spot. The outfield swung to the right for Berra, a dead pull hitter.

This time, though, Berra hit a high fly down the left field line. It was not hit with his usual authority. Podres's first reaction, in fact, was that it would be an ordinary fly ball, and he reached down for the rosin bag, to prepare for the next hitter, Bauer.

In the Yankee dugout, though, the reaction was different: Players were on their feet, screaming, because they were certain the ball would fall in for a double, and both Martin and McDougald would score.

McDougald, who had the same line on the ball as the players in the Yankee dugout along the first base line, felt the same way. He started running, intent on scoring behind Martin.

Martin was more cautious. He came halfway down the line between second and third, far enough that he could score if the ball dropped in but not so far that he couldn't get back if the ball were caught.

By this time, Podres had looked up again and he now saw that the ball was slicing toward the left field line. He realized that Amoros had a very long run coming from left center, and his heart went to his throat. This could be the ball game, he thought.

"I'll tell you," he said later, "that's a helpless goddamned feeling, standing on the mound at a moment like that."

Amoros just kept running and running and running. At the last possible moment, he stuck out the glove on his right hand and the ball fell into it, just before he ran into the fence. It was a catch made possible only because he was left-handed; the right-handed Gilliam, even if he had got there, would have had to reach across his body and could never have made the catch.

As soon as he straightened up, Amoros fired the ball into the cutoff man, shortstop Reese. Martin had safely retreated to second, but McDougald, who had been around second when the ball was caught, was still far from first base. The ever alert leader of the Dodger infield whipped it to Hodges, and the Dodgers had a double play.

"Boy, did that juice me up," said Podres, who got Bauer to ground out to end the inning. In the seventh, he mowed the Yankees down, 1–2–3, including Mantle as a pinch hitter. In the eighth, he gave up a one-out single to McDougald but then got Berra on a fly to short right and struck out Bauer.

Now he needed just three outs. He got the first one on a Skowron grounder to the mound, the second on a Bob Cerv fly to left. Howard was the next batter and Podres wanted to finish with a flourish, striking him out. He threw fastball after fastball to Howard, but Howard kept fouling them off.

Finally, shaking off Campanella for the only time in the game, he went to his change-up, and Howard hit it to Reese at short. The anxious Reese threw the ball low to Hodges at first, but Gil scooped it up for the third out.

Pee Wee Reese, "The Little Colonel," played a steady shortstop and was a reliable hitter for the Dodgers in World Series play. (George Brace)

And the Dodgers were finally World Champions.

The borough of Brooklyn threw a party that lasted for days and Podres, of course, was the focal point—or, at least, he assumes he was.

"A lot of what happened is a blur," he said later. "I wish I could remember it all, because I'm sure I had a hell of a good time."

18. Perfecto for Larsen

It was the fifth game of the 1956 World Series between—who else?—the New York Yankees and the Brooklyn Dodgers, and the Autumn Classic was tied at 2–2. Dodger manager Walter Alston picked Sal Maglie as his starter.

Maglie? Of course. That made sense. Although Maglie, the feared "Barber" because of his habit of throwing fastballs close to a batter's chin, was on the downside of his career, he had won 13 and lost only five for the Dodgers after they had picked him up before the start of the season. He had pitched a no-hitter in the closing weeks of the 1956 season, and he was always at his best in clutch situations. He had, indeed, already won one game in this Series.

For the Yankees, the starter was Don Larsen, and that choice seemed to make no sense at all. Larsen had won only 11 games in the regular season, and he had been bombed in an earlier Series start. "He wasn't throwing in Brooklyn, he was just pushing the ball up there," said Yankee manager Casey Stengel about that game. "Maybe he was worried about the fences. He can pitch better."

Not everybody was as optimistic as Stengel about Larsen's chances, however. One doubter was Chief Justice Earl Warren, an avid sports fan who seldom missed a big sports event.

Chief Justice Warren was in New York and he stopped off at Toots Shor, a famous meeting place for sports personalities. In the back of the room that night was Larsen, quietly drinking with Shor.

When Shor spotted Warren, he came over to say hello, and was surprised to hear Warren say that he was heading back to Washington, D.C., that night.

"But the game tomorrow, Chief. You won't want to miss that," said Shor.

"Why should I stay over another day to see Larsen pitch if he's going to stay up all night drinking with you?" asked the Chief Justice.

Warren's skepticism seemed deserved. Larsen had spent most of his baseball career wasting his potential, chiefly because he was more interested in pursuing pleasure than excelling on the field.

Larsen's career had been more often measured in potential than performance. Signed out of a San Diego high school by the St. Louis Browns (now the Baltimore Orioles), he had pitched four years in the minors, his only good season in 1948, when he was 17–11.

After two years in the military, Larsen came out in 1953 and was 7–12 for the last place Browns. The next year (the Browns were in Baltimore by then), he won only three games and led the league with 21 losses.

After the season, the Orioles traded Larsen, pitcher Bob Turley, and shortstop Billy Hunter to the Yankees for outfielder Gene Woodling, pitchers Harry Byrd and Jim McDonald, catchers Gus Triandos and Hal Smith, and shortstop Willy Miranda. Later, to complete the deal, four minor leaguers from the Baltimore system went to New York and three Yankee farmhands went to Baltimore.

Turley, a hard-throwing right-hander who was to become a major disappointment to the Yankees (although he won 21 games one season, Turley won only 82 in eight Yankee seasons), was the key man in the deal. But Larsen was also important; Yankee general manager George Weiss had insisted he be included in the trade.

"When we got Turley and Larsen," said Weiss, "we plugged the major weakness of the Yankee club. They are two of the finest and fastest young right-handers in the game."

In Larsen's first season with the Yankees, he was 1–1 in early season and so ineffective the Yankees farmed him out to Denver of the American Association. He was 9–1 at Denver and when he returned to the Yankees, won eight of nine decisions; for the season, major and minor, he had a combined 18–3 mark.

That showing encouraged Stengel to say in spring training before the 1956 season: "See that big feller out there. He can throw, he can hit, he can field, he can run. He can be a big man in this business—any time he puts his mind to it."

Larsen wasn't ready to put his mind to it, though. A few days later, he crashed his car into a telephone pole—at 5:00 A.M. "Not only did I get the telephone pole," said Larsen, "but you should have seen what I did to the mailbox."

What was he doing out at that long-past-curfew hour? "He was mailing a letter," said Stengel, sourly.

In that 1956 season, Larsen was 11–5, but his last four games had been impressive, a three-hitter and three four-hitters. That would earn him a chance in the Series.

The Series started in Brooklyn that year, and Whitey Ford and Maglie were matched in the opener. Mickey Mantle hit a two-run homer in the first inning to give Ford, a 19-game winner during the regular season, the early lead, but it wasn't enough.

In the second, the Dodgers tied the score when Jackie Robinson homered, Gil Hodges singled, and Carl Furillo doubled. In the third, Hodges hit a home run to follow singles by Pee Wee Reese and Duke Snider, and Ford was taken out. The Dodgers coasted to a 6–3 win.

Don Newcombe, still looking for his first World Series victory, was the Dodger starter for the second game. Newcombe had had his finest season, winning 27 games and losing only seven, but he proved again he couldn't handle the special pressure of the World Series as the Yankees knocked him out with a six-run second, keyed by a grand-slam homer by Yogi Berra.

Even in Ebbets Field, a pitcher should be able to hold a 6–0 lead, but Larsen couldn't. In the bottom of the second, the Dodgers tied the score and knocked out Larsen, and they went on to a 13–8 win, the second straight for them.

"When Casey came to take the ball away from me, he was mad," said Larsen later. "That made two of us because I was mad, too. I was still boiling in the clubhouse. I figured I had blown my chance. I was sure I'd never get another chance to start in that Series."

Larsen's failure seemed very costly to the Yankees, who were down 2–0 as the Series shifted to Yankee Stadium. But because the second game of the Series had been delayed a day by rain, Ford (who had pitched so briefly in the opener) was able to come back in the third game for a 5–3 Yankee win. The key to the victory was a three-run homer by 40-year-old Enos (Country) Slaughter, hero of the 1946 Series, in the sixth inning.

The Yankees, behind Tom Sturdivant, squared the Series at 2–2 the next day with a 6–2 win. Mantle hit a lead-off homer in the sixth, the second of three he would hit in this Series and the seventh he had hit in Series competition—and, he thought, the hardest yet.

Although nobody knew it at the time, the Yankee victory set the stage for history.

On what would be the biggest day of his athletic life, Don Larsen arose about 8:00 A.M., not by choice. He preferred to sleep until noon, but Stengel had ordered him to be in the Yankee clubhouse by 10:00 A.M.

Meanwhile, umpire Babe Pinelli was debating whether he could make it for the game. Pinelli, who had played eight years in the major leagues as a third baseman, would be umpiring behind the plate for the last time. Before the start of the Series, he had told the National League office that he was retiring, though he hadn't made a public announcement. In the fourth game, he had been hit just below the belt by a foul line drive by Gil McDougald of the Yankees, and he was hurting. But, he finally decided he could make it for this game, a decision he never regretted.

Larsen had had only a cup of tea when he got up, but by the time he got to the clubhouse, he was still not hungry and refused a can of fruit juice offered to him by clubhouse worker Pete Previte.

Through the first three innings, neither Larsen nor Maglie allowed a hit. The closest to a hit was a line drive by Robinson in the second which hit off the heel of Yankee third baseman Andy Carey's glove and caromed directly to McDougald at shortstop. McDougald's throw just nipped Robinson at first; a younger, fleeter Jackie probably would have beat it out.

The capacity crowd of 64,519 at Yankee Stadium felt something in the air. So did Pinelli, who had worked four no-hit games—all by Dodger pitchers—before. "The atmosphere carries you right along," he said. "You can tell by the way the players act and the noises from the fans when you've got a no-hitter going."

There had never been a no-hitter in World Series play, and only three pitchers had pitched even a one-hitter. Ed Reulbach of the Chicago Cubs had been the first, yielding only a seventh-inning single in the 1906 Series. Claude Passeau had pitched to only 28 men for the Cubs in the 1945 Series, blanking Detroit, 4–0 (one runner who had walked was eliminated in a double play). But the one hit Passeau yielded had been in the second inning, so there had been no real no-hit suspense, though Passeau's win was probably the best pitched game in a Series to that point.

The closest to a no-hit game had been the weird 1947 game pitched by Bill Bevens of the Yanks against the Dodgers. Bevens, as related in an earlier chapter, had one out in the ninth before pinch hitter Cookie Lavagetto broke up the no-hitter and won the game with a double off the right field wall.

Now, there was no-hit suspense on both sides of the field, but any thought of a double no-hitter ended with one swing of Mantle's bat in the fourth. With two outs, Mantle worked the count to 2-and-2 and then lined a high fast ball down the right field line to put the Yankees on the board for the first time. Mantle's homer was no surprise. He was coming off a Triple Crown season in which he had hit .353 with 52 homers and 130 RBIs—overall, the best season of his career.

Often in baseball it seems that a player who makes a brilliant play in the field will be up at bat in the next inning. This time, it was just the reverse. With one out for Brooklyn in the top of the fifth, Gil Hodges lashed a long drive to left-center that appeared to be not only a hit but one for extra bases. But Mantle, running at full speed, made a lunging backhanded stab of the ball for the second out.

The inning, Larsen's shakiest, wasn't over yet. Sandy Amoros, hero of the 1955 Series, hit a line drive into the right field seats—but it curved foul by a few feet. Larsen then got Amoros to ground out, and he was back in control.

Behind the plate, Pinelli thought Larsen's control made the difference between his failure in the second game and his brilliance in this one.

"He was a master of control that day," said Pinelli later. "His change of pace, particularly to the right-handed hitters, was great, because it kept curving away from them, but the biggest thing was the way he was pinpointing his pitches. He wasn't an overpowering pitcher that day, but he was making them hit his pitch."

The Yankees scored their second, and what would be their last, run in the sixth inning. Carey led off with a single, only the second hit off Maglie to that point, and Larsen sacrificed him along, bunting successfully on a two-strike count.

Hank Bauer singled to left to score Carey, and when Joe Collins followed with another single, sending Bauer to third, Alston came out to talk to Maglie.

Sal convinced the Dodger manager that he should stay in, and then, he got a big boost from his defense. Mantle ripped a one-bouncer to Hodges at first. The nimble-fielding Hodges, who had become the National League's best first sacker after being converted from a catcher early in his career, stepped on first and then fired home. Bauer was trying to score but he had to backtrack; catcher Roy Campanella and third baseman Robinson got him in a rundown and Robinson finally tagged him out.

Maglie allowed only one more hit after that inning, a two-out single to Billy Martin in the seventh. He pitched a five-hitter and finished with a flourish, striking out the side in the eighth; the Yankees, as home team, didn't bat in the ninth.

It was a fine effort that would have won most games, in the Series, or in regular competition, but it was not good enough on this day because Larsen was great.

By the time the Yankees got their second run in the sixth, everybody realized that Larsen was pitching not only a no-hitter but a perfect game; not a man had reached base in any way. Tension crackled in the Stadium, as each pitch became important. Fans leaned forward in their seats and cheered each out with the enthusiasm usually reserved for long home runs or strikeouts that end a rally.

There were no easy outs in this Dodger lineup. Six Dodgers had been in double figures in home runs during the season, topped by Snider's 43, which led the league. As a team, they had hit 179 homers. But they all looked the same to Larsen on this day of special magic.

Junior Gilliam, at an even .300 the top Dodger in hitting percentage during the season, led off the seventh. He took a strike and a ball, lashed a foul strike down the left field line and then grounded out to shortstop.

Reese hit a foul ball and then flied out to center. Snider, one of the most dangerous hitters in Series history, took a ball and flied to left. The seventh inning was history for the Dodgers.

Robinson led off the eighth and, though Jackie was long past his prime, he was still at his most dangerous in the clutch. This time, he took a strike, fouled off another pitch, and then grounded back to the mound.

Hodges made Larsen work, running the count to 2–and–2 before he lined to third. Amoros took one strike and then flied to center. One more inning.

By now, the pressure was almost unbearable, for everybody but most especially for the tall (6–4) right-hander on the mound for the Yankees.

"I'm not what you call a real praying man," said Larsen later, "but in the ninth inning, I said to myself, 'Help me out somebody.'"

Carl Furillo, leading off for the Dodgers in the ninth, fouled off Larsen's first two pitches, took a ball and then fouled off two more. By now, the fans were holding their breath on every pitch, exhaling loudly on each swing.

Finally, Furillo flied to Bauer in right field, a few feet in front of the fence. Two outs away. Larsen took off his cap to wipe away some sweat, took a deep breath, and looked in at the plate again.

The batter was Roy Campanella, who had hit 20 homers for the Dodgers in what was his next-to-last season. He lined a pitch down the left field line but foul by quite a bit, and then grounded to second. One more out.

Maglie was the next scheduled hitter but Alston sent up Dale Mitchell as a pinch hitter. Those with long memories thought back to 1947, and Beavens' ruined no-hitter. Like Lavagetto, Mitchell was in his last season, but he was still dangerous. A lifetime .312 hitter, Mitchell had hit .292 in 19 games, primarily as a pinch hitter, after being picked up by the Dodgers in late season.

He was also the worst kind of hitter for Larsen to face in this situation because he was a contact hitter; he struck out only 119 times in an 11-year career, fewer times than many sluggers do now in one season.

The first pitch to Mitchell was a ball, which dismayed Larsen. "Oh, no," he thought. "All day I've been getting ahead of the hitters and now I have to get behind on the last batter."

Larsen threw two strikes, and then Mitchell fouled a pitch back to the backstop. Finally, he put a fastball low and outside. Mitchell started to swing, then held up. But Pinelli shot his right arm into the air. Mitchell was out, the ball game was over, and Larsen had his perfect game.

Mitchell turned around angrily to argue with Pinelli. "He thought it was a lousy call," said Pinelli later, "but he was crazy to take it. Pictures later proved that it was a strike."

At any tate, Mitchell had nobody to argue with. Pinelli had already turned around to head for the dugout to take off his plate umpiring gear for the final time.

Yankee catcher Yogi Berra had run out to the mound and jumped up into Larsen's arms. The incongruous combination of the lanky Larsen and the stubby Berra, at least eight inches shorter than the pitcher, made a memorable picture that appeared in newspapers across the country the next day.

Players and fans were swarming around the mound. Elsewhere in the country, millions were still mesmerized by the picture they saw on the television set; the time had not yet arrived when every home had at least one TV set, so most people were gathered around sets in bars, meeting rooms, or college student lounges—or watching from sidewalks in front of stores.

In the dressing room, Yankee owners Dan Topping and Del Webb came by to

Lightly regarded Don Larsen became the first pitcher to throw a World Series no-hitter—and he did it with a perfect game in 1956. *(George Brace)*

shake Larsen's hand, in between questioning by the press; baseball commissioner Ford Frick also congratulated Larsen.

Robinson and Maglie came over from the Dodger dressing room. Maglie told Larsen, "I felt sorry for you in the ninth, because I knew what was going through your mind. You were the best and there was nothing we could do about it."

Stengel was interrupted as he was undressing, he said later, by a writer who asked timidly, "Is that the best game you've ever seen Larsen pitch?" That question, though, may well have been a whimsical invention by Casey, because nobody ever identified the writer who supposedly asked the question. Of course, any writer who did would certainly seek anonymity.

Among the thousands of congratulatory telegrams was one from President Dwight D. Eisenhower; the Presidential practice of phoning locker rooms had mercifully not yet begun.

Ike's message came right to the point:

Dear Mr. Larsen:

It is a noteworthy event when anybody achieves perfection. It has been so long since anybody pitched a perfect big-league game that I have to go back to my generation of ball players to recall such a thing—and that is truly a long time ago.

This note brings you my very sincere congratulations on a memorable feat, one that will inspire pitchers for a long time to come. With best wishes,

Sincerely,
Dwight D. Eisenhower
President of the United States

Larsen answered:

Dear Mr. President:

I can't begin to tell you how much I appreciated your recent letter. And if anyone were to ask me now what is the greatest thrill I've ever experienced, I'd certainly find it difficult trying to decide between the no-hitter and the congratulatory note I received from you. . . .

A World Series doesn't stop, even for a perfect game, and this one continued on to game six in Brooklyn. The impact of Larsen's perfect game, though, was so strong that the rest of the Series faded into anticlimax, to the point that many fans recall Larsen's game as being either the first or the seventh game of the Series.

Larsen's outstanding game also overshadowed a great pitching performance by Clem Labine for Brooklyn the next day, as the Dodgers evened the Series at 3–3.

For nine innings, Labine and Bob Turley matched zeroes, Labine yielding only seven hits and Turley just four, while striking out 11. It was one of the few times Turley, considered the fastest American League pitcher since Bob Feller had been in his prime, had lived up to his great promise.

In the tenth, Labine set the Yankees down 1–2–3 in the top of the inning. With one out in the bottom of the inning, Gilliam walked and was sacrificed to second by Reese. Snider was intentionally walked for the second straight time, and then Robinson lined a ball to left field. Slaughter misjudged the ball because of the sun (left field is notoriously hard to play in Yankee Stadium, particularly in October when the sun and shadows make it almost impossible to pick up the ball) and started in. Realizing his error, he backtracked and leaped for the ball, but it went over his head and the Dodgers scored the only run they needed.

In 1955, Alston had gone to Johnny Podres for the seventh, and winning, game, but Podres was not available this time. The reason? Probably his fame of the previous season.

In 1952, Podres had been classified 4–F because of a back problem. But after his Series fame of 1955, he was reexamined and reclassified 1A. His back was no better, though; in boot training for the Navy, it went out again. Meanwhile, he missed the entire 1956 season, including the Series.

Alston went back to his ace, Newcombe, for big Newk's fifth Series start, but by now, Newcombe couldn't have beaten the Yankees if they'd gone up swinging brooms. He lasted only one batter into the fourth. Berra hit a two-run homer in the first and another in the third, and when Elston Howard led off the fourth with a solo homer, Newcombe was gone.

Meanwhile, Johnny Kucks, getting his first start in the Series, pitched magnificently, three-hit shutout ball for nine innings. Bill Skowron hit a grand-slam homer off reliever Roger Craig in the seventh as the Yankees romped, 9–0.

Despite the loss, it had been a great decade for the Dodgers, who had made it to the Series six times. Although nobody could know it then, it would be the last time Brooklyn was represented in the Series; the next time the Dodgers got there, they would be in Los Angeles.

Larsen? He lasted only three more years with the Yankees and, though he pitched in the majors through 1967, finished with only 81 wins (and 91 losses). But for two hours and six minutes, and 97 pitches, on October 8, 1956, nobody has ever been as good in a World Series.

19. Casey Makes an Exit

The New York Yankees were in the World Series in 1960 which, considering the Yankees' four-decade record, should not have been a surprise. But it was both a surprise and an embarrassment to the club ownership.

The year before, the Yankees had finished a badly beaten third, their 79–75 record the worst under Casey Stengel. Yankee co-owner Dan Topping, who was becoming more and more active in the workings of the organization, wanted to replace Stengel and general manager George Weiss.

Stengel's replacement would be Ralph Houk, a coach with the club. Ironically, it had been Stengel who had originally encouraged Houk by making him a coach in 1953. Before that, Houk had been one of the many catchers who had come to the Yankees and found Yogi Berra an impossible roadblock.

Houk had become a minor league manager in 1955, for the Yankees' farm club in Denver, where he won a Junior World Series. He returned to the Yankees as coach in 1958.

Meanwhile, the young Yankee players had become increasingly resentful of and hostile toward Stengel. Mantle, a player Stengel had nurtured into stardom, talked behind Stengel's back and criticized him for not keeping the press off his back. Other players laughed at Casey, 69 in 1959, when he dozed on the bench. Now, they would talk back at him, and criticize his strategy.

Stengel had never been one to praise players overly much; in that, in fact, he was very much like John McGraw, who had been the biggest influence on his life. But times had changed. Players once accepted criticism as part of the game and were satisfied with rare bits of praise. Now they expected more praise and less criticism.

"In 1960 I hated the man, I really did," said Clete Boyer, then a young third baseman and later a coach, who later realized that Stengel was just trying to win. "Why didn't he explain it? I was young. I was sensitive."

There was one particularly telling incident, a game in which Boyer was at third, Tony Kubek at shortstop, and Bobby Richardson at second base. All three made errors in the game, and Casey called them "My air-conditioned infield."

Houk was much more sympathetic to the young players and an obvious favorite. Topping didn't want to take a chance on losing Houk to another team, so he decided Houk would replace Stengel. The only question was when.

Stengel's contract ran through 1960. Topping considered paying him off for 1960 and bringing in Houk at that point, but he finally decided it would be better to let Stengel go through one more year—which Topping assumed would be another bad (by Yankee standards) one. Houk would then be brought in, and Roy Hamey would replace Weiss as general manager.

But Weiss fouled up that cozy little timetable by trading for Roger Maris, a good outfielder with the Kansas City A's whose left-handed pull-hitting style was ideally suited for Yankee Stadium. Maris hit 39 homers and knocked in a league-leading 112 runs; Mantle won the home run title with 40 and had 94 RBIs. Maris and Mantle finished 1–2 in the Most Valuable Player voting, and the Yankees won the pennant.

That didn't change Topping's plans. He had had his partner, Del Webb, speak to Stengel during the season. Webb spoke of an annuity for Stengel. "Why did I need an annuity if I was working," Stengel said later in his inimitable style, "so I got the hint I wasn't."

None of this was made public, however, as the Yankees swept to the flag and went on to meet up with the Pittsburgh Pirates, a team they had last seen, and demolished in four games, in the 1927 World Series.

The Pirates were an interesting story, too, the last of the teams to feel the influence of Branch Rickey. Rickey had not been able to work immediate magic with the Pirates as he had with the Cardinals and Dodgers. The Pirates of 1952, in fact, were one of the worst teams of all time, and even before the 1960 season, they had been expected to finish no higher than third. Instead, they won easily, finishing seven games ahead of Milwaukee.

The Pirates were a solid team, defensively and offensively. Defensively, shortstop Dick Groat and second baseman Bill Mazeroski were especially adept at the double play; there has probably never been a second baseman who made the double-play pivot and throw faster than Mazeroski.

Bill Virdon was an excellent center fielder, and Roberto Clemente was sensational as a right fielder. The starting pitching was strong; Vern Law won 20 games, which earned him the Cy Young Award, and Bob Friend won 18. Behind them in the bull pen was Elroy Face. The year before, Face had been an astounding 18–1. In 1960, his winning percentage was ordinary (10–8), but he was probably more effective, saving 24 games.

The Pirates were not a power-hitting team, especially compared to the Yankees;

they rang up only 120 homers (the Yankees smashed 193) and only Dick Stuart, who had 23 homers, was a legitimate power hitter.

But they had a balanced lineup, with no automatic outs, and two high percentage hitters in Dick Groat, who led the league with a .325 mark, and Clemente, who came in third with an average of .314.

The Series that matched these two teams was one of the strangest in history. The Yankees set all kinds of offensive records. As a team, they batted an astounding .338 on 91 hits and scored 55 runs, with ten home runs. Elston Howard hit .462, Mantle .400, Bill Skowron .375, and Richardson .367. Richardson knocked in 12 runs, Mantle 11.

In contrast, the Pirates hit only .256 and Mazeroski was the individual leader at .320. They scored only 27 runs, fewer than half the Yankee total. "If this had been medal play," said golfer Arnold Palmer, "the Yankees would have won in four."

The Yankees, in fact, trailed in only one statistical department: games won. The Pirates took four, which is the only statistic that counts.

The Achilles' heel for the Yankees that year was their pitching. Arm trouble had limited staff ace Whitey Ford to 192 innings, and Ford had been only 12–9. Art Ditmar had been the big winner for the Yankees with a 15–9 record; on most of the great Yankee teams, Ditmar would have been no better than the fourth starter.

Stengel went with Ditmar in the first game, and Maris staked him to an immediate lead with a two-out, upper-deck homer in the top of the first off Pirates starter Vern Law.

But Ditmar couldn't hold the lead for even an inning. Virdon led off for the Pirates with a walk, stole second, and went to third as Berra's throw sailed into center because nobody covered the base.

Groat followed with a double to right, scoring Virdon, and Bob Skinner singled in Groat. Skinner then stole second and scored on Clemente's single, and Ditmar was relieved by Jim Coates.

In the fourth, the Yankees got one run back and would have had more but for a great defensive play.

Maris singled and Mantle walked with nobody out, and Berra drove a ball deep to right-center. But Virdon, who played an exceptionally deep center field, caught up with the ball and made a great leaping catch at the 420-foot mark. Maris went to third on the play and scored on Bill Skowron's single, but Law was then able to get out of the inning when Gil McDougald fouled out to third baseman Don Hoak and Richardson flied to center.

The Pirate lead went to 5–2 in the bottom of the inning when Mazeroski homered after a walk to Hoak, and the Pirates added a sixth run in the sixth when Mazeroski singled, was sacrificed to second, and came in on Virdon's double off the screen in right.

Meanwhile, Law had been holding the Yankees in check, but just barely. He had yielded only two runs, but he gave up eight hits in his first seven innings and had needed the big catch by Virdon to save him in the fourth.

When Law yielded singles to Hector Lopez and Maris leading off the eighth, Pittsburgh manager Danny Murtaugh had seen enough. He brought in Face, his bull pen stopper.

A wispy 5'8", Face hardly looked the part of a baseball hero, and he relied more on deception than speed. Ironically, his best pitch was one he had learned from the Yankee fireman of the late '40s, Joe Page.

Face was being sent back to the minors in 1954 to learn a change-up to go with his fastball and curve, but before he left, he talked to Page, who was attempting a comeback after three seasons away from the majors.

Page taught him the forkball, a pitch delivered by wrapping the index and middle fingers around the ball where there are no seams. (The same pitch later thrown by Bruce Sutter was called a "split-fingered fastball," just as Christy Mathewson's "fadeaway" became Carl Hubbell's "screwball.")

When he threw it high, Face's forkball would break sharply in toward a left-handed hitter. Thrown low, it would break sharply down, much like a spitter. Because of the way it was delivered, it would float to the plate with almost no rotation on the ball, almost like a knuckler.

The amount of break in a forkball depends on the speed with which it is thrown. Face usually threw it hard, so there was a sharp break.

Although he was only 12–11 with New Orleans of the Southern Association that year, Face gained the confidence that he could make it in the majors. And the pitch he had learned to complement his fastball and curve actually became his main pitch, the one he used to get batters out in tight situations.

Brought back up in 1955, Face was used both as a starter and as a reliever that first year, but by 1956, he was a full-time reliever, and he remained that until the end of his career in 1969.

Now he was in a position familiar to relief pitchers: instant pressure. It didn't bother him. Mantle took a called third strike, Berra flied out, and Skowron struck out swinging, and the Pirates were out of the inning.

The Yankees roughed up Face a little in the ninth when McDougald singled and Howard belted a two-run homer as a pinch hitter. But Lopez grounded into a double play, started by Mazeroski, and the Pirates had won the first game.

The second game was an entirely different affair. This time, the Yankees romped to a 16–3 rout. Friend was taken out after four innings when he was trailing, 3–0, and the Yankees then slammed five Pittsburgh relievers for 13 more runs. Face was not one of the relievers; Murtaugh used him only in situations where the Pirates had a chance to win the game, and this was emphatically not such a situation.

It was like batting practice for the Yankees, who had 19 hits, good for 30 total bases.

Mickey Mantle didn't hit for average, but he set World Series records for home runs and RBIs. *(New York Yankees)*

Mantle hit two home runs, including a three-run blast in the seventh that went an estimated 475 feet, and drove in five runs. Richardson and Kubek each had three hits and scored three times.

When the Series shifted to Yankee Stadium two days later, the barrage continued. This time, the Yankees won, 10–0, with 16 hits. The biggest hitter was Richardson, who had a grand-slam homer in the first and singled home two runs in the fourth, setting a Series record with six RBIs in a game. It was an unlikely performance for Richardson, who had hit just one homer all year.

Mantle, who was expected to do such things, hit his third homer of the Series in the fourth inning.

Meanwhile, Ford was sailing along with a four-hit shutout, though he hardly needed to be that sharp.

But the Pirates were not ready to quit, and they came back to tie the Series with a 3–2 win in the fourth game. This one belonged to Law, who picked up his second win of the Series and also got two hits, while scoring the winning run.

Skowron opened the scoring with a solo homer in the fourth, but the Pirates bounced back with a three-run inning in the fifth.

Gino Cimoli opened the inning with a single off Yankee starter Ralph Terry, and then Smokey Burgess hit a grounder to Skowron at first; both runners were safe when Skowron tried to make the play at second and was late with his throw.

Hoak and Mazeroski both popped out, but Law then doubled into the left field corner, scoring Cimoli. Virdon singled to center and both Burgess and Law scored, Law just beating Mantle's throw to the plate.

The Yankees rallied in the seventh and it took a combination of Face and Virdon to hold them off.

Skowron led off with a ground-rule double into the right field stands, moved to third on McDougald's single, and scored when Richardson grounded into a force play. When pinch hitter John Blanchard singled, Murtaugh again brought in Face.

Bob Cerv lined a Face pitch deep to right-center where Virdon made another fantastic leaping catch. That was the Yankees last shot. Face got Kubek to ground out to end the inning and then shut down the New Yorkers, 1–2–3, in the eighth and ninth.

Amazingly, the Pirates, so thoroughly bombarded in games two and three, took the lead in the Series with a 5–2 win in the fifth game.

It was the same pattern as the other Pirate victories: Get an early lead and then bring in Face. Harvey Haddix allowed the Yanks only three hits in the first six innings—one a homer by Maris—but when Kubek and Lopez singled with one out in the seventh, Murtaugh immediately brought in Face.

For the third time in the Series, Face saved the victory, retiring eight Yankees in order; he had retired 18 of the last 19 Yankee hitters he had faced, going back to the last inning of the first game.

Coming back to Forbes Field, the Pirates anticipated wrapping up the Series. Instead, they again ran into an incredible bombardment from the Yankees, losing, 12–0. As they had in the second game, the Yankees knocked out Friend early, this time in the third inning, as they were in the process of scoring five runs.

The Yankees got 17 hits, three each by Maris, Berra, and Blanchard. Richardson got two triples, driving in his 11th and 12th runs of the Series.

Once again, Ford was the beneficiary of the Yankee power, and once again, he pitched a shutout, this time allowing seven Pittsburgh hits.

That set the stage for the seventh game, one of the most bizarre and certainly most exciting in World Series history.

The Pirates took the early lead, scoring two runs in the bottom of the first with two outs, as Skinner walked and Rocky Nelson homered into the right field seats.

Pittsburgh got two more in the second when, with the bases loaded and two outs, Virdon singled to right.

The Yankees scored for the first time in the fifth on Skowron's solo homer and captured the lead in the sixth. Richardson started the rally with a single and Kubek walked, and Murtaugh again went to Face, relieving Law, who was trying for his third Series win.

Face got Maris to pop out, but his magic was gone, either because the Yankees were beginning to time the forkball or because the law of averages was catching up to Elroy.

Mantle singled to center, scoring Richardson, and then Berra followed with a three-run homer down the right field line into the upper deck, putting the Yankees on top, 5–4.

With Face still in the game, the Yankees increased their lead in the eighth when, with two outs, Berra walked, Skowron beat out an infield hit, Blanchard singled, and Boyer doubled. The Yankees had a 7–4 lead in this topsy-turvy game, but it wasn't over yet—not by a long shot, it wasn't.

In the eighth, the Pirates got one of those breaks that can often decide a Series. After Cimoli, batting for Face, had singled, Virdon hit a shot to Kubek at shortstop.

The ball should have led to a double play, but it took a strange bounce on the rock-hard Pittsburgh infield and struck Kubek in the throat. Both runners were safe, and Tony, his uniform soaked with blood, was forced to leave the game.

Groat singled to score Cimoli, and Stengel brought in Coates in relief. Skinner then sacrificed the runners into scoring position, but Nelson flied to short right and both runners had to hold their bases. The Yankees very nearly got out of the inning without further damage when Coates got Clemente to roll down the first base line, but the fleet Roberto beat Skowron to the bag and Virdon scored on the play.

And then, on a 2–2 count, Hal Smith homered over the left field wall and, just like that, the Pirates were ahead again, 9–7. Whew!

But it wasn't over yet, on this wild Day of the Hitters. Richardson led off the ninth with a single to left. Pinch hitter Dale Long singled to right, and Murtaugh brought in Haddix.

Haddix got Maris to foul out, but then Mantle singled to center, scoring Richardson and moving Long to third. McDougald, representing the tying run, ran for Long.

Berra grounded to Nelson at first base for what could have been a Series-ending double play. But Nelson stepped on first and threw to second and the quick-thinking Mantle, realizing the force was no longer on, dived back into first base as McDougald crossed the plate with the tying run. Finally, Haddix induced Skowron to bounce to short to end the inning.

The Yankees had made a classic mistake: They had only tied the score. On a day when pitchers simply could not contain hitters on either side, that was certain to be fatal and it was. Just two pitches into the bottom of the ninth Mazeroski slammed a Ralph Terry fastball over the left field fence and Pittsburgh had taken the game, 10–9. For the first time in 35 years, Pittsburgh had won the World Series, and fans celebrated well into the night throughout the city.

In the Yankee clubhouse after the game, Kubek lay on a training room table, blood seeping out of a towel around his neck. Mantle wept, and Terry sat immobile, his face buried in his hands.

Stengel parried questions from reporters about his future, waiting for a press conference to be held five days later in New York, which turned out to be a fiasco. Topping had wanted Stengel to announce that he was resigning, but Casey was too honest for that and the reporters got the message: He was being forced out.

For all their brilliance on the field, the Yankees have long had a public relations touch as heavy as that of the Soviet government. This time, they were forced into a public position of firing a man who had won an unprecedented ten pennants in 12 years and eight World Series, including five in a row, because they wanted a younger man.

Would it have made a difference if the Yankees had won the World Series? Bob Fishel, then the publicity director for the club, didn't think so.

"I think their minds were made up," said Fishel. "You can feel change around a ball club. All of a sudden in the final weeks of that season, important people began ignoring him."

An era had ended with the departure of the 70-year-old Stengel and Weiss, who was 66. As usual, Casey summed it up best: "I'll never make the mistake of being 70 again."

20. Sandy Wows 'Em

Sandy Koufax had one of the strangest careers a star player ever had. Koufax never pitched an inning in the minor leagues, but for six years—half of his 12-year career—he was in and out, spectacular one day, or one inning, terrible the next three or four games.

Koufax had one of the great fastballs of all time; he ended his career with an average of more than a strikeout per inning, which is an incredible feat. But early in his career, he never knew where that fastball was going. When it was on, he was capable of such feats as striking out 18 Giants in a 1959 game; when it was off, he was capable of walking himself, literally, right out of the game.

Several times, the Dodgers were on the brink of giving up on him and trading him to another team. They held off, always hoping, hoping he would someday find the plate on a steady basis. Until then, manager Walter Alston could only keep his fingers crossed every time he sent Koufax to the mound, never knowing whether he would overpower the other team or look like a left-handed Rex Barney.

Then, in spring training in 1961, catcher Norm Sherry suggested to Koufax that he ease up just a bit on his fastball, so he could control it. That one bit of advice turned Koufax into a pitcher, instead of a thrower.

The difference was as night and day. Koufax won 18 games that year, struck out a league-leading 269 in 255 innings, and walked only 96. And he was just warming up.

Although injuries cut short two of his next five seasons, he won 111 games in that time, losing only 34. Three times he had earned run averages under two runs a game and once just over, at 2.04. Three times he took the strikeout title, setting a record of 382 (since broken) in 1965.

And then, at the age of 31, he retired, his arm throbbing with arthritic pain that he could no longer take. His early retirement prevented him from reaching high career figures—he finished with 165 wins—but he had so impressed the writers who had watched him in that period that he was voted into the Hall of Fame in 1971, the first year he was eligible.

For five years, Koufax was as dominant as any pitcher who ever lived. Walter Johnson and Christy Mathewson had better records, but they were pitching in an era when the ball was so dead, it was rarely hit out of the park. Koufax operated in an era when .210 hitters could muscle up and hit a careless pitch out, and he was under constant pressure because he was pitching for a team which seldom got him many runs.

In the lively ball era, only Lefty Grove had a better five-year period, winning 128 games in the 1929–33 stretch. But Grove had a much better hitting team behind him (the 1929–31 A's were just about the equal of any team in history) and his other statistics—strikeouts, hits per inning, ERA—aren't close to Koufax's.

The 1963 season was typical of Koufax in that stretch: 25–5, 1.88 ERA, 306 strikeouts, 11 shutouts. He was making his second World Series appearance but he had been only 0–1 in 1959. This time, he would be overpowering; the 1963 World Series was the Sandy Koufax Series.

He and the Dodgers were meeting a New York Yankee team that was on the way down, though that wasn't obvious yet. The Yankees had won the Series the year before from the San Francisco Giants and they would win one more pennant, their fifth straight, in 1964, but the magic was gone. They would not win another pennant until 1976, and they would go 15 years in between Series triumphs.

The Yankees missed George Weiss. The dour, unlikeable Weiss had run a farm system that had been so rich in prospects that starting players were always looking nervously over their shoulders. But the supply had dried up, and the Yankees were still basically the team Weiss had left behind.

Weiss, too, had been able to make strategic trades to strengthen weak points, and since 1920, the Yankees had always had at least one super player to whom everybody could look—a line stretching from Babe Ruth to Lou Gehrig to Joe DiMaggio to Mickey Mantle. But Mantle was at the end of the line and, hobbled by the injuries which plagued him throughout his career, he had played only 65 games that year. He would, in fact, have only one more year in which he hit more than 30 home runs or knocked in more than 100 runs.

But the aura surrounding the Yankees was still mystical, and Yankee Stadium still seemed the only place to hold the World Series, so Koufax was nervous and excited as he warmed up before the first game.

Koufax held a different view of the Series than many other players did. He felt that the real pressure came in the pennant race, and that the Series provided great excitement but not that type of pressure. He was looking forward to enjoying himself in the Series.

And as he warmed up that October afternoon, he felt especially good because his fastball was moving, his curve ball dropping as sharply as it ever did. He felt this might be one of those five or six times a year when he was capable of pitching a great game.

It certainly seemed that way as he took the mound in the bottom of the inning and struck out Tony Kubek on four pitches. Bobby Richardson was the next hitter, and Koufax quickly went to an 0–2 count on Richardson.

Richardson was a hitter who seldom struck out; only 22 times in 630 at-bats in the 1963 season. He was also a hitter who loved a high fastball.

But, as Koufax explained later, sometimes on an 0–2 count, it's a good idea to throw the hitter a bad pitch in his strength to see if he'll chase it. Sandy threw a fastball that was up around Richardson's chin and Bobby bit, swinging and missing.

It was a significant pitch because the Yankees thought Koufax was giving them a message: that he could pitch to their strength and beat them. The Yankees knew they were in trouble.

The trouble didn't stop with the next batter, Tom Tresh, a switch-hitter who batted right-handed against Koufax. The book on Tresh was that he was a fastball hitter, so Koufax curved him on 2–2 and got him on a called third strike. Koufax had struck out the side, and on just 12 pitches.

It seemed an epic pitchers' duel was looming because Whitey Ford, coming off his second-winningest season (24–7) had retired the Dodgers easily in the first inning. But

Whitey Ford broke Babe Ruth's record for consecutive scoreless innings in the World Series and also won a record ten games. *(George Brace)*

in the second inning, Ford made some uncharacteristically bad pitches and was hammered for four runs.

The worst pitch was probably a chest-high fastball to Frank Howard, leading off the inning. Howard was an erratic hitter who would chase low outside pitches, but he absolutely destroyed fastballs out over the plate. He drove this one on a line over Mantle's head to the center field wall, 460 feet away, and he was singled in by Bill Skowron, an ex-Yankee who had come to the Dodgers in an inter-league trade.

Dick Tracewski followed with another single and then John Roseboro, who often didn't even play against left-handed pitching, jumped on a hanging curve ball and drove it down the line for a home run. It was the first home run he had hit off a left-hander all year.

Just like that, it was 4–0, shocking everybody, most especially Ford. This was a man who was at his best in Series play; Ford had pitched a record 33 consecutive scoreless innings in the 1960–62 World Series.

Koufax got two more strikeouts leading off the bottom of the second, getting Mantle looking and Roger Maris swinging. Elston Howard broke the strikeout streak but accomplished nothing else, fouling out to Roseboro in front of the Yankee dugout.

In the top of the third, Skowron singled in another run and now Koufax had a 5–0 lead, a luxury he seldom experienced at any time during his career, let alone in the Series.

For the first time in the game, Koufax fell behind in the count to Joe Pepitone leading off the bottom of the third, at 2–1, but he threw two strikes and got Pepitone swinging, his sixth strikeout in seven batters. Clete Boyer then grounded out, and Ford popped out.

In the fourth, Koufax got Richardson and Tresh on strikeouts again, giving him eight in four innings. Remarkably, he had thrown only 42 pitches (just 11 of them balls), a very low total for a pitcher getting so many strikeouts.

Not until the fifth, by which time Koufax had retired the first 14 men to face him, did the Yankees get a hit, a two–out single by Elston Howard. Pepitone followed with another single, a ground ball that just eked through the infield, and Boyer popped a ball up just past the infield that second baseman Tracewski got a glove on but couldn't quite catch. Tracewski was able to keep Howard from scoring, but the Yankees had the bases loaded.

Yankee manager Ralph Houk sent up Hector Lopez, a tough, contact hitter. Koufax resolved to show him almost nothing but fastballs, reasoning that a pinch hitter is coming up cold and will have a tough time adjusting. After three fastballs that made the count to 1–2, Koufax wasted a curve and then came back with an inside fastball that got Lopez swinging.

Then, Koufax said later, his rhythm deserted him. He thought it was because he had gotten tired and he was trying to throw the ball too hard. Finally, in the eighth inning, he relaxed a bit and his rhythm came back. Ironically, that was the only inning the Yankees gave him trouble.

Koufax started the inning impressively by striking out Phil Linz, a pinch hitter. Kubek reached base on an infield single, but then Richardson struck out—for the third time. At this point, Koufax was just trying to get the ball over the plate so he didn't walk anybody, not with a five-run lead, and he made a pitch too good for Tresh, who homered over the left field fence. The Yankees were finally on the board, but still trailing by three.

Then Koufax did exactly what he didn't want to do: He threw four straight balls to Mantle, bringing up Maris. Maris, who had hit 61 home runs in the historic 1961 season, had a left-handed swing perfectly grooved to drive the ball down the short right field line in Yankee Stadium. If he did it in this spot, the Yankees would trail by only 5–4.

He didn't. On a 1–1 count, Maris grounded out to Tracewski to end the inning, and the only suspense left in the game was whether Koufax would set a World Series strikeout record. His strikeout of Richardson had brought him to 14, tying Carl Erskine's mark.

Although Sandy had known he had a lot of strikeouts, he hadn't known how many until it was flashed on the scoreboard as he walked off the mound at the end of the eighth inning. At any rate, that was secondary in his mind; the important thing was getting the win, which would be his first in Series competition.

Howard, known for his first-ball hitting, did it again in the ninth, leading off with a line drive out to Tracewski at second. Pepitone, hanging in there against a left-hander better than he normally did, went to 2–2 and then lifted a pop foul back to the screen. The fans yelled, "No, no," as Roseboro chased it, hoping it would hit in the screen so Koufax would get another chance at the 15th strikeout. They got their wish—but then Pepitone singled.

Boyer was up next and he lofted a fly ball to Willie Davis in center field—the only Dodger out recorded by an outfielder that day. Houk sent up pinch hitter Harry Bright, a journeyman who had bounced around, playing for four teams after coming up with the Pittsburgh Pirates in 1958.

Dodger manager Walter Alston came to the mound to ask Koufax if he knew anything about Bright. "He likes the off-speed pitch," said Sandy. "He won't get one."

In fact, Koufax—mindful also of the shadows coming out to the mound and making it difficult for a hitter to pick up a fastball—threw Bright nothing but fastballs on the outside. Bright took two for strikes, another two that were balls, and topped Koufax's fifth pitch foul down the third base line.

The crowd was roaring on every pitch, which upset Bright. "I'd dreamed all my life about playing in a World Series," he said later, "and now my own fans were rooting for me to strike out."

Sandy Koufax was at his overwhelming best in the 1963 World Series, striking out 15 to set a one-game record. *(George Brace)*

Unfortunately, for Bright, he did strike out on the next pitch, another fastball low and outside. The Dodgers had won the first game, and Koufax had his record.

Erskine was watching the game; the two men had actually been teammates for the last four years of Erskine's career and the first four years of Koufax's. Erskine had great respect for Koufax. In 1959, the first year of his retirement, he had watched Koufax strike out two men in the first inning of a World Series game against the Chicago White Sox and had turned to his wife and said, "You don't mind losing that record today, do you?" But Koufax hadn't lasted in that game; this time, he had.

"I suppose I should thank you for letting me hold the record for another four years," Erskine joked as photographers posed the men together in the dressing room.

"When it got to 14," Koufax said, "I thought that it was enough."

Koufax's pitching was one indication this would not be the Yankees' Series; an even better indication came from the way the Yankees played the next day.

Maury Wills opened the game for the Dodgers with a single and was caught leaning off first base by left-handed pitcher Al Downing. Wills was so far off, in fact, that he made no attempt to return to first, heading instead for second base. But Pepitone's throw to second was high, pulling second baseman Richardson away from the play, and Wills dived headfirst into the base, safely.

Junior Gilliam followed with a single lined so hard to right that Wills had to hold at third but Maris, who was usually a very reliable fielder, threw too high to the cutoff man and Gilliam was able to take second.

And then, when Willie Davis hit a line drive to right field, Maris slipped as he turned for the ball and Davis had a double, scoring two runs.

That was all the Dodgers would have needed on this day because Johnny Podres allowed just one run to the Yankees, on four hits. The Dodgers got two more runs, one on a fourth inning homer by Skowron, to win, 4–1. Maris hurt his arm running into the fence in the fourth inning and was replaced by Lopez, who went on to get two doubles, the only extra-base hits off Podres.

Don Drysdale was superb for the Dodgers in the third game, striking out nine and allowing just three hits in blanking the Yankees, 1–0.

The Yankees again contributed to their downfall in the first inning, when the Dodgers scored their only run. Gilliam walked, took second on a wild pitch by Yankee starter Jim Bouton (later to become more famous as the author of *Ball Four*), and scored on a single by Tommy Davis.

The game was typical of Drysdale, who was in the midst of a four-season stretch, 1962–65, in which he won 85 games. He was an excellent pitcher for the Dodgers, winning 209 games in his 14 seasons, three times leading the league in strikeouts. On almost any other staff, he would have been the leader. On the Dodgers, he took second billing to Koufax.

It was the same again in this Series, as Koufax closed the Autumn Classic with a dramatic 2–1 win over Ford in the fourth game.

This was the duel everybody had expected in the first game. Ford pitched a two-hitter and would have won on almost any other day. But this was a Series in which the Dodgers could do nothing wrong, and there was no better example of that than in the fifth inning. Pitching to Frank Howard, Ford threw exactly the kind of pitch he was supposed to throw to the big strong man, a fast-ball so low on the outside corner that Howard wound up swinging with one hand. With that one hand, he hit the ball into the second deck of the left field bleachers.

Koufax admitted after the first game that he had twice gotten fastballs up over the plate against Mantle and gotten away with it because Mickey had just fouled the ball back.

Koufax did it again in the seventh inning of this game, but this time, Mantle drove the fastball deep into the left field stands. The game was tied.

The Dodgers got that run back in the bottom of the seventh, and the way they did it says all you need to know about the way this Series went.

Gilliam led off by hitting a high bouncer to third base. Boyer, an excellent fielding third baseman, made a leaping grab of the ball and threw to first for what should have been an out. But as Pepitone was reaching for the ball at first base, the sun reflected off something in the stands—a belt buckle, a woman's compact?—and blinded him. The ball hit his wrist and rolled down the right field line. Gilliam went to third and scored moments later on Willie Davis' line drive to right center.

Koufax and Yankee reliever Hal Reniff matched zeroes in the eighth, and Sandy went out for the ninth with a one-run lead which seemed very precarious when Richardson opened with a single. Barring a double play, Koufax would have to face Mantle with the tying run on base.

Tresh struck out, and up came Mantle. Koufax crowded him with a fastball, high and inside, and Mantle fouled it off. Sandy came back with the same pitch; this time, Mantle missed it completely.

Koufax thought this might be the time for a surprise, a slow curve when Mantle would probably be looking for another fastball.

Sandy hesitated, wondering how he would defend himself against the second-guessers if Mantle hit the pitch out of the park. He looked in at Roseboro. The Dodger catcher was signalling for a curve and waggling the two fingers, meaning that it should be a slow one.

The strategy worked perfectly: Koufax's curve broke slowly into the strike zone and Mantle watched it in wonderment.

But the game wasn't over. Richardson was still on first base. Elston Howard hit a Koufax pitch into the hole at shortstop and Wills grabbed it with his bare hand, throwing to Tracewski at second. The umpire started to signal out, and then changed his call when Tracewski bobbled the ball.

A hit would score the tying run now, and Lopez was at the plate, Koufax threw him the perfect pitch in the circumstances, a fastball on his fists. Lopez could manage only a ground ball to Wills, and this time Tracewski hung on to the throw.

The Dodgers had swept the Series and, most amazingly, the four games had taken only eight hours and 17 minutes.

21. The Dream Becomes Impossible

For the Boston Red Sox, 1967 was the year of the Impossible Dream come true.

Nobody ever made a more dramatic turnaround from one season to the next than that Red Sox team, which had finished ninth—and only half a game out of tenth place—in 1966 but sprung to the pennant in 1967.

There were several reasons for the Red Sox resurgence. New manager Dick Williams had changed the atmosphere of the club, from the notorious "country club" for which the Red Sox had long been known to a competitive, driving bunch. Pitcher Jim Lonborg had a great year, winning 22 games and taking the Cy Young Award.

But the biggest single reason for the Red Sox pennant drive was Carl Yastrzemski, who had the kind of season players dream about. Every time the Red Sox needed a hit, a catch, or a throw, Yastrzemski was there to make it. Williams, who had played on the great Brooklyn Dodger teams of the '50s, said he had never seen one player carry the team as Yastrzemski did that year.

Yastrzemski had had the misfortune of being billed as "the next Ted Williams" when he came to the majors in 1961, and he had spent most of his first six seasons disappointing the Boston fans.

Then, after the 1966 season, he went to a strenuous off-season workout program to build up his strength, and he changed his batting style to produce more power.

He had never hit more than 20 homers in a major league season nor batted in 100 runs, but he hit 44 homers and knocked in 121 runs in 1967. And he did it without sacrificing his percentage; he led the league with a .326 average, highest of his career at that point, thus winning the Triple Crown. In all, he led the league in six offensive categories: average, RBIs, homers (tied with Harmon Killebrew), runs (112), hits (189), and slugging percentage (.622).

And in the final two weeks of the season, when the pennant was up for grabs, Yastrzemski hit an incredible .522, with five homers and 16 RBIs.

Going into the final weekend of the season, the American League standings read: Minnesota, 91–69; Detroit, 89–69; Boston, 90–70. The Red Sox were scheduled to play two games in Boston against the Twins; because Thursday and Friday games had been rained out, Detroit had to play back-to-back doubleheaders at home against California.

The Red Sox beat Minnesota the first day, 6–2; Yaz knocked in the go-ahead run with a single and hit a three-run homer in the seventh. Detroit split, so the Twins and Red Sox were tied, the Tigers a half-game back.

The Red Sox won the Sunday game, too, 5–3, behind Lonborg; Yastrzemski singled in two runs and made a great throw in the eighth to get Bob Allison trying to stretch a single into a double, which ended the inning and the Twins' hopes. When Detroit lost the second game of its doubleheader with the Angels, the Red Sox were league champions.

Hero of the 1967 season, Carl Yastrzemski continued his great play, though in a losing cause, in the World Series. (Boston Red Sox)

But if they thought the season was an impossible dream, wait until they tried to hit Bob Gibson's fastball in the World Series.

Gibson was nearly as overpowering as Sandy Koufax had been in his prime. A great athlete (he had played basketball in college) with an overwhelming fastball, he was also an incredible competitor. In the 1967 season, he had suffered a broken leg on a line drive hit through the box—but he had finished pitching the inning before collapsing in the dugout.

The broken leg had limited Gibson to 175 innings and a 13–7 record, the only year in a six-year span, 1965–70, in which he did not win at least 20 games. But he had come back in September to prove that he was as good as ever, pitching the game that clinched the pennant for the Cardinals on September 18, and he was ready for the Series.

The Red Sox ace, Lonborg, was not ready because he had been used in the final game of the season. Williams chose Jose Santiago, who pitched a strong game but not strong enough to beat Gibson.

In this game as in the Series as a whole, Gibson shared top billing with Lou Brock, the swift outfielder who had come to the Cardinals in 1964 from the Chicago Cubs for pitcher Ernie Broglio in one of the most lopsided trades of all time.

Brock would go on to set both a single season stolen base record (since broken by Rickey Henderson) and a career mark, and his 52 stolen bases that season, though the National League high, paled in comparison with some of his other seasons; he had ten in which he stole more frequently.

But a word needs to be said about that mark to put it in perspective. Most top base stealers are singles hitters. Second base is both the easiest to steal and the most logical, because getting to second puts a man in scoring position. So, when a hitter singles, he is in position to steal.

Brock, at that stage of his career, was not a singles hitter. He had 32 doubles, 12 triples, and 21 home runs among his 206 hits. That meant that on 65 of his hits he had basically removed any chance he would steal, which made his league-leading mark all the more impressive.

He had had what was probably the best all-round season of his career, hitting .299 and leading the league with 113 runs scored, and he continued his fine play in the first game of the Series and right through to the end.

In that first game, he scored both Cardinal runs in a 2–1 victory. The first came in the first inning when he singled, went to third on a double by Curt Flood, and scored when Roger Maris grounded out.

In the third inning, Santiago lifted a ball into the screen atop Fenway Park's famed left field wall, also known as the Green Monster, and the score was tied.

The Cardinals had many scoring opportunities throughout the game, getting ten hits, and eventually, they had to break through. They did it in the seventh. Brock got his

Record-setting slugger Roger Maris played in five World Series for the Yankees and a final one for the St. Louis Cardinals. *(New York Yankees)*

fourth hit of the game, a single, and stole second for the second time. He moved to third when Flood grounded out, which brought up Maris again.

Maris had been traded by the Yankees before the start of the 1967 season. Bone chips in his right hand had robbed him of his strength and he was no longer a home run threat; he had hit only nine during the regular season. But he had provided the Cardinals with steady outfield play and he was always a smarter player than most people realized. He knew that in this situation he needed only get the ball on the ground to the right side to score Brock, and he did that, grounding out to second as Brock scored what would be the winning run.

Yastrzemski was so irked by his failure to hit Gibson in the first game that he stayed to take batting practice when it was over. Whether that made the difference or not, his batting stroke was definitely on target in the second game the next day, as he hit two home runs. The first one, in the fourth, gave Boston its first run and he added a three-run homer in the seventh off Joe Hoerner.

Meanwhile, Boston's other superstar, Lonborg, was pitching brilliantly, setting the Cardinals down in 1–2–3 order for the first six innings. He'd been helped by excellent defense. Second baseman Jerry Adair had made two fine plays on ground balls by Brock to keep the speedy outfielder off the bases, and shortstop Rico Petrocelli had taken a hit away from Dal Maxvill in the sixth.

The Boston sky turned dark at the start of the seventh and a light rain began to fall, and the lights were turned on. Lonborg got the first man, making it 19 in a row that he had retired, and Red Sox fans thought back to Don Larsen's perfect game in the 1956 Series.

Flood worked the count to 3–2, the fourth time Lonborg had gone that far on a hitter. The first three times he had gotten the hitter; this time he lost him, walking Flood.

So the perfect game was gone, but he still had a no-hitter intact, and he preserved it for the seventh by getting Maris to fly out and Orlando Cepeda to ground into a force out, Petrocelli making a good play to grab the hard-hit ball behind second base.

The rain stopped at the top of the eighth, and Lonborg seemed very much in control as he got Tim McCarver and Mike Shannon to ground out. He was only four outs from the second no-hitter in World Series history.

But then he hung a curve ball to Julian Javier, who lined the ball into the left field corner for a double.

Lonborg retired the last four men to face him and walked off the mound with a 5–0 victory that seemed anticlimactic after he had come so close to the no-hitter.

The Series shifted to St. Louis for the third game, where it had been oversold. The Cardinals solved that problem by putting folding seats in the aisles, and any complaints that might have occurred diminished when the Redbirds wrapped up a 5–2 win early.

This game and the next one exposed a major problem for the Red Sox: lack of starting pitching. Williams had done a masterful job of juggling his pitching all year because, behind Lonborg, he had very little. Santiago and Gary Bell were his next two starters, each with just 12 regular season wins. Retread John Wyatt had pitched well in relief, winning ten games and saving 20, and that had been enough for the Red Sox in the regular season. It wasn't in the Series.

Bell was the logical choice for the third game, but he was hammered, lasting less than two innings. Shannon homered, the ubiquitous Brock tripled and singled, and Nelson Briles got the win.

Santiago, who had done a good job of holding the Cardinals in the first game, was no mystery at all in the fourth as St. Louis knocked him out with a four-run first inning.

One run would have been enough because Gibson was pitching. He allowed only five hits, gave up no runs, and came home an easy winner, 6–0.

Again, Brock played a big role, with a single, double, and stolen base. Maris, Cepeda, and Javier all had doubles.

But the Red Sox weren't dead yet, not as long as they could run Lonborg out there again. In the fifth game they got a single run in the third off young Steve Carlton, who would become an outstanding pitcher with the Philadelphia Phillies in later years, and then posted two more in the ninth on a bloop single by Elston Howard, finishing out his career in a Red Sox uniform.

Lonborg was almost as impressive as in his one-hit shutout in game two, allowing only two hits and no runs until there were two outs in the ninth. Then Maris, reaching back in his memory to remind himself how it was done, crashed a home run to right field. That only ruined the shutout, not Lonborg's composure, as Jim got the third out for a 3–1 win that made a sixth game, and a trip to Boston, possible.

The return to friendly Fenway seemed to revitalize the Red Sox bats. Petrocelli opened the scoring with a solo homer into the left field screen in the second inning of the sixth game, and then Yastrzemski, Reggie Smith, and Petrocelli all hit home runs in the fourth to give Boston a 4–0 lead.

Williams had seen enough of Bell and Santiago to realize they weren't the answer against the St. Louis hitters, so he surprised everybody by starting rookie right-hander Gary Waslewski, who had won just two games and pitched only 42 innings in the regular season.

Waslewski pitched six shutout innings before the Cards bounced back to tie the score with four runs in the top of the seventh. But the determined Red Sox scored four of their own in the bottom of the inning and went on to an 8–4 triumph, Wyatt picking up the win in relief.

Even in defeat, Brock was magnificent, with a single, homer, and yet another steal.

The Boston win had tied the Series at 3–3 and set up what seemed to be a classic confrontation. Gibson and Lonborg had yet to pitch against each other and they had both been overwhelming against lesser competition. This time, with the Series on the line, they would both be out there.

The two pitchers had come from entirely different backgrounds. Lonborg had come from Stanford, which prides itself on being the western equivalent of an Ivy League school, and it had taken him a while to realize his potential.

He had always had a live fastball and good control, but he was no more than an average pitcher for his first two seasons with the Red Sox, 9–17 as a rookie in 1965, 10–10 the next year.

Perhaps it was the change of managers that turned Lonborg around. Perhaps it was emotional maturation. But, whatever the reason, his emotional change was the key to his physical improvement. Before 1967, the word around the league was that you could crowd the plate on Lonborg because he wouldn't brush back hitters.

In 1967, he started moving hitters back with inside fastballs, and that made his pitches on the outside corner much more effective. Early in the season, when an opposing pitcher dusted off a Red Sox batter in a game he was pitching, Lonborg asked Williams, "Who do you want me to get?"

A skiing accident after the 1967 season would change the course of his career and Lonborg, though he lasted another 11 years, was never again quite the pitcher he was in 1967. But when the Red Sox concocted their miracle, he was a most important part, leading the league with 22 wins, 39 starts, and 246 strikeouts and yielding only 228 hits in 273 innings.

Gibson had been overcoming obstacles all his life. He had grown up in an Omaha ghetto, where he'd had his ear bitten by a rat when he was a baby. He'd had rickets, and he was asthmatic.

Like Koufax, he pitched with an arthritic elbow that required cold applications after he pitched. "But you don't hear about it because he doesn't talk about it," said Sandy, who knew the pain Gibson was suffering.

Gibson was a magnificent athlete, a switch-hitting catcher and shortstop in high school. The first black to play basketball for Creighton University, he jumped so high his elbow very nearly touched the rim.

Like many fastball pitchers, he had had control problems early in his career, but once those were behind him, he was on his way, winning 181 games from 1963 through 1972.

St. Louis writer Bob Broeg feared that it was a bad omen when he saw a surly Gibson climb onto the bus to go to the park for the final game.

Because the breakfast room was overcrowded that morning, Gibson had had nothing to eat; a piece of burned toast was all that was offered him, and he rejected that in anger.

Broeg, who had visions of a hungry Gibson tiring in the late innings, got off the bus at a cafeteria and ordered two ham-and-cheese sandwiches to go, and brought them via taxi to Gibson at the park.

Gibson ate just one of the sandwiches and then went out to shut down the Red Sox on a three-hitter, but Lonborg was finally unable to meet one last challenge. The Red Sox ace was pitching his fourth game in 11 days, all of them pressure games, and he simply ran out of gas.

The Cardinals opened the scoring as early as the third when Maxvill, leading off, tripled deep to center. That was an indication that Lonborg didn't have it; Maxvill had hit just .227 that year and was a lifetime .217 batter.

Lonborg managed to retire two batters while holding Maxvill on third, but then Flood scored Maxvill with a single, went to third on a single by Maris, and came home on a wild pitch by the rapidly tiring Lonborg.

Gibson got himself a run with a homer in the fifth, and then it was Brock's turn on stage; Lou singled, stole second *and* third, and then scored on a fly by Maris.

The game and the Series was lost for the Red Sox, a point that was underscored when the Cardinals scored three more times in the sixth. Williams allowed Lonborg to finish out the inning, so he was spared the humiliation of being lifted during the inning; Lonborg, who had done so much for the team during the season and the Series, deserved that. In the bottom of the inning, Williams lifted him for a pinch hitter, but the game was gone beyond recall. Gibson relaxed enough to allow a couple of runs but coasted to a 7–2 triumph.

It had been a colorful Series with several heroes. Lonborg, before his demise in the

Lou Brock was a spectacular player for the St. Louis Cardinals in three World Series. *(St. Louis Cardinals)*

Bob Gibson was the most overpowering pitcher of all time for the St. Louis Cardinals in the World Series. *(George Brace)*

final game, had allowed just four hits in two wins. Yastrzemski had carried his hot bat into the Series, finishing at .400 (10–for–25) and hitting three home runs.

Brock had topped even Yastrzemski, leading both clubs with runs (8), hits (12), and average (.414) and stealing a Series record seven bases.

But, start and finish and in between, Gibson was the main man. He had pitched three complete games and won them all, giving up only 14 hits and three runs, while striking out 26. It didn't quite match Christy Mathewson's three shutouts in 1905, but Mathewson never pitched with a ball whose rabbit heart was beating as he held it on the mound, either.

And as he savored the final win, Gibson ate Broeg's second sandwich—washing it down with champagne.

For his exploits, Gibson won two cars: *Sport* magazine gave him one as the outstanding player of the Series, and KMOX in St. Louis told him he could pick out whatever he wanted at an automobile showroom.

But the finest tribute to Gibson came from Boston's George Scott, who had hit safely against Gibson in all three games.

"The thing is," said Scott, "he'll never give in. He'll always challenge you. He'll throw the ball across the plate with something on it and say, 'There it is. See if you can hit it.'"

Tom Seaver was Joe Hardy come to life as the Amazin' Mets won the 1969 World Series from Baltimore. *(George Brace)*

22. Joe Hardy Lives

Life imitated art in 1969. In his novel, *The Year the Yankees Lost the Pennant* (later made into the play and movie, *Damn Yankees*), Douglass Wallop had his hero, Joe Hardy, sell his soul to the devil for one great baseball year. In 1969, it seemed the entire New York Mets team had sold its collective soul.

Star pitcher Tom Seaver had a slightly different slant. During the World Series, Seaver was asked if he thought God was a Met. "No," said Seaver, "but I think he has an apartment in New York."

It had been an incredible year for the Mets, leading up to the World Series. Since the team had been formed in 1962, it had been the symbol of ineptitude. That very first team had lost 120 games, which was and probably always will be a record. Manager Casey Stengel moaned, "Can't anybody here play baseball?"

Although the Mets didn't lose as many games in subsequent years, their improvement was negligible. In their first seven years, the Mets lost a total of 737 games, another record. They finished ninth or tenth in the expanded National League every year of the seven.

The wise guys said 1969 would be the year the Mets climbed to sixth place—because the league, expanding again to 12 teams, would be divided into two six-team divisions.

Instead, the Mets climbed all the way to first place, beating out the Chicago Cubs in one of the strangest pennant races of all time. In early August, Leo Durocher had the Cubs leading the Mets by 9½ games. By September 8, the Mets had climbed to within 2½ games. They swept a two-game series from the collapsing Cubs at that point, moved into first place with a win on September 10, and eventually finished eight games ahead of the Cubs.

The Mets' 100 victories were 27 more than they had won in any other season of their existence, and they seemed to do it with mirrors. True, they had some standouts.

Seaver, baseball's best pitcher that year with a 25–7 record, was one; Cleon Jones, a .340 hitting outfielder, was another.

But Seaver and Jerry Koosman, 17–9 with a 2.28 ERA that was just behind Seaver's 2.21, were the only reliable starters. (Nolan Ryan was on that team but was only 6–3, though he struck out 92 batters in 89 innings.)

Manager Gil Hodges did an excellent job of juggling his talent, and the Mets continually came up with the key hit, though they hit only .242 as a team, with 109 homers; maybe there was something to the theory that they'd sold their soul to the devil.

Because the leagues had split into divisions, the Mets had to battle the Atlanta Braves, winners in the National League West, for the right to play in the World Series. Few thought they could beat the Braves, who were overwhelming favorites—but the Mets swept Atlanta, 3–0.

In the World Series, though, they would face the Baltimore Orioles, who had swept the Minnesota Twins in their playoffs. This time, thought the experts, the Mets' luck would run out.

The 1969 Baltimore Orioles were probably one of the ten best teams of all time; baseball historian Donald Honig has so nominated them.

The Orioles would go on to win two more American League pennants, and this was

Frank Robinson was the team leader of the Baltimore Orioles during the 1966–71 period, which began with their World Series sweep of the Dodgers in 1966. *(Baltimore Orioles)*

probably the strongest of the three teams. They won 109 games and finished 19 games ahead of the second-place Detroit Tigers, a winning margin second only to the 19½ game spread posted by the 1936 New York Yankees.

The Orioles were great in every measurement of a baseball team. Hitting? Boog Powell hit 37 home runs and knocked in 121, Frank Robinson had 32 homers and an even 100 RBIs to go with a .308 average; the Orioles had four hitters with at least 23 home runs. And yet, Baltimore batters recorded the fewest strikeouts of any team in the league.

Fielding? Paul Blair in center field continually turned drives that looked like doubles or triples into outs. Most baseball people ranked him with Willie Mays as a defensive center fielder.

At third base, Brooks Robinson was probably as good as anybody who ever played the position. Early in his career, when Robinson was hitting under .200, pitchers begged then-manager Paul Richards not to farm him out.

Shortstop Mark Belanger was considered the premier defensive shortstop in the league. Second baseman Dave Johnson was near the top at his position. Powell made only seven errors in 144 games at first base.

"Hitting a ball through the Baltimore infield," said Detroit manager Mayo Smith, "is like trying to throw a hamburger through a brick wall."

The Baltimore pitching was excellent, too. Southpaw Mike Cuellar, obtained in an off-season trade from the Houston Astros, won 23 games to anchor a staff that led the league in earned run average. Another lefty, Dave McNally, won his first 15 games and finished 20–7. Jim Palmer, who had won 15 games and pitched a shutout in the 1966 World Series before succumbing to arm trouble in 1967 and 1968, bounced back with a 16–4 mark.

To top it off, the Birds were managed by Earl Weaver, who would go on to gain a reputation as the best manager in the game by the time he retired from the Orioles after the 1982 season.

But the Orioles were about to learn the bitter lesson that had been taught earlier to the 1906 Chicago Cubs and the 1914 Philadelphia Athletics, also among the best teams of all time: The best team does not always win the World Series.

Unlike those two teams, the Orioles won the first game of the Series and, in fact, did it so easily that it seemed they might be on their way to a sweep.

As Seaver had left his Baltimore hotel for the first game, his wife, Nancy, said to him, "Good luck. I hope you make history today."

"I did," said Seaver later. "I became the first New York Mets pitcher to lose a World Series game."

Indeed, Seaver showed little of the stuff that had made him so overpowering to National League hitters during the regular season. On just the second pitch of the

Earl Weaver was regarded as the best manager of his time as his Baltimore Orioles played in three consecutive World Series, 1969–71. *(Baltimore Orioles)*

game, 5'7" Don Buford, whose goal usually was to get on base so the power hitters could drive him home, homered over the right field fence. "That's one way of getting a new ball in play quickly," said Seaver, wryly.

The Orioles made it 4–0 in the fourth inning, and once again, Buford played an important role. Interestingly, too, the big Oriole hitters—Powell and Frank Robinson—were not a part of the scoring binge.

With two outs, Elrod Hendricks singled, Johnson walked, and Belanger singled in Hendricks, with Johnson going to third. Then pitcher Cuellar also singled, scoring Johnson, and Buford doubled down the right field line sending Cuellar home. Seaver finally got the third out when Blair grounded to third.

Seaver came out for a pinch hitter after five innings, in which he had given up six hits and four runs.

His teammates got their only run of the game in the seventh. Donn Clendenon opened the inning with a single and Ron Swoboda walked. After Ed Charles flied out, Jerry Grote singled, loading the bases, and Al Weis hit a sacrifice fly to get the run across.

The Mets reached Cuellar for six hits, but Clendenon's two-out double in the fourth was the only one for extra bases and only in the seventh were they able to get more than one hit in an inning.

With their good team speed, the Mets had gotten a lot of infield hits during the regular season, but their soft infield rollers were eaten up by Brooks Robinson in this game, as Robinson threw out six Mets from his position at third base.

"If the infield grounder is their best shot," needled Weaver, "they're in trouble, because we've got the best infield in baseball."

But a strange thing happened in the aftermath of that game: The Mets realized the Orioles could be beaten.

"The feeling we had," said Seaver, "was that they had just barely beat us. Never mind the score; a team knows if they've been badly beaten or outplayed, and we felt we hadn't been."

The Mets knew they had been just a hit or two away from getting right back in the game, and they felt they could do it. "We're going to kick hell out of those guys," said Clendenon, walking around the clubhouse.

Sometimes, players make statements like that because of sheer bravado, realizing at least subconsciously that they can't back up the statement with deeds. But the Mets believed. This was their year, they knew, even if others doubted.

The tide of the Series changed in the second game, as Koosman pitched a two-hitter, both singles and both coming in the seventh inning.

Koosman had to be good because McNally was pitching almost as well for Baltimore, allowing just six hits and striking out seven.

Clendenon gave the Mets their first lead of the Series with a home run in the fourth, but Baltimore came back to tie it in the seventh. Blair led off the inning with the Orioles' first hit, a single to left. After Frank Robinson had lined to center and Powell had popped to short, Blair stole second and scored on Brooks Robinson's single.

In the top of the ninth, with two outs, Charles and Grote got consecutive singles, with Charles going to third on the second hit. Then Al Weis singled in Charles. During the season, Weis was a .21 hitter, and if you want to know how improbable the Mets' win really was, that tells it all.

After getting the first two men Koosman ran into trouble in the bottom of the inning when he pitched too carefully to Frank Robinson and Powell and walked both men. Hodges brought in ace reliever Ron Taylor to face Brooks Robinson, right-hander against right-hander, and the percentage move paid off as Robinson grounded out for the final out of the game.

Back home at Shea Stadium for the third game, after a day of travel (for television purposes, of course, since a trip from Baltimore to New York is hardly enervating), the Mets seemed more confident than ever.

Just as Buford had for Baltimore in the first game, Tommie Agee led off the Mets in the first inning with a home run off Palmer, and the Mets stretched their lead to 3–0 in the third when Grote walked, Bud Harrelson singled, and pitcher Gary Gentry doubled—another indication of the kind of year the Mets were having.

As important as Agee's homer had been, he would soon make even bigger contributions in the field. The first one came in the fourth inning.

With one out for Baltimore, Frank Robinson singled to left and Powell singled to right, Robinson going to third. Brooks Robinson then struck out, but Hendricks hit a slicing line drive to deep left-center that seemed certain to score both runners. The ball was moving away from Agee as he raced toward the fence, but he caught up with it just as he bounced into the wall. The white of the ball showed above the webbing of his glove, but he hung on and the inning was over.

In the sixth, the Mets took a 4–0 lead when Ken Boswell singled and Grote doubled him home, but that lead seemed about to disappear in the Baltimore half of the seventh when, with two outs, Gentry loaded the bases by walking Belanger, pinch hitter Dave May, and Buford.

Hodges brought in Ryan, throwing heat and more heat at the Orioles; although Gentry was known as a fastball pitcher, nobody has ever thrown faster than Nolan Ryan.

Paul Blair wasn't intimidated. He jumped on one of Ryan's blurring fastballs and drove it into the gap in right-center. The Oriole runners were all off with the crack of the bat, and Blair was whipping around the bases, too, heading for what seemed a sure triple.

As he started for the ball, Agee punched his glove, as he always did when he thought he had a chance to catch the ball. Nobody else thought he had a chance as he ran and ran and ran. As the grass gave way to the red dirt track which ran in front of the outfield fence, Agee saw he couldn't quite reach the ball running, so he dove and put out his glove. The ball landed in it. Nobody had seen that kind of outfield play in New York since before Willie Mays moved west to San Francisco with the rest of the Giants team in 1958.

The inning was over, and the Orioles' chances with it. Ed Kranepool hit a solo homer in the bottom of the eighth to make the final score 5–0.

After the game, all the talk was about Agee's catches. He thought himself that his first catch was the toughest; Hodges voted for the second.

Weaver said he thought the catches cut off seven Baltimore runs, not just the five that obviously would have scored if the drives had fallen safely. "If those runs score," said Weaver, "don't you think Hendricks and Blair score, too?"

Writers asked Frank Robinson if he believed in the Mets as a team of destiny. "When I see them fly," said Robinson, "I'll believe it. Have you seen them fly?"

Those who had just seen Agee's catches thought they had indeed seen the Mets fly, and there would be even more conclusive proof the next day.

Seaver started the fourth game for the Mets, and this time, he was the great pitcher he had been during the season. Going into the ninth, he had shut out the Orioles on just three hits, walking just two men. Only once had Baltimore gotten a runner past first base.

Meanwhile, the Mets had gotten the only run of the game when Clendenon had led off the second inning with a home run.

In the top of the ninth, Seaver got Blair to fly out for the first out, but he still had the meat of the Baltimore order—Frank Robinson, Powell, Brooks Robinson—coming up.

He'd had good success with Frank Robinson, pitching outside; Frank hadn't gotten a hit off Seaver in either of Seaver's two starts. Thinking Robinson would be expecting to be pitched away again, Seaver decided to come inside—and Robinson ripped it to left field for a base hit. "You just can't mess around with those great hitters," Seaver said later.

Then Powell bounced a single over Kranepool's head and Robinson, always a great base runner as well as hitter, raced all the way to third base.

Brooks Robinson followed with a line drive to right field, where Ron Swoboda was stationed. The prudent move would have been for Swoboda to let the ball bounce, conceding one run but forcing Powell to stop at second—especially because Swoboda was, at best, an erratic fielder.

But this was a year in which logic didn't apply to the Mets. Swoboda came galloping in gracelessly, stuck his glove out, and fell down, sliding on his stomach—but the ball stuck in his glove.

Frank Robinson alertly scored after the catch, tying the score, but the Orioles could manage no more. Without Swoboda's catch, the Baltimore rally might have lasted long enough for the Orioles to take the lead.

The Mets couldn't score in the bottom of the inning and the game went into extra innings, but luck started turning their way again in the bottom of the tenth.

Grote led off with what should have been an ordinary fly ball but Baltimore right fielder Buford, normally a good defensive outfielder, misjudged the ball, breaking first toward the fence and then coming back—as the ball landed in front of him. Grote reached second with a gift double, and Rod Gaspar went in to run for him.

Al Weis was intentionally walked to set up a double play possibility, and then pinch hitter J. C. Martin, batting for Seaver, laid down a sacrifice bunt. Baltimore pitcher Pete Richert threw errantly to first base and hit Martin, the ball bouncing nearly to second base as Gaspar came around third base to score the winning run.

The Orioles claimed Martin had run out of the base lines, and pictures the next day seemed to prove that. But by that time it was too late. The umpires' decision stood, the Mets had won the game, 2–1, and they had a 3–1 lead in the Series.

Even the Orioles were beginning to sense that this wouldn't be their Series, but they didn't give up. In the third inning of the fifth game, the Orioles struck for three runs as pitcher McNally hit an unexpected home run after Belanger's single and then, with two outs, Frank Robinson hit a solo homer.

But the Mets came back, starting with a bizarre play in the sixth inning. Cleon Jones, leading off the inning, was hit on the foot by a McNally pitch, but the plate umpire didn't see it. He called the pitch a ball and ordered Jones back into the box, but then, Mets' manager Hodges came out of the dugout and demanded to see the ball. A spot of shoe polish was on the ball, proving irrevocably that Jones had been hit.

Given first base, Jones soon came all the way around on Clendenon's homer, his third of the Series.

The improbable continued in the seventh when Weis led off with a home run that tied the score. In his entire ten-year major league career, Al Weis hit only seven home runs, but it figured that this would be the Series in which he would hit a crucial one.

The tide was obviously turning, and the Mets made it official in the eighth inning. Jones led off with a double off reliever Eddie Watt and, after Clendenon grounded out, Swoboda knocked in Jones with the run that gave the Mets their first lead of the game.

After Charles flied out for the second out, the demoralized Orioles committed two errors on one play, giving the Mets their final run. Powell fumbled Grote's grounder, allowing Grote to reach base safely, and when he finally threw late to first base, Watt fumbled the throw, allowing Swoboda to come all the way home from second base.

Koosman walked Frank Robinson leading off the ninth but then got the next three

Brooks Robinson had a bad World Series against the Mets in 1969 but an incredible World Series in 1971 against the Pirates, both at bat and in the field at third base. *(Baltimore Orioles)*

hitters to nail down the 5–3 win, his second of the Series. The Mets were World Champions.

The statistics showed just how improbable a Series it had been. The great Oriole hitters had been shackled—Powell had hit .263, Frank Robinson .188, and Brooks Robinson just .053.

Meanwhile, Clendenon, a .252 hitter with 12 homers in the regular season, had hit .357 with three homers in five games. Weis, a .215 hitter, had led everybody with .455 in the Series. Swoboda, a regular season .235 hitter, had hit .400 and made a great defensive play.

Joe Hardy couldn't have done it better.

Vida Blue was the most spectacular of the Oak-land pitchers during their three consecutive Series triumphs. *(Jonathan Perry)*

23. Victory for the Moustache Gang

The 1972 Oakland A's won the first American League pennant in 41 years for the nomadic franchise, which had started in Philadelphia and stopped in Kansas City en route to Oakland, but they failed to win the respect of their baseball colleagues.

The A's were a hard team to take seriously. They were outfitted in garish green-and-gold uniforms which seemed more suited to a men's softball league than a baseball team. Owner Charles O. Finley had given bonuses to those players who grew moustaches for a 1971 promotion, and many of the players had liked their moustaches so much that they had kept them. Thus, the team had the look of an 1890s road show, and the A's were widely known as "The Moustache Gang."

The team seemed rent with dissension. Players fought openly in the clubhouse, not just in 1972 but in later years, as the A's kept winning. Reggie Jackson and Bill North fought over a young woman. On the eve of the 1972 World Series, Vida Blue (who had been relegated to the bull pen), asked Blue Moon Odom why "you starters can't finish" and made the "choke" sign, putting his hand to his throat. The enraged Odom had to be grabbed by teammates as he tried to go after Vida.

Blue had been in the middle of a continuing controversy himself. After his great 24–8 season in 1971, he had held out for much more money, a dispute that was not settled until well after the season had started. Emotionally upset and lacking the physical conditioning he would have gotten in spring training, Blue had slumped to 6–10 in 1972.

Convinced (probably correctly) that Finley had told manager Dick Williams not to start him in postseason play, Vida was bitter in his public comments about Williams. "He never says anything to me," Blue complained. "The only way I find out what I'm going to do is by reading the newspapers."

Finley was a constant source of irritation—to his players, to writers, to others in baseball. He had a million ideas, all of them borrowed and some of them good. He

Controversial Charles O. Finley owned the colorful Oakland A's, who won three consecutive World Series, 1972–74. *(Jonathan Perry)*

campaigned for the designated hitter and night mid-week World Series games, both of which came to pass. He also campaigned for designated runners, orange baseballs, and three-ball walks and two-strike strikeouts, none of which were seriously considered.

He had had four managers since coming to Oakland, and Williams was the first to last two full seasons. (John McNamara had managed the last 13 games in 1969, after the firing of Hank Bauer, and a full season in 1970.)

Williams was an excellent manager who had won a pennant with the Boston Red Sox in 1967 and a divisional title and pennant in his two seasons in Oakland. But Finley was convinced he needed to help Williams, and he constantly gave orders to the manager.

It was a tribute to Williams and the A's that they were able to win despite Finley's interference, because the owner's ideas were often bizarre.

It was Finley, for instance, who came up with the idea of rotating second basemen, pinch-hitting early for the weak bat of second baseman Dick Green. That had almost cost the A's the American League playoff because catcher Gene Tenace had wound up at second base and made a critical error which cost the A's a game.

It was Finley who insisted that the A's use sprinter Allen Lewis, though Lewis was a weak hitter ("He hit .300 as a switch-hitter," said Williams dryly, ".150 right-handed and .150 left-handed") and not even a good base runner. Finley dubbed him "The Panamanian Express" but writer Herb Michelson renamed him "The Panamanian Local" because, Michelson explained, "he stops at every base."

Most of all, Finley had alienated his players. He held down salaries (this was before the end of the reserve clause, of course), insulted players publicly, and, thought the players, used broadcaster Monte Moore as a pipeline from the clubhouse.

One time I commented to Jackson that, because of a critical column in *The San Francisco Chronicle,* Finley had not spoken to me in two years. "I wish I could be that lucky," said Jackson.

The inner turmoil on the club often obscured the fact that the A's were a solid team where it counted, on the pitching mound and in the field.

Catfish Hunter, who had pitched a perfect game in 1968 and was one of those rare major leaguers never to play in the minors, had had an exceptional year, 21–7 with a 2.04 ERA. Hunter was not an overpowering pitcher, but he had great control, which enabled him to make the batters hit the pitch he wanted.

Rollie Fingers was a dominant relief pitcher for the A's in three World Series before going as a free agent to San Diego. *(San Diego Padres)*

Ken Holtzman, obtained in an off-season trade, had won 19 games, and Odom had won 15. Rollie Fingers, perhaps the best relief pitcher of all time, had won 11 games and saved 21. (An oddity: Holtzman, Odom, and Fingers all had ERAs of 2.51.)

Defensively, the A's had good gloves everywhere—at least, when a Finley-dictated move didn't catch them with an out-of-position player at second base. Offensively, they were not overwhelming, but they had a knack for getting the clutch hit. (Their averages, too, were artificially depressed because they were playing in the Oakland Coliseum, which was a bad park for hitters, mostly because of its huge foul areas.)

But they were also going into the '72 World Series with their most dangerous hitter, Jackson, sidelined by a pulled hamstring and calf muscle; Reggie would not be able to even pinch-hit.

Even with Jackson, the A's would have been considerable underdogs. Their opponents, the Cincinnati Reds, seemed a great team, with future Hall-of-Famers like catcher Johnny Bench, second baseman Joe Morgan, and the versatile Pete Rose, playing in the outfield that season.

Offensively, the Reds were very well balanced. The first three hitters—Rose, Morgan, and Bobby Tolan—got on base, and the next two, Bench and Tony Perez, knocked them in. Morgan led the league with 155 walks and 122 runs scored and Rose had a league-leading 198 hits and brought home 107 runs; Bench led the league with 40 homers and 125 RBIs, while Perez had 21 and 90.

Morgan and Tolan stole 100 bases between them, Morgan having 58, and the Reds were a blur on the base paths, routinely going from first to third on singles. There probably hadn't been a National League team with as much overall speed since the St. Louis Cardinals of 1942—and this Reds team had far more power.

The feeling in baseball was that the National League was much the superior, and that the real World Series had been the NL playoff between the Reds and the Pittsburgh Pirates, a monumental struggle that had gone five games before the Reds had won.

The bitter Blue agreed. In a television interview, Vida said, "I don't think Oakland has the best club in baseball. I'd rate Cincinnati and Pittsburgh better."

The Reds themselves were so confident, quipped Oakland baseball writer Ron Bergman, "they thought they'd win in three."

But, even for those who thought the Series was a physical mismatch, it was an interesting pairing—"The Hairs Vs. the Squares."

The A's, of course, were the hairy ones, with a variety of moustaches and sideburns, presaging the era when long hair would become the norm, not the exception. The Reds, representing the heartland, were clean-shaven and short-haired—by club edict.

The contrast extended to the managers. Williams, going with the trend, had a moustache and long hair, and he had learned to live with the variety of opinions expressed by his players—and owner.

Cincinnati manager Sparky Anderson, though the youngest in the majors at 38, seemed much older because of his homely appearance and his outlook on life, which would not have been out of place had he been managing Cincinnati's first National League team in 1876.

To reinforce the contrast, two banners were towed by airplanes over Cincinnati's Riverfront Stadium for the first game: "Oakland has weird uniforms" and "Women's Lib will destroy the family."

But, when all the imagery was laid aside, what followed was an exceptionally close seven-game Series, with an unlikely winner and an even more unlikely hero.

Before the first game, the A's players were kidding around about which of them would be the Series Most Valuable Player, winning the car awarded by *Sport* magazine.

Relief pitcher Darold Knowles had a bizarre suggestion: Gene Tenace.

At that point, only the most avid baseball fans would have been able even to identify Tenace. A versatile player (he would eventually play most of his career at first base), Tenace had been only a backup catcher for most of the season. In August, when the A's had slumped, Williams had put Tenace into the starting lineup.

Tenace had hardly become an overnight star. He had finished the season hitting just .225 with only five homers in 82 games, and he had followed that with a dismal one-for-17 showing in the American League playoff against Detroit.

Still, Knowles was convinced he had spotted something. "I like the way he's swinging the bat," he said.

Tenace himself wasn't so impressed; he had felt he was pressing in the playoffs. As he waited in the on-deck circle, while George Hendrick batted, in the second inning of the opening game, different thoughts and emotions streamed through his mind. He remembered, for instance, that Cincinnati scouts had watched him play in high school in Lucasville, Ohio (not far from Cincinnati), and said he'd never make it. But mostly, he was awestruck at the thought of the 50,000 fans watching the game and the millions more seeing it on television.

Hendrick walked and Tenace came to bat. Gary Nolan was pitching for Cincinnati. Nolan was brilliant when healthy; he had been 15–5 with a 1.99 ERA that season. But he also had a history of arm trouble, and his fastball wasn't what it had been. He tried to get one past Tenace; Gene, trying only to make contact, he said later, hit it over the left field fence to give his team a 2–0 lead.

Cincinnati got one run back off A's starter Holtzman in the third on singles by Bench and Perez, a walk to Denis Menke, and a forceout by Dave Concepcion.

The Reds tied it in the fourth when Bench walked, went to third on Perez's single, and scored on a force play off Menke's grounder.

But Tenace came to bat again in the fifth inning, one out, nobody on. This time, Nolan threw him a curve. "It hung like a feather," Nolan said later. Tenace slammed it

Using a fastball almost exclusively, Ken Holtzman was a key in the A's World Series run. *(Oakland A's)*

Catfish Hunter was a key pitcher for the A's in the World Series wins and a controversial figure in the 1977 Series, when he was pitching for the Yankees. *(Oakland A's)*

into the left field stands, just inside the foul pole. He had become the first batter to hit home runs in his first two at-bats in a World Series.

As Tenace came across the plate, Bench was considering the irony of the situation. "I had kinda hoped," he said later, "that if a catcher hit two home runs in a game, it would be me."

The A's had an anxious moment left. Nursing a 3–2 lead, Williams had brought in Fingers for Holtzman in the sixth and Blue for Fingers in the seventh, and Vida was still pitching when Hal McRae opened the Cincinnati ninth with a pinch-hit single.

Concepcion sacrificed pinch-runner George Foster to second, and Foster went to third on a groundout by pinch hitter Julian Javier. Rose was the next batter. After a bunt attempt went foul, Rose topped a ball to the right side. A's second baseman Ted Kubiak charged the ball and just got the flying Rose at first to end the game.

The A's win didn't shake the Reds' confidence, though, and especially not that of Rose.

"I'm not impressed with the A's," said the always forthright Rose. "Outside of Gene Tenace, they didn't do much. They got only four hits, so I can't be impressed with their offense. They had a couple of shots at double plays and they didn't make them, so I'm not impressed with their defense. And Johnny Bench threw out the only two guys who tried to steal, so I'm not impressed with their base running. And Holtzman didn't throw as hard as he had with the Cubs."

Joe Rudi made a key catch that started the Oakland A's on their way to an upset win in the 1972 World Series. *(Oakland A's)*

It was hard to tell who had won the game.

The A's didn't impress Rose the next day, either, even though they won their second game from the Reds.

In the second inning, singles by Sal Bando, Green, and Hunter got one run across, and the A's lead went to 2–0 on a solo homer by Joe Rudi in the third.

Meanwhile, Hunter muffled the Cincinnati bats, yielding only four hits over the first eight innings. Perez singled for the fifth hit off Hunter to lead off the ninth, and then the A's underrated defense went to work.

Menke hit Hunter's next pitch deep to left field; he thought it was a home run, which would have tied the game. But Rudi ran full-out to the fence, jumped at the last possible moment, crashed into the 12-foot fence chest first and made a backhanded catch. He pulled away from the fence, held up the ball to indicate he'd caught it, and fired it to the infield. Perez had rounded second, confident the ball was at least off the fence, and only a headfirst dive back into first prevented a double play.

Cesar Geronimo then lined a ball toward right field. A's first baseman Mike Hegan dived to his right and caught the ball. It popped loose when he hit the ground, but he picked it up and crawled to first base to make the putout. Had the ball gone through, it would have been at least a double and Perez would have scored.

Perez did finally score when the next batter, McRae, singled, and Williams brought in Fingers, despite Hunter's protests that he was still throwing well. Williams didn't want to test his fielders any more.

Fingers quickly got pinch hitter Javier to foul out, and the A's had won again, 2–1—and were going home to Oakland.

"It happened so fast," Rudi said of his catch, "that I didn't even know what happened. But I figure that any ball I can reach, I can catch."

Williams called it, "the best catch I've ever seen."

Rose? "Hunter's not a super-pitcher," snapped Pete. "If they don't get those two plays in the ninth, he's just a super-loser."

And winning didn't make the A's less contentious. Hegan was in the lineup because Mike Epstein, the starter at first base, had been removed for pinch runner Lewis. Epstein wasn't happy about the attention Hegan was getting. "The play Hegan made was a beauty," Epstein said, "but I could have done the same thing if I had been on first base. I might have even held on to the ball for a double play."

Nobody who had seen Epstein play first base thought that, however.

On the plane ride home, Epstein yelled at Williams, "You don't appreciate me. I've been busting my ass and I don't want this to happen again."

"I'm the manager," Williams said. "I'll do whatever I want."

Meanwhile, Finley was walking up and down the aisle. He paused and put a hand on Duncan's shoulder. "I know you, Dave Duncan. . . ."

"Bullshit!" snapped Duncan. "You don't know me because you've never taken the trouble to know me."

Just another day in the lives of the happy-go-lucky A's.

Blue, who was doing more talking than pitching, told a reporter, "We're handling Cincinnati easier than we did the Texas Rangers."

"Before the Series is over," said Anderson, "we'll thank Vida Blue. I've always heard that when you've got an athlete down, let him sleep. Don't wake him up."

The Reds' chance for revenge was delayed another day because of a strange rainstorm that hit the Oakland Coliseum and nowhere else in the area. The next day, the game that was played was a travesty. For the purpose of television, it was scheduled at 5:30 P.M.—prime time of 8:30 A.M. Eastern time but twilight in California. In the poor light, hitters seemed helpless. Cincinnati got the only run of the game, and there were 21 strikeouts in the game, 11 of them registered by Oakland starter Odom.

Even the one Cincinnati run almost didn't make it. In the seventh, Perez led off with a single, only the second hit for the Reds, and Menke sacrificed him to second.

Geronimo hit a ball off his fists into center field. Hendrick picked up the ball in center and threw to shortstop Campy Campaneris. Perez, rounding third, fell on the wet grass by the coach's box but Campaneris didn't realize that. Campy had already conceded the run and was simply making certain Geronimo didn't advance to second—so Perez picked himself up and ran in to score.

To his chagrin, Bench fell for an A's ruse in the eighth that prevented another Cincinnati run. With Tolan on second and one out, Fingers went to 3–2 on Bench. Williams rushed to the mound, gesturing toward first base as if Bench should be given an intentional fourth ball. Actually, he was telling Tenace to pretend to be taking the fourth ball but to jump back behind the plate so Fingers could throw a strike.

It worked to perfection, Fingers throwing what he later called the best slider of his career as Bench watched a third strike. After the game, as Williams answered questions about the play, Tenace said he had never heard of the play before. Fingers couldn't resist needling Williams, though. "I've known about the play for years," he said. "Our Little League coach taught it to us."

Tenace had cooled off since the first game, going hitless in his last eight at-bats as he came to the plate in the fifth inning of the fourth game. The slump ended quickly as he belted his third homer.

The Reds bounced back to take a one-run lead in the eighth inning as Blue, coming on in relief of starter Holtzman, yielded a walk to Morgan and a two-run double to Tolan.

It had been a strange Series. The home team had lost the first three games, and now it appeared the home team would also lose the fourth. But that trend was about to stop.

With one out in the bottom of the ninth, Gonzalo Marquez singled up the middle as a pinch hitter for Hendrick. Lewis went in to run. When the count reached 2–1 on Tenace, Anderson yanked Pedro Borbon and brought in Clay Carroll, who had set a major league record with 37 saves that year. But, on Carroll's second pitch, Tenace singled.

Williams sent up another pinch hitter, Don Mincher, and Mincher singled. Lewis scored the tying run, and Tenace went to third. The Reds' infield came in to try to cut off the winning run as Williams used his third pinch hitter of the inning, Angel Mangual.

The position of the infielders was critical. Mangual hit a ball just to the left of second baseman Morgan that could have been a double play ball if Morgan had been in normal position. Instead, it went through for a hit, and Tenace scored the deciding run in a 3–2 game. The A's were up, 3–1, in the Series.

There hadn't yet been a moment, though, when either team could relax in this Series, and that continued through the fifth game.

Rose got the Reds off winging in this one with a homer leading off the first against Hunter, but the ubiquitous Tenace hit a three-run shot in the second. It was his fourth homer of the Series; only Babe Ruth, Lou Gehrig, Duke Snider, and Hank Bauer had done it before Tenace. Gene Tenace and Babe Ruth? Get serious.

Manke hit a solo homer to close the gap to 3–2 in the top of the fourth, and the A's got the run back on another pinch hit by Marquez in the bottom of the inning.

But the A's were in trouble in this one because Fingers was understandably tired as he made his fifth straight Series appearance and seventh in the last ten postseason games the A's had played. Coming on in the fifth to stop a Reds' rally by striking out Bench, after Morgan had scored from first on a Tolan single, Fingers couldn't hold the A's one-run lead.

In the eighth, the Morgan–Tolan combination worked again for the Reds. This time Morgan walked and stole second ahead of a Tolan single, tying the game.

In the ninth, Geromino singled and was sacrificed to second, and then Rose singled in Geromino for the deciding run. The Reds had won, 5–4, and the Series would go back to Cincinnati.

Before the sixth game, a woman standing in line outside the stadium heard a man say, "If Tenace hits another homer, he won't walk out of this ball park." Acting on the woman's tip, police arrested the man.

After the game, the A's joked about that. "If you got to go, Geno," Jackson told him, "at least it will be on national television."

"No one would even bother shooting me," said Epstein, who was 0–for–16 in the Series.

That threat to Tenace capped an absolutely miserable day for the A's. The first five games of the Series had all been one–run games, but in the sixth game, the Reds had bombed the A's, 8–1, evening the Series and giving new hope to their fans. Interestingly enough, it was the first Series game the Reds had won at home since 1940.

The lopsidedness of the win was made possible in part by a decision by the A's manager, Williams—one that was virtually forced on him.

Because of the rainout earlier in the Series, the teams had played on Friday, which would normally have been a travel day. Saturday was a natural for television, of course, so the travel day was eliminated; the sixth game was played instead.

The A's pitching staff was worn down. Williams decided to start Blue, and he resolved that he would not use Fingers, Hunter, Holtzman, or Odom. He had to think ahead, to a possible seventh game.

Williams lost the battle but he won the war. For the seventh game, he would have all four of his top pitchers available—and he used every one, starting Odom and using Hunter, Holtzman, and finally Fingers in relief.

For the seventh game, Williams made some significant changes. To improve his defense, he put Duncan behind the plate and switched Tenace, who had not been able to stop the Reds' runners, to first base. He also moved Tenace up in the batting order, from seventh to fourth.

Tenace repaid Williams's faith in his hitting immediately. With two outs and Mangual on third, after a three-base error by Reds' center fielder Tolan, Tenace ripped a grounder to third that hit the seam of the artificial turf and bounced over the head of third baseman Menke, knocking in the first run of the game.

The defensive move also paid off. With one out in the fourth inning, Morgan walked. Odom, though right-handed, had an excellent move toward first and had boasted that the Reds would not steal on him. He threw once, twice . . . eventually seven times to first before pitching to Tolan. Twice, his throws almost got Morgan, and he gradually drove Joe back. Morgan had started with a lead which took him onto the artificial turf; after the seventh throw, he was back on the dirt, closer to the bag. On the second pitch to Tolan, Morgan took off, but Duncan threw him out at second, a play that many thought later was one of the keys to the game.

With one out and two men on in the fifth, and a 2–1 count on Concepcion, Williams brought Hunter in for Odom. Hunter completed the walk and then pinch hitter McRae smashed a line drive to deep center. For a moment, it seemed that it would hit the fence, but Mangual caught the ball right at the base of the fence. Perez scored easily from third base to tie the game, 1–1.

In the sixth, Campaneris singled and was sacrificed to second by Mangual, bringing up Tenace. By now, the Reds should have known enough to pitch around Tenace, but Borbon came in with a fastball and Tenace lined a double into the left field corner, scoring Campy.

Williams then made a surprise move, taking out Tenace for pinch runner Lewis, who scored when Sal Bando followed with a double. The A's led, 3–1.

Rose led off the eighth with a single and Williams, pulling out all the stops, brought in Holtzman to pitch against the left-handed hitting Morgan. But Morgan never had any problems hitting left-handers, and he lined a shot down the first base line, just past the diving Hegan at first base. The ball was pulled so sharply that Rose had to hold up for a moment to avoid being hit, and he then had to jump over Hegan, slowing him

Campy Campaneris was a triple threat for the A's—hitting, fielding, and base running—and an integral part of the three-time World Series champions. *(Jonathan Perry)*

down for crucial moments. As he rounded third, Rose was waved back by third base coach Alex Grammas. Had he continued, Rose would have scored easily because right fielder Matty Alou, conceding the run, had thrown to third to try to keep Morgan from advancing there.

Now Williams brought in Fingers, his finisher, and Rollie got pinch hitter Joe Hague on an infield fly. Williams then made a move that was more dangerous than the one in which he removed Tenace: He ordered Bench walked intentionally to load the bases.

That was violating one of baseball's hoariest rules—don't put the leading run on base—but Williams was determined he was not going to let Bench beat him with one swing of his powerful bat.

The strategy worked. Although Rose came home on Perez's sacrifice fly, Fingers got Menke on a fly to left for the third out. The A's still had the lead, 3-2.

Gene Tenace was the surprise hero of the '72 World Series, hitting four home runs and winning the Most Valuable Player award for the Series. (Oakland A's)

It stayed that way, though the Reds had one last shot in the ninth. With two outs, Fingers threw a slider that hit Darrel Chaney, pinch hitting for reliever Tom Hall, and Williams came to the mound, thinking of bringing in Blue to pitch to Rose.

Duncan talked his manager out of it, and Fingers then got Rose to hit his first pitch to Rudi in left field for the final out. The A's had won by a single run for the fourth time, and the six one-run games in the Series had set a record.

For Tenace, it had been a Series for which incredible is too weak a description. He had tied a record with his four home runs, had hit .348, and had led all the hitters with nine RBIs and a remarkable .913 slugging average. None of his teammates had knocked in more than one run.

As the A's went on to win three straight World Series—a feat nobody other than the Yankees has ever accomplished—their 1972 win seemed less of a fluke than it did at the time. Maybe they looked funny, but they knew how to play the game of baseball.

24. The Best Series Ever?

The Big Red Machine has an automatic choke.

The Cincinnati Reds were tired of hearing that taunt. They had been the dominant team in the National League in the '70s, but they had not erased the final doubt in the minds of baseball people. Despite their undeniable talent, the Reds had consistently faltered in postseason play, losing in the World Series in 1970 and 1972 and, shockingly, in the National League playoffs in 1973 to a much inferior New York Mets team.

Now, in 1975, the Reds were better than ever. After splitting their first 40 games, the Reds had gone on a tear, winning 41 of their next 50. Eventually, they had won 108 games and finished a shocking 20 games up on the second-place Los Angeles Dodgers in the NL West. In the playoffs, they had demolished Pittsburgh in three straight.

The old Reds' stars—Johnny Bench, Joe Morgan, Pete Rose, Tony Perez—were still going strong. Morgan, in fact, had had his best season, winning the first of what would be two consecutive Most Valuable Player awards as he hit .327 with 17 homers, 94 RBIs, 107 runs scored, a league-leading 132 walks, and 67 stolen bases, while playing his second base position better than anybody else.

To that group had been added George Foster, a power-hitting outfielder who had socked 23 homers in 1975 and would two seasons later set a club record with 52, and Ken Griffey, a .305-hitting outfielder who could flat-out fly on the bases.

Manager Sparky Anderson had become known as "Captain Hook" because of his tendency to go early to his bull pen—the Cincinnati starters had only 22 complete games—but Anderson knew what he was doing. Relievers Rawly Eastwick, Will McEnaney, Clay Carroll, and Pedro Borbon often successfully bailed out the Reds' starters, saving 49 victories that season.

If the Reds, who had not won a World Series since 1940, had something to prove, so did their opponents, the Boston Red Sox, who had not won a World Series since 1918.

The Red Sox, who had captured their division by five games over Baltimore and then disposed of the Oakland A's in three straight in the playoff series, were decided underdogs in the Series.

From the start, this promised to be a provocative matchup because the two franchises were among the richest in history in all of baseball. Cincinnati, of course, had been the very first baseball franchise, predating even the beginning of the National League. The Red Sox could not trace their lineage back that far but they had won the very first World Series, when they were still known as the Pilgrims.

The parks the teams played in were important, too. Cincinnati played in one of the modern multipurpose stadiums, a designation which usually means that the stadium is designated for football with baseball as an afterthought.

Riverfront Stadium had artificial turf, a field ideally suited to the Reds because it rewarded speed, and the Reds were blessed with an abundance of it.

Fenway Park, in contrast, was the best of the old parks, a small, cozy park in which spectators sat so close it seemed they were on the playing field—especially to those players they were throwing insults at.

The park, of course, was most famous for the Green Monster, the left field wall which was only 315 feet down the line but stretched 40 feet high. The wall altered the game because high flies that would be outs in other parks went for home runs, while line drives that would have been doubles or even triples in other parks sometimes were turned into singles when the left fielder played the carom perfectly.

Because of the wall, Boston teams traditionally had a collection of right-handed sluggers who could loft the ball over the fence—but who suffered on the road in less-hospitable parks. Left-handed pitchers had nightmares about the park, and the Red Sox seldom had had good left-handed pitching over the years.

Defensively, too, the wall was a factor because the ball bounced erratically off it. As the Reds prepared for the Series, they devised a plan for balls hit off the wall: shortstop Dave Concepcion would race out in case the carom got by left fielder Foster and headed back toward the infield, and center fielder Cesar Geronimo could come over to get any balls that bounced toward him. "That's the only way to play the wall," said manager Anderson. "You have to surround it."

Sometimes, the hoopla surrounding a World Series makes the games seem almost anticlimactic, especially in the era of television. Not this time. The 1975 World Series had everything: big home runs, controversial plays, and one game—the sixth—which will never be forgotten by anybody who watched it, in person or on TV.

The 1975 Series, in fact, was probably the best ever played.

It started with an immediate controversy. Luis Tiant, the Red Sox starter who admitted to 34 years (some thought he had his digits reversed), had a motion unlike anybody's in baseball. With nobody on, he turned his body completely toward second base before reversing himself and pitching to the plate. Pitching from the stretch with men on base, he had a variety of twitches and shrugs which disguised an excellent move to first.

Tiant had never been called for a balk, but before the Series had started, there had been a rumor that Anderson had sent film on Tiant to the umpires to check whether Tiant was balking. Anderson denied that, but he had planted the thought in everybody's mind. And in the fourth inning of the first game, with Morgan on first base, first base umpire Nick Colosi, working his first Series, called a balk.

Tiant charged the umpire, shouting in Spanish. It seemed Anderson's ploy had worked. But Tiant understood what was happening. "I realized while I was arguing that this is just what Cincinnati wants me to do," said Tiant later. "I just told myself not to get mad and to get back to thinking about pitching."

Which he did, magnificently. Although the Reds were hitting the ball hard, it was usually right at a Boston fielder. Inning after inning, the colorful Cuban right-hander kept the Reds from scoring.

For six innings, Don Gullett was matching him zero for zero. Gullett, a left-hander who threw as hard as anybody in the game, had won 15 games for the Reds during the season, despite missing nearly two months because of a sore arm.

In the seventh, though, Gullett faltered and, ironically, it was against his pitching rival, Tiant, who had not batted in two seasons—because of the American League's designated hitter rule. Gullett got two strikes on Tiant with fastballs and then made a classic mistake, throwing an off-speed pitch, a forkball. Weak hitters lap up off-speed pitches (the fact that they can't hit fastballs is what makes them weak hitters) and Tiant hit this one to left field for a single.

Dwight Evans laid down a sacrifice bunt and Gullett, a good-fielding pitcher, got to it quickly. Bench yelled at him to throw to second for the force. But the grass was slippery because of an earlier rain and Gullett's feet slipped as he started his throw. "I had nothing on it," he said later.

The throw to second was too late to get Tiant, and when Denny Doyle followed with a single, the bases were loaded, the slow Tiant having to stop at third.

Carl Yastrzemski followed with a single which scored Tiant with the first run of the game, and the only one he would need, as it turned out. Anderson took out Gullett and brought in Carroll, who walked Carlton Fisk, forcing in another run. Anderson went to his bull pen again, bringing in McEnaney, who struck out Fred Lynn. But then Rico Petrocelli and Rick Burleson singled and Cecil Cooper hit a sacrifice fly, and the Red Sox were up, 6–0. It ended that way.

Rose, who never believes that any pitcher can get him out, was not impressed by Tiant. "I would not mind hitting against Luis Tiant every day," he said. "I might go 0-for-100, but I wouldn't mind hitting against him."

The first game had been played in dark, gloomy weather. For game two, there was also a light drizzle. A regular season game would probably have been postponed but because this was the Series—and on national television—it was played.

For a time, it seemed the Red Sox would go up, 2–0, taking a 2–1 lead into the ninth inning. The irrepressible Boston left-hander, Bill Lee, had pitched a four-hitter over the first eight innings.

Bench led off the ninth, and the Boston infield over-shifted for him, second baseman Doyle actually playing to the left side of second. Lee threw a low fastball on the outside corner to Bench. A lesser player, with the left field wall beckoning, would have tried to pull the ball—and probably hit a harmless grounder to the left side. Bench went with the pitch and belted a double down the right field line.

"Why don't you hit the ball where you're supposed to?" said Doyle as Bench stood on second base.

Perez grounded to short, Bench moving to third, but Foster's fly to left was too short to score Bench. It was up to Concepcion, who had made the final out of the first game. This time, the Cincinnati shortstop hit a high-bouncing grounder up the middle. Doyle grabbed it but had no play. Concepcion was safe and Bench had scored the tying run.

Fisk had thrown out the only two Cincy base-runners who had tried to steal—Foster in the first game, Morgan in the second—but Anderson sent Concepcion, anyway, and Davey reached second safely, though he overslid. If Doyle had tagged him again, he'd have been out, but Concepcion reached back for the base before the Boston second baseman could react.

Moments later, Griffey slashed a double to left center that gave the Reds a 3–2 win.

After the game, a writer asked Lee how he characterized the Series so far.

"Tied," said Lee.

The third game, back in Cincinnati, was a wild one, with each team getting three home runs—by Bench, Concepcion, and Geronimo for the Reds and Evans, Fisk, and Bernie Carbo (as a pinch hitter) for the Red Sox.

But, in the tenth inning, it was a disputed call by plate umpire Larry Barnett (another umpire in his first World Series), which was the crucial play. Rather, it was Barnett's noncall that was critical.

Geronimo singled to lead off the inning and Ed Armbrister batted for Eastwick. Armbrister's sacrifice bunt went straight down and up in front of the batter's box. Fisk leaped out from behind the plate as Armbrister took one step and stopped. Fisk collided with Armbrister, shoved him back with his gloved hand and then threw to second base, trying to get Geronimo for what would have undoubtedly been the start of a double play.

But Fisk's throw sailed wildly into center field. Geronimo went to third, and Armbrister sped all the way to second.

Fisk and Boston manager Darrell Johnson argued that Armbrister had interfered with Fisk and should thus be called out, with Geronimo having to return to first. But Barnett said it had not been an intentional collision—there was no doubt, as the many TV replays showed, that Fisk and Armbrister had collided—and thus, he would not rule interference.

Baseball rules are quite clear on this. There are, in fact, three different rules (2.00 a, 6.06 c, and 7.09, if you want to look them up) which say that a batter is out if he interferes with a fielder—and there is nothing which says it has to be intentional.

But the league offices had sent umpires a "supplemental instruction" memo on the interference rules which said, "When a catcher and a batter-runner going to first have contact when the catcher is fielding the ball, there is generally no violation and nothing should be called."

Barnett had had that memo in mind when he made his call, and he would not change his mind. When the argument at home plate had ended, Rose was intentionally walked to load the bases and pinch hitter Marv Rettenmund took a called third strike.

But then, Morgan hit a ball over center fielder Fred Lynn's head—officially a single, because of scoring rules—and the Reds had won, 6–5.

The loss was a particularly bitter one for the Red Sox because they had battled back from a 5–1 deficit; Evans' two-run, one-out homer in the ninth had finally tied it at 5–5. Some players thought manager Johnson had not argued hard enough.

Johnny Bench, a great power hitter and an outstanding defensive catcher, won honors as the all-time World Series catcher. *(Cincinnati Reds)*

"If it had been me out there," said Lee, "I'd have bitten Barnett's ear off. I'd have van Goghed him!"

It was Tiant's turn again for the Red Sox in game four, but it was quickly evident that this was not the same Tiant who had bewildered the Reds in the first game.

Rose singled to lead off the bottom of the first for the Reds and Griffey followed with a double that scored Rose, though Griffey was thrown out at third trying to stretch his hit into a triple.

Morgan walked and went to second as Perez grounded out, and Bench's double scored Morgan with the second run of the inning, before Foster grounded out to end the inning.

In the fourth inning, though, the Red Sox broke through for five runs, knocking out Cincy starter Fred Norman. Fisk and Lynn started the rally with singles and, after Petrocelli popped out, moved up on a wild pitch and scored on an Evans triple.

Burleson doubled in Evans before Anderson brought in Borbon in relief, an unusually slow move by Captain Hook, but the Red Sox weren't finished. Tiant singled up the middle and Juan Beniquez was safe when Perez fumbled his grounder, Burleson scoring.

Doyle fouled out but Yastrzemski singled to right, scoring Tiant with the fifth run of the inning, before Fisk, batting for the second time, flied out for the third out.

The Reds battled back with two runs after two were out in the bottom of the inning, on an infield hit by Foster, a bloop double by Concepcion, and a triple by Geronimo into the right field corner.

And then, amazingly, the pace of the game changed completely. It was 5–4 Boston after four innings and it was still 5–4 as the Reds came to bat in the bottom of the ninth. The gutty Tiant was still in there, and Eastwick, who had won the previous two games in relief, had pitched the final three scoreless innings for the Reds, making Anderson wish he had brought him in earlier.

In the ninth, Geronimo led off with a single and once again, Armbrister was called on to bunt as a pinch hitter. This time, he laid one down without incident, Geronimo going to second.

Rose walked, and Johnson came out to the mound to talk to Tiant, surprising everybody by leaving him in. Griffey went to a 3–2 count and then lashed a long drive to the deepest part of the ballpark. For a few moments, it seemed it was a drive that would knock in both runs, but Boston's Lynn, probably the best outfielder in the game that year, went all the way to the fence to haul it in.

That still left Morgan, the most dangerous hitter in baseball in a clutch situation. But Tiant got Morgan to pop to first, and the Red Sox had tied the Series.

"Never mind his age," said Morgan in admiration of Tiant, who had thrown 163 pitches. "Being smart, having an idea—that's what makes a pitcher."

Morgan has a confidence which borders on arrogance—until you see him back up his words with deeds. As Dizzy Dean once said, "It ain't braggin' if you do it."

Joe felt he should have gotten a hit in his last at-bat in the fourth game, and he was determined he'd do something to help win the next one. He did. He changed the whole rhythm of the game in the sixth inning, just by being Joe Morgan.

The Reds led, 2–1, going into the inning, one of the runs coming on a fourth-inning home run by Perez that had ended an 0–for–15 drought.

Morgan led off with a walk. In the first inning he had singled and stolen second, so Boston pitcher Reggie Cleveland was determined not to let Morgan steal again.

Before he threw a pitch to Bench, the next batter, Cleveland threw over to first seven times. Then he threw a strike to Bench. He threw four more times to first base and then threw another pitch, fouled off by Bench. Cleveland threw another five times to first base, and then pitched a ball to Bench.

None of the throws to first had come close to getting Morgan, nor to bothering him. Each time he got up and took the same lead, and each time the ball was delivered to home plate he made a feint at going to second.

On the fourth pitch to Bench, Morgan feinted again—and second baseman Doyle started for the bag to cover. Bench hit a grounder through the right side that would have been at least one out and maybe the start of a double play, but with Doyle out of position, it went through for a base hit, and Morgan sped to third.

The flustered Cleveland then gave up a three-run homer to Perez, who had broken his slump in a big way, and the Reds breezed to a 6–2 win behind Gullett.

That brought up game six, one of the most dramatic in Series history—but not quickly. A nor'easter hit Boston, and for three days, there could be no baseball in Fenway Park. But the rains stopped on the fourth day and the setting was perfect for this theatrical game, clear skies and a lush harvest moon overseeing the field.

As dramatic as game three had been, this one was even more so, and its finish was a magnificent one, not clouded in controversy as the earlier game had been.

The Red Sox struck first in the bottom of the first inning as Lynn homered behind singles by Fisk and Yastrzemski.

It stayed 3–0 until Cincinnati tied it with a three-run fifth. With one out, pinch hitter Armbrister walked and Rose singled, his second straight hit off Tiant, going again for the Red Sox because he had gotten his rest during the three-day rain out.

Griffey lined a ball to left center that Lynn made a courageous try for, but the ball bounced off the fence as Lynn crashed into it and crumpled to the ground. Both runners scored and Griffey got a triple before Yastrzemski could run the ball down and throw it in. Lynn, though shaken, remained in the game.

Morgan popped out, but Bench singled off the wall in left field to score Griffey before Perez struck out.

In the seventh, the Reds took the lead when Foster hit a double that knocked in Griffey and Morgan, who had singled, and the Cincinnati lead went to 6–3 when Geronimo homered in the eighth.

In the bottom of the inning, Lynn opened with a single off Borbon's leg and Petrocelli walked. Anderson brought in Rawly Eastwick, his sixth pitcher of the night. Captain Hook wasn't slow in this game.

Eastwick, throwing nothing but heat, struck out Evans and got Burleson to fly out. Red Sox manager Johnson sent up Carbo, who had hit a home run as a pinch hitter in the third game and had complained ever since because he wasn't playing more.

Anderson had a decision to make. He could bring in McEnaney to pitch to Carbo, left-hander to left-hander. But he knew what would happen.

"If I had," he said later, "they would have pinch-hit with Juan Beniquez. With that wall in left field, any right-handed hitter is a dangerous hitter. If Beniquez had come up and hit one over the wall, I'd have been sick."

So he left Eastwick in the game to pitch to Carbo, who had once played for Cincinnati and had, in fact, been one of Anderson's favorite players.

Eastwick, Cincy's premier reliever, made Carbo look very bad on an inside fastball. But then he got a fastball out over the plate and Carbo hit it long and far into the night, over the center field fence. The score was tied.

The Red Sox had a chance to win the game in the ninth. Doyle led off with a walk and went to third on a Yastrzemski single, and Anderson brought in McEnaney. Fisk was intentionally walked to set up a force at any base. Lynn flied to Foster, and Doyle tried to come home on the catch. But Foster's throw was perfect, and Doyle was nailed at the plate. Petrocelli then grounded out, and the game went into extra innings.

The Reds had a chance to win the game in the tenth when, with one out, Concepcion singled and stole second. But Red Sox reliever Dick Drago got a strikeout against Geronimo and a fly out from pinch hitter Dan Driessen.

In the 11th, Rose was hit by a pitch and then forced at second on an attempted sacrifice by Griffey. The ever-dangerous Morgan lined a ball to right field that seemed on its way out of the park, but Evans raced to the wall and stuck out his glove at the last moment, grabbing the ball just when it seemed about to go over the fence.

It was one of the great fielding plays in Series history, and it wasn't over. Griffey had taken off the moment the ball was hit, confident it would at least be off the fence. When Evans recovered and threw back to first, Griffey was easily doubled off.

By the bottom of the 12th inning, the game had gone well into the morning hours in Boston. Time to end it, and Fisk did. On the first pitch from Pat Darcy, the record eighth pitcher for the Reds, Fisk slammed a towering drive into the night, momentarily out of sight as it went far above the lights.

As it dropped back into sight, it was obvious the ball was hit far enough for a home run—but would it be fair or foul? Fisk took just two steps out of the batter's box and

Pete Rose was the engine for the Big Red Machine, the Cincinnati Reds, who won the '75 and '76 World Series and were probably the best National League team of all time. *(Cincinnati Reds)*

Joe Morgan got the hit that scored the winning run in the final game of the 1975 World Series, perhaps the best ever. (Cincinnati Reds)

then gyrated wildly, moving his body as if he were trying to pull the ball into fair territory. Finally it landed in the foul screen, just fair, and the Red Sox fans went wild.

After a game like that, the seventh game was almost anticlimactic but it, too, like all of the Series, was a fine game, one with its own special excitement.

The Red Sox jumped out to a 3–0 lead in the third inning, primarily on the wildness of Gullett, who walked four men, the last two forcing in runs.

But this was not a Series in which early leads held up, and the Reds came back with two in the sixth, helped by an errant Boston defense.

Rose, who got on base 11 of his last 15 appearances in the Series, led off with a single. After Morgan had flied out, Bench hit a double-play grounder to Burleson. But Rose slid hard into Doyle, making the pivot, and Doyle heaved the ball into the Boston dugout. That gave Cincinnati another chance, and Perez made the most of it, hitting a Lee curve ball far over the left field wall to make the score 3–2.

The Reds tied it in the seventh on walks to Griffey and Armbrister and a single by Rose, and you could feel the momentum changing. The Red Sox had squandered scoring opportunities—stranding nine men in the first five innings—and now the Reds were at a point where Anderson could go with his bull pen, rather than his less reliable starters.

Finally, in the ninth, Griffey led off with a walk off left-handed rookie Jim Burton and was sacrificed to second. Burton got pinch hitter Driessen on a groundout and walked Rose. That brought up Morgan.

Burton pitched as well as he could to Morgan, getting to a 1–and–2 count and then throwing a near-perfect slider, low and away. Morgan barely got his bat on it, but that was enough. He hit a soft liner into short center that dropped in front of the frantically-rushing Lynn, and the swift Griffey scored with the lead run. The Red Sox went down, 1–2–3, in the ninth, and the Reds had won the Series.

With that behind them, the Reds went on to sweep through postseason play in 1976 and establish themselves as probably the best National League team of all time, bowling over the New York Yankees in four games in the World Series.

But the 1975 Series is the one they'll remember, and so will everybody else.

25. Reggie, Reggie, Reggie!

For most of his career, Reggie Jackson has been the most controversial player in baseball. He seems certain to make the baseball Hall of Fame one day, and yet, there are many who regard him as scarcely more than an average player.

Why this disparity of thought? For openers, there is his playing style.

When Jackson first came to the majors for 35 games at the end of the 1967 season, the A's last in Kansas City, he had everything—size, speed, strength. He was a dangerous base runner, with as many as 28 stolen bases in a season, and an outfielder who could make exceptional plays because of his speed, though he also messed up routine plays.

But injuries and age gradually robbed him of much of his speed, and weak eyesight deprived him of consistency at the plate. Not until his 13th full season did he hit .300. He became a slugger who was always dangerous and capable of hitting incredibly long home runs—but a slugger who was also capable of striking out frequently; he set club strikeout records for two teams.

The complex Jackson personality also divides people into two camps: You either love Reggie or you hate him.

Having dealt with Jackson since his early playing years in Oakland (where he still makes his home), I've found Reggie a thoughtful, articulate man who can analyze not only his play but that of others. He is also a man who is generous of time and money for charity causes, and one who often lavishes money on clubhouse attendants and less fortunate friends.

But Reggie is also a moody man, overly sensitive to criticism. To mask that, he often makes bombastic statements; when he joined the Yankees as a free agent, he proclaimed that, "I'm the straw that stirs the drink," meaning that he would be the player who made the Yankees champions. He was right, but he enraged Yankee team captain Thurman Munson, and other Yankee players, with the remark.

Even players who like Reggie will needle him. Catfish Hunter, a teammate on both the A's and the Yankees, once said that Reggie would give you "the shirt off his back." But, added Hunter impishly, "he'd call a press conference to do it."

One point about Jackson is not arguable, however: Wherever he plays, championship flags fly. When he played in Oakland, the A's won five consecutive divisional titles and three World Series. (Jackson missed the first of those Series because of an injury, but he was the Most Valuable player in the third one, in 1974.)

When he went to the Yankees, they won two straight World Series. Finally, when he moved on to the California Angels in 1982, they won a divisional championship.

None of this was coincidental. Jackson always has hit best down the stretch in a pennant race, and his World Series performances won him the nickname, "Mr. October."

And in 1977, Reggie Jackson put on a World Series performance like no hitter—not Babe Ruth, not Lou Gehrig, not Duke Snider—had ever done. In the final game, he took just three swings and hit three home runs, and his team won the Series. It was a fantastic finish to a tumultuous year.

Jackson had come to the Yankees that year as a free agent. In many ways, it was a dream come true for Reggie, who had once boasted, "If I played in New York, they'd name a candy bar after me."

He was expected by Yankee owner George Steinbrenner—and himself—to be the difference for a Yankee team which had won the American League pennant the previous year but had then been embarrassed by a four-game sweep by the Cincinnati Reds in the World Series.

It would not be easy. Controversial enough without any help, Jackson was placed in the middle of a struggle between Steinbrenner and manager Billy Martin. Martin had not wanted the Yankees to sign Jackson, and he did everything possible to demean Reggie when he came to the club, including batting him fifth and sixth, instead of in the cleanup position which was natural.

There are many theories about Martin's dislike of Jackson. Having known both men, I think it can simply be ascribed to jealousy on Martin's part.

As insecure as Jackson, but without Reggie's mitigating generosity of spirit, Martin was not willing to share the spotlight, especially in New York, where he had been greeted as the conquering hero.

The culmination of Martin and Jackson's feud came in a June 18 game in Boston, televised by NBC. A fly ball hit by Jim Rice dropped in front of Jackson and went for a double, in a game Boston went on to win, 10–4.

Martin was enraged because he felt Jackson had not made a good effort for the ball, and he sent Paul Blair out to take Reggie's place in the field, humiliating Reggie.

As Jackson jogged into the dugout, the cameras following, Martin screamed at him, "You show me up, I'll show you up."

Jackson screamed back, and the two moved at each other. Pitcher Mike Torrez told Jackson in Spanish, "Go inside, cool off."

That night, Steinbrenner talked separately to both Martin and Jackson. He was close to firing Martin but had no replacement for him. Finally, Jackson told the club owner, "I don't want to be the cause of a manager's firing. Don't fire him."

The tension remained between the two, but in August, Martin for the first time put Jackson's name in the fourth spot in the batting order, where it had always belonged. Jackson responded by knocking in 50 runs in his last 49 games, and the Yankees won the American League East by 2½ games over Baltimore.

When the Yankees won the divisional title, the two drank champagne from Jackson's bottle, but Martin hadn't relented. He had one final humiliation for Reggie: In the fifth game of the American League playoff series, Martin benched him because Kansas City pitched left-hander Paul Splittorff.

It was an understandable move from the standpoint of baseball percentages. "We looked up the records," said Martin, "and they showed that Reggie doesn't hit Splittorff."

Still, when Martin explained it to Steinbrenner, the Yankee owner was very upset. He saw Hunter walking by and yelled at him, "Hey, Cat, can Reggie hit Splittorff?"

"Not with a paddle," said Hunter, confirming Martin's judgment.

Jackson came up as a pinch hitter against Doug Bird in the eighth inning and hit a two-strike single to knock in a run. The Yankees won, 5–3, to take their second straight AL pennant.

"I love to hit when the pressure's on," said Jackson. "I enjoy the excitement. I try harder. I concentrate more."

Steinbrenner praised Jackson for not sulking when he was benched. Martin's reaction wasn't recorded, but it was no doubt ambivalent. Billy was happy his team had won, but Jackson's hit had revived the talk of "Mr. October." That was a title Martin thought he deserved for his excellent World Series performances as a Yankee player.

Perhaps that was still in Martin's mind when he told reporters Jackson would start the first game of the Series "because Splittorff isn't pitching for them [the Dodgers]."

The Series was a well-played one starting from the first game at Yankee Stadium. The Yankees took a 3–2 lead into the ninth before the Dodgers tied it and sent it into extra innings. But Sparky Lyle held the Dodgers at bay until the 12th, when Willie Randolph doubled and Paul Blair singled to win it for the Yankees.

The next day, Martin started Hunter, a questionable decision. Hunter had been the best pitcher in the league in the mid-'70s, but injury and illness had turned him into a mediocre pitcher in '77, just 9–9. The Dodgers blasted him for four home runs and coasted, 6–1.

"How could the son of a bitch pitch the man [Hunter]?" Jackson asked writers the next day before a workout at Dodger Stadium, which would be the site of the next three games. "How could they embarrass him like that?"

Martin told writers he had gambled on Hunter to save his other starters, tired by the stretch drive and the extended playoff series against Kansas City. "Let him worry about playing right field and I'll do the managing," he said of Jackson. "Where the hell does he come off saying something like that?"

Media watchers were amused. The Yankees were acting as they had always acted during the Steinbrenner era, snarling at each other. It wasn't just Jackson and Martin; Thurman Munson was also threatening not to play because his Series tickets were in a bad location.

At various times during the Series, Munson, Mickey Rivers, and Ed Figueroa all said they wanted to play somewhere else the next season. A magazine story quoted two anonymous Yankee players as telling Steinbrenner in mid-season that Martin should be fired.

Meanwhile, the Dodgers kept their disagreements, if any, private. Dodger players are instructed in the fine art of public relations, and the organization's relationship with the community is as good as any in sports.

The team stressed "family." Manager Tom Lasorda talked of the "Big Dodger in the Sky," and the influence of Hollywood and the entertainment business was obvious: Lasorda talked of having dinner with Frank Sinatra and trading jests with Don Rickles.

The Yankees, however, scored one for disharmony as they won the next two games in Los Angeles, 5–3 and 4–2. Mike Torrez and Ron Guidry both went the distance, justifying Martin's decision to start Hunter in the second game.

Jackson got a second-inning double and sixth-inning home run in the fourth game win, but the Dodgers felt the key to the game was Lou Piniella's leaping catch in the fourth inning of a Roy Cey drive. The catch robbed Cey of a home run that would have tied the score at 3–3 and changed managerial strategy on both sides.

"I thought the ball was out, sure," said Cey. "That would have given us a tie and the momentum. I never like to lose a home run, particularly a home run that would have been as important as that."

Jackson had had his best day yet in the Series, and he said he wanted to come back to the Yankees. "I'm planning on playing in New York next year. I'm looking forward to it."

He admitted he was tired of the battles with Martin. "They wear on me mentally," he said. "They make me older faster. It's very trying. Sometimes you wonder if it's worth it. I don't think Joe DiMaggio ever squabbled when he was playing ball. You never heard a word from Sandy Koufax. I don't think you have to be a 'bitcher' to be a good ball player."

But the controversy returned again after the fifth game, in which Jackson hit his

Fireballing Ron Guidry was the staff leader as the Yankees took the '77 Series. *(New York Yankees)*

second home run but the Dodgers won easily, 10–4, returning the Series to Yankee Stadium.

Time magazine had a story which said Jackson had told Steinbrenner he would not play another season under Martin. Although Reggie tried to deny the story, he had told the writer that several weeks before, when he was at a low point. Now he didn't feel that way—but that didn't change the story.

The New York Times ran a front-page story the morning of the sixth game headlined, "Steinbrenner Plans to Keep Jackson With Yankees in '78." Steinbrenner would not say, however, that he planned to have Martin back, insisting that was a decision that would have to be made by general manager Gabe Paul. Hours after the *Times'* story had appeared, Paul called a press conference to announce that Martin, too, would be back.

And that cleared the deck for the sixth game, which would become one no baseball fan would ever forget.

It started poorly for the Yankees with the Dodgers getting two unearned runs in the first. Shortstop Bucky Dent fumbled Reggie Smith's grounder, Cey walked, and Steve Garvey tripled them both home.

Jackson came to bat for the first time against Dodger starter Burt Hooton, famed for his "knuckle curve," in the second and drew a leadoff walk on four straight balls. Chris Chambliss followed with a home run deep into the right field seats for a 2–2 tie.

Reggie Smith sent the Dodgers ahead again at 3–2 in the top of the fourth with a home run off Yankee starter Torrez. The drive was Smith's third of the Series and one of nine the Dodgers hit during the six games, but it would soon be forgotten because the other Reggie, Jackson, was about to take center stage.

There is a frame of mind that athletes sometimes call being "in the zone" when everything goes right for them. They are moving swiftly and smoothly, everything in perfect synchronization, and their reflexes are so quick that everything else seems to be happening in slow motion.

Jackson was "in the zone." He had hit home runs in each of the last two games, and he had been crushing the ball in batting practice. He was ready.

Reggie's next at-bat came in the bottom of the fourth, after Munson had singled. On Hooton's first pitch, he swung and drove the ball into the right field stands to put the Yankees up for the first time, at 4–3.

Yankee Stadium exploded, and the Yankee dugout was almost as riotous. The crowd yelled, "Reggie, Reggie, Reggie," until Jackson came back out of the dugout and tipped his cap to the fans.

When he returned to his defensive position in right field at the start of the fifth inning, fans threw several objects, including a toy football and toilet tissue, onto the field. (Asked after the game what he thought of the Yankee fans, Steve Garvey

Reggie Smith looked like the hero of the 1977 World Series for the Dodgers—until another Reggie stole the show. *(Los Angeles Dodgers)*

commented, "Well, throwing things on the field is not my idea of a well-rounded human being.")

Jackson again doffed his hat to the fans. *San Francisco Chronicle* baseball writer Bob Stevens compared Reggie to a bullfighter standing over his kill.

In the fifth inning, Jackson came to bat again, with two outs and Willie Randolph on second. By this time, reliever Elias Sosa was on the mound for the Dodgers.

When Sosa had come to the mound in the fifth, Jackson immediately called upstairs to scout Gene Michael (later to become a Yankee manager). "He told me I'd see fastballs," said Jackson.

He saw only one. Swinging on the first pitch again, Jackson lined a drive hit even harder than the first one into the right field stands. Although the ball was hit so low that it appeared from the press box at first that it might fall in for a single, it was hit with such authority that right fielder Smith, who had the best look at it, hardly moved, realizing very quickly that it was gone.

That made the score 7–3 Yankees and effectively removed any doubt about who would win the game. Again, Reggie was called out of the dugout to acknowledge a standing ovation from a crowd which realized the first World Championship in 15 years was soon to come to the Bronx. Again, litter descended on the field as Jackson went out at the conclusion of the inning. It seemed a strange way to celebrate a joyous occasion, but that's New York.

Jackson wasn't through yet, and his next—and last—swing was even more magnificent than the first two. This time, the pitcher was knuckleballer Charlie Hough. It is difficult to hit knuckleballs great distances because they are relatively slow pitches, which means a batter must supply his own power. Jackson supplied plenty of it to the first pitch he saw from Hough, sending the ball 450 feet into the center field stands. As Reggie rounded first base, Garvey clapped into his mitt. "I don't think anybody saw that one," Garvey said later. "I had to applaud him. He just beat us single-handedly."

Reggie's performance defied belief. He had set Series records of five homers, 25 total bases, and ten runs scored. Babe Ruth had hit three home runs in a Series game twice, in 1926 and 1928, but his homers had not been on consecutive at-bats, and neither splurge had been decisive in the games.

Moreover, Reggie's fifth game home run had been in his last at-bat. Since he did not take a swing in getting his first inning walk, that meant that his last four swings in the Series had resulted in four home runs.

No precise statistics are kept on this, but it seems safe to say that nobody in major league history, let alone in the World Series, had ever hit four home runs on consecutive swings.

Even Martin was willing to put aside his dislike of Reggie in his awe of Jackson's performance. Although Reggie would normally have been replaced by Paul Blair for defensive purposes at that stage of the game, Martin left Jackson in.

Steve Garvey was an important figure on the Dodgers' World Series teams of the '70s—and a sportsman who clapped for an opponent. *(Los Angeles Dodgers)*

"I wanted him to get the ovation," said Martin.

Jackson got his ovation—and more litter. He finally came back into the dugout for a batting helmet to wear in the field, to protect himself against all the objects that were being thrown out there.

The Dodgers, down 8–3 in the ninth, didn't go down quietly. Garvey and Dusty Baker singled, Garvey going to third on Baker's hit, and pinch hitter Vic Davalillo beat out a bunt that scored Garvey for 8–4, though with two outs.

Since giving up Smith's homer in the fourth, Torrez had pitched magnificently, yielding only one hit over the next four innings. He was struggling a bit now, and he had thrown 118 pitches.

Martin went to the mound to talk to Mike. Sparky Lyle, who had had a great season (13 wins, 26 saves, 72 games) was ready in the bull pen. But Martin decided to let Torrez pitch to one more batter.

That was all it took. Lee Lacy tried to bunt, and the ball looped lazily out in front of the mound. Torrez moved off and caught it. The Yankees were World Champions.

Fans poured onto the field, and Jackson had to do some artful dodging to get safely to the dugout. "You gotta watch out for yourself in this town—no matter what the situation," he said.

"He's the MVP, you bet, and his most impressive move all night was the broken field

The incomparable Reggie Jackson hit home runs on four consecutive pitches in leading the Yankees to a triumph in the 1977 World Series. *(New York Yankees)*

run he made to get back to the dugout and escape those crazies," said Dodger pitcher Don Sutton. "He could help the New York Giants."

The Dodgers were as impressed as anybody else by Jackson. Lacy summed up the game: "Reggie Jackson . . . Reggie Jackson . . . Reggie Jackson."

"I think he was able to release all his emotional tension of the entire season in this one game," said Garvey. "It was just a tremendous performance."

As usual, Reggie had the last word. "For one night," he said, "I might have reached the level of that overrated word, 'superstar.'"

Indeed he had.

26. The Tide Turns Again

In 1983, the American League made a comeback.

The proud American Leaguers had been eclipsed by the National League for nearly three decades. The turning point had been the 1954 World Series, when the New York Giants had swept the Cleveland Indians, who had won an AL record 111 games.

The National League clubs had been ahead in signing black and Latin players, and most of the big names of the ensuing 29 years had been National Leaguers. The National League had dominated the All-Star Game and had won 17 of the 29 World Series, the most legitimate competition between the leagues.

But in 1983, the American League won the All-Star Game, and it climaxed a season of triumph when the Baltimore Orioles won decisively in the World Series.

Fittingly enough, the Orioles' competition in the Series was the Philadelphia Phillies. No team represented the immediate glorious past of the National League better than the Phillies, who had four players who would certainly make the baseball Hall of Fame eventually: pitcher Steve Carlton, second baseman Joe Morgan, first baseman Pete Rose, and third baseman Mike Schmidt.

But of the four, only Schmidt was in his prime. Carlton had won the 300th game of his career during the season—he would be the first 300-game winner in the World Series since Grover Cleveland Alexander in 1928—but he had relinquished his spot as the staff leader to John Denny.

Morgan, beset by injuries for most of the season, had hit only .200 until September; finally healthy, he had spurted to raise his batting average to .230 and was a prime factor in the Phils' stretch drive to a pennant. Rose, finishing the season only 201 hits away from the record he cherished, Ty Cobb's career mark of 4191 hits, had been benched for much of the late season.

The 1950 Phillies had been known as the "Whiz Kids" for their youth. In an obvious play on that nickname, these Phillies were known as the "Wheeze Kids." Four

Steve Carlton was the first 300-game winner to pitch in the World Series in 57 years, but he couldn't bring the Phillies home a winner. *(Philadelphia Phillies)*

Phillies—Rose, Morgan, Tony Perez, and Ron Reed—were over 40 (no other Series team had ever had more than two in that age category) and Carlton was only 14 months away from his 40th birthday.

The Phillies didn't act their age in the first game, though, and they raised some questions in the minds of those who had made the Orioles strong favorites to win the Series.

The Orioles got off quickly in front of their Baltimore fans when Jim Dwyer hit a tailing fastball by Denny for a solo homer in the first inning.

Dwyer was an excellent example of how Baltimore had become successful. He had been only a utility outfielder for five other clubs since first coming to the majors in 1973, but that was fine in Baltimore: The Orioles thrived by using "role players," guys who played only part-time but made the critical play when they were called on. Used only against right-handed pitchers, Dwyer had been an important factor in the Orioles' drive to the pennant.

But his homer would be overlooked as the Phillies bounced back in a game played in terrible weather for baseball. John Lowenstein of the Orioles called it "despicably difficult" to hit in a fine mist that fell from the second inning on. "Wouldn't it be nice," said Baltimore shortstop Cal Ripken, "if they played a World Series in sunny, 80-degree weather?"

After Dwyer's homer, the only Baltimore threat came when Al Bumbry hit a two-out double in the eighth inning, before being stranded. Otherwise, Denny held them in check.

"He's always been good," Ripken said of Denny. "When he's got that big, overhand curveball going, he's extremely tough. Even if you wait on that pitch, it's tough to hit."

In the early going, Scott McGregor was even tougher for the Orioles. The Phillies liked to hit fastballs, but McGregor is a pitcher who gets by more on his guile. He will show a batter a fastball just out of the strike zone, and then make him hit a breaking pitch.

But in the guessing game between hitter and pitcher, experience can often make the difference. Morgan had seen an awful lot of curve balls during his career. He popped up against McGregor in the first inning (the ball was dropped by Baltimore third baseman Todd Cruz) but he had hit a single to center in the fourth. He was beginning to time McGregor's curve, and he told Rose in the dugout before he came up in the sixth that, if McGregor threw him another curve, he would hit it out.

McGregor got the count to 1–2 on Morgan but, in the TV booth, former Orioles manager Earl Weaver, now doing color on the games for ABC, noted that Morgan was hanging tough against the left-handed McGregor and getting good swings.

On the next pitch, McGregor came in with another curve. True to his word, Morgan hit it out of the park. Not by much. He ran full out until he neared second and saw the ball disappear into the stands, and then he raised his arms in triumph. "The balls were dying out there in batting practice," he said later. "I would have enjoyed a nice home run trot, but I didn't think it was going out."

The score stayed at 1–1 until Garry Maddox led off the eighth. McGregor had been ready to start pitching to Maddox when an ABC representative waved him off; the network wanted more time because Howard Cosell was interviewing President Reagan.

Although McGregor didn't use that as an excuse, it may have affected his concentration. Maddox is notorious for looking for a fastball to hit on the first pitch, but McGregor threw him one, anyway. Maddox hit it out.

Maddox had never been known as a power hitter (his major league high was 14 homers in the 1977 season), and he was as surprised as anybody. "I visualize a lot of

Garry Maddox surprised even himself with a home run in the 1983 World Series opener. *(Philadelphia Phillies)*

things," he said. "Usually, a great catch in the outfield, something like that. A game-winning home run in the World Series? Never."

After Bumbry doubled with two outs in the eighth, Philadelphia manager Paul Owens brought in reliever Al Holland, an exuberant, extroverted pitcher who challenges hitters with a steady diet of fastballs.

Holland got pinch hitter Dan Ford on a fly ball to end the inning. In the ninth, the Orioles had the heart of their batting order coming up and, if any of them got on, Baltimore manager Joe Altobelli was ready to use Ken Singleton, the Orioles' designated hitter for most of the season, as a pinch hitter.

But Holland got Ripken on a pop fly, Eddie Murray on a strikeout, and Gary Roenicke, a right-handed pinch hitter, on a fly to left, and the Phillies had won the first game, 2–1.

Morgan again looked like a hero in the second game when he reached back into the past for the kind of performance that had made him such a great player. In the fourth inning of a scoreless tie, he hit a Mike Boddicker changeup to left field and then stole second on the first pitch to Rose.

Rose bunted but went the wrong way with it, to the third base side. Morgan held second as catcher Rick Dempsey pounced on the ball and, after looking at second, threw Rose out at first.

With Schmidt up, Morgan gambled again, going to third on a routine grounder to shortstop. Perhaps he distracted Murray. At any rate, Murray, a perennial Gold Glove winner at first, dropped the throw and Schmidt was safe. So, when Joe Lefebvre hit a fly ball, it was only the second out, and Morgan scored.

But this was to be the Orioles' night—and especially Boddicker's. The rookie was baffling the Phils with his variety of off-speed pitches, and his teammates were getting him the runs he needed to win.

In the fifth, Lowenstein hit a solo homer against the Phils' Charles Hudson, another rookie. Rich Dauer singled to left and, on a bunt by Todd Cruz, Morgan was slow to cover first and everybody was safe. Dempsey doubled down the right field line to score Dauer, and then Boddicker (who had only two professional at-bats because of the DH rule) hit a sacrifice fly to make it 3–1.

Although Ripken singled in a fourth run for the Orioles in the seventh, Boddicker didn't need it. He pitched a three-hitter, the best effort by a rookie pitcher since Dickie Kerr had thrown one in the 1919 Series, and left the Phillies wondering what had happened.

"I can't compare him to anybody in our league," said Morgan. "In fact, I haven't seen a pitcher like him since Stu Miller and that was a long time ago." (Miller's career had ended in 1968.)

"It's not so much that he throws a lot of curve balls," said Schmidt. "He throws 'em at different speeds, and never the same place twice in a row. The good curve ball pitchers in our league—Neil Allen, Nolan Ryan—throw it consistently hard."

But if the second game loss was a disappointment to the Phils, the third game was a crusher, because it demonstrated so graphically that their aging greats couldn't beat the Orioles' role players.

The game started in controversy because Phillie manager Owens, who had started the season as general manager and had taken over when manager Pat Corrales was fired, benched Rose in favor of Perez. As a youth movement, it fell somewhat short; Rose was 42 and Perez 41.

"We've got eight hits in two games," explained Owens before the game. "We need more offense, and Perez has hit (Orioles starter Mike) Flanagan well in the past (when Perez played for Boston). That's all there is to it."

For the singleminded Rose, it was the supreme insult. He stomped around the dugout and announced that the thing he'd remember about this Series, win or lose, was that he was benched.

It didn't seem to bother the rest of the team, at least, at first. Gary Matthews hit a home run off Flanagan in the second inning and Morgan, having a great Series in what would probably be his last shot, homered in the third to make it 2–0.

Meanwhile, Carlton was magnificent in the early going. He was beating the Orioles just as he had beaten so many National League teams, throwing the fast slider that had made him the all-time career strikeout leader.

"You're supposed to lay off that pitch," said Ripken. "Sure, that's easy to say. It comes up looking like a fastball, then it's gone, and you're totally helpless."

Ripken was speaking from experience; he had struck out on a futile check-swing in the first inning.

In the sixth, Dan Ford came to the plate for Baltimore. Just batting was an act of courage for Ford. Two nights earlier he had been hit on the helmet by a Willie Hernandez fastball and, though he got a tremendous headache out of it, stayed in the game and belted a base hit.

"If I'd come out of that game," said Ford, who had lain on the ground for several minutes after being hit, "it might have been a tough road back. But by staying in and getting a hit the next time up, I totally erased the fear from my mind."

Now Ford was simulating hitting against Ron Guidry, the Yankee left-hander the Orioles feel pitches much like Carlton. He was determined to hit Carlton's slider.

Hit it he did, driving it high and deep down the left field line for a home run that cut the Phils' lead to 2–1. "That changed everything," Ripken said. "We figured, 'Maybe this Carlton's human, after all.'"

In the seventh, with two outs, Dempsey came to bat. The previous time, Dempsey had hit a hanging curve for a double. This time, Carlton threw him a low fastball—and Dempsey smashed another double.

Carlton went to 3–0 on pinch hitter Bernie Ayala, including a wild pitch that sent Dempsey to third, but Ayala wasn't looking for a walk; he fouled off the 3–0 pitch. "I'll get one good fastball if I'm patient," he thought.

He got the fastball and drilled it to left to score Dempsey and tie the game at 2–2.

Holland came in for Carlton, but this time, the Orioles knew what to expect. John Shelby singled to left and Ford hit a sharp grounder to shortstop that kicked off Ivan DeJesus' glove for an error ("There was a wet patch of turf right in front of me, and the ball skidded," said DeJesus later), the ball going far enough away that Ayala scored with the go-ahead run.

The Phillies' aging stars were frustrated the rest of the way. Morgan drew a lead-off walk in the seventh but was caught trying to steal second. Rose was called on to pinch-hit in the ninth, but grounded out. The Orioles won, 3–2.

Interestingly enough, the winning pitcher for Baltimore was Jim Palmer, another sure Hall-of-Famer in years to come. Palmer had had a poor year, winning only five games and at one point going to the minors to work out his problems. He admitted he didn't bring his good stuff with him in this game, either, but he survived two shaky innings to pick up the win.

In the clubhouse after the game, Perez was asked how it felt replacing Rose, who had been his teammate on the great Cincinnati teams of the '70s.

Morgan blew up when he heard the questions. "How can you ask that petty stuff?"

Mike Schmidt was the MVP of the 1980 World Series for Philadelphia but a big bust three years later as the Phillies lost. *(Philadelphia Phillies)*

he yelled. "We're trying to win a World Series and he's trying to do a job, and you ask him that? Why don't you buy the ball club and make out your own goddamn lineup?"

But the next day, Morgan himself was critical of Rose, his long-time friend. (The two had had side-by-side lockers at Cincinnati.)

"I told Pete he should've handled it better," said Joe. "I think I would have. No way he should have embarrassed Tony like that. Tony Perez has 2500 hits in this league, too. It was ridiculous to put Tony in that situation [having to watch Rose's reaction] and I told Pete so. We ought to be thinking about winning instead of who's playing."

Perez was embarrassed. "I didn't want to play at Pete's expense," he said. "You'll never hear me ask to replace him."

Rose was back in the lineup for the fourth game and went 2–for–3 with an RBI, but the Phillies still lost.

It is often true in the World Series that stars will have slumps, and this one was no exception. The Orioles' big gun, Eddie Murray, hadn't hit safely since his first at-bat. For the Phillies, Mike Schmidt was even worse, having gone hitless.

The difference was that the Orioles could win without Murray but the Phillies couldn't win without Schmidt. Oh, it was certainly easier for the Orioles when they had Murray hitting three-run homers. But when he didn't, they won with those role players who never show up in an All-Star lineup but still win a lot of games for the Orioles. In the fourth game, they showed how.

After three scoreless innings, the Orioles struck for two runs in the fourth. They loaded the bases with nobody out on consecutive singles by Dwyer, Ripken, and, yes, Murray. After Lowenstein struck out, Rich Dauer hit a two-run single to right. "All year we've been trying to get him to go the other way, and today he finally did it," said an Oriole scout.

Rose started a Phillie rally in the bottom of the inning with a single and went to second when Schmidt broke his 0–for–13 streak with a blooper that shattered his bat; he still wasn't swinging well.

Joe Lefebvre doubled down the line in right to score Rose and Matthews walked. But the rally ended when Greg Gross grounded into a double play.

The Phillies took a 3–2 lead—it would be their last of the Series—on a double by Bo Diaz, a wild pitch, a single by Denny, and a double by Rose.

But, noted Philadelphia owner Bill Giles, "It seems that every time Denny runs the bases, he doesn't pitch well the next few innings."

Giles' fears were realized in the next inning, as Lowenstein singled and Dauer doubled, Lowenstein holding third.

At this point, Baltimore manager Joe Altobelli sent up four consecutive pinch hitters, a Series record. It startled some observers, who thought Altobelli would have forgotten classic baseball strategy because the American League used the DH. But others who had seen him as manager of the San Francisco Giants in the late '70s remembered that Altobelli loved to juggle players, seldom using the same lineup two days in a row and making hunch changes. In San Francisco, he didn't have the talent to make that system work; in Baltimore, he did.

The pinch hitters: Joe Nolan was walked intentionally to load the bases; Singleton walked to force in a run; John Shelby, facing reliever Hernandez, hit a sacrifice fly that forced Matthews to make a spectacular leaping catch, the go-ahead run scoring; and Ford struck out.

Sammy Stewart held the Phillies in relief for 2⅓ innings, the O's stretching their lead to 5–3 with a seventh inning double by Dwyer and single by Dauer, and ace reliever Tippy Martinez came on in the ninth.

The Phillies gave their fans some hope by scoring once on a single by Diaz, a ground out by DeJesus, and another single by Ozzie Virgil. "I was only trying to create a little excitement, sell some hot dogs," quipped Martinez after the game. But with two outs and the tying run on, Martinez threw a great curve to Morgan and Joe popped weakly to second for the out.

Was the Series over? The Orioles weren't ready to say so. They had had a 3–1 lead in the 1979 World Series and lost it to Pittsburgh, and that memory sobered them. "The last time we were in this position," said Stewart, "we were counting our Series shares and seeing those rings on our fingers. Not this time, though."

And for the fifth game, the real Eddie Murray, not that imposter who had been swinging harmlessly for the rest of the Series, would stand up.

Murray is a man who sets his own pace and he didn't even take batting practice before the game. "When you're 2-for-16," he said, "you get to thinking about bad habits. Sometimes, your head needs a rest."

Murray came to bat for the first time in the second inning, in a setting that was difficult for hitters. To avoid head-to-head competition with the bulk of the NFL schedule that Sunday, ABC had decreed that the game would start at 5:00 P.M., and the twilight was a nightmare for the hitters. Philadelphia starter Charles Hudson thought he could throw a fastball past Murray.

Nope, Murray smacked it 400 feet into the right field seats, and the Orioles were on their way.

It went to 2–0 in the third when Dempsey hit a shot down the left field line. The Orioles' dugout erupted in joy at this unexpected turn of events.

Dempsey was a good defensive catcher but no great hitting threat, with a .242 lifetime average. But he was no more improbable than some earlier World Series heroes—remember George Ruhe? Two innings later he would hit his fourth double of the Series and, with his .385 average on 5-for-13, he was a natural choice for the Series Most Valuable Player.

The Philadelphia fans, quick to boo even their own (Schmidt got a terrible roasting during the Series), had shouted, "Eddie, Eddie, Eddie," derisively at Murray during

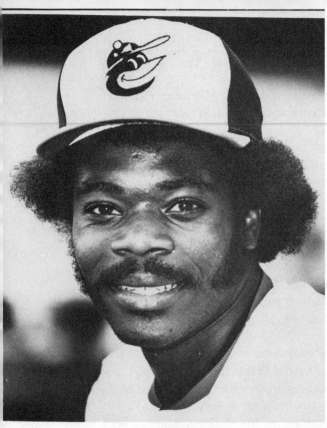

Eddie Murray blasted two home runs in the fifth game as Baltimore won the 1983 World Series. *(Baltimore Orioles)*

games three and four because of his ineffectiveness. Some of them had been silenced his first time up; his second time would take care of the rest.

With Ripken on base after a lead-off walk, Hudson tried to throw a curve to Murray, and the ball hung there, shoulder high. Murray hit an enormous drive to right center that bounced off the scoreboard.

"Did you notice how quiet the place got?" Lowenstein said later. "Eddie just took the air right out of the stadium. We knew it would be terribly difficult for the Phillies to win. The sleeping giant had awakened, and Mr. McGregor was throwing a shutout."

The Phillies were dying. Rose got a couple of hits, but Schmidt had another hitless game. (The scouting report on Schmidt was that he would chase high fastballs, and the Oriole pitchers did that to him for the whole Series.)

Morgan hadn't conceded. In the eighth inning, the Phillies trailing, 5–0, he lashed a drive down the right field line and hustled all the way to third, belly-flopping into the base.

But when Rose followed with a fly ball that should have scored Morgan, Joe hit some soft dirt just as he started out and fell flat. He had to scramble back to the base to avoid being doubled off, and that was the last Philadelphia scoring threat. In its way, it epitomized the frustration of the Series for the Wheeze Kids.

Despite Murray's final game heroics, he and Ripken, the two most dangerous hitters in the Baltimore lineup, had batted only a collective .210. But the lesser-known players had picked up the slack, just as they had so many times in the season. That is the key to the Baltimore success.

That and, of course, their pitching. The Orioles' collective 1.60 earned run average was the best since 1966, when another Baltimore staff had allowed just one earned run in four games in sweeping the Dodgers. In a five-game Series, you had to go back to the New York Yankees of 1943 to find a better ERA.

Although the Orioles had been consistent contenders and occasional league champions, this was their first World Series win since 1970. "Finally," said Flanagan, "we've got a highlight film with a happy ending."

The Orioles had won without one of their big weapons, the designated hitter, because this was a year in which National League rules applied in the World Series.

They had won four straight after the opening game loss. They had beaten the Phillies all three games in Philadelphia. Although the games, except for the finale, had been close, it was a decisive win for the Orioles, who were clearly the better team.

The American League was back.

27. The All-Time Team

The World Series is not the regular season, a point that needs emphasizing when an all-time World Series team is picked.

Some of the greatest players in the game's history did not do well in the World Series: Ty Cobb played in three and did not excel in any, Honus Wagner was little more than average in the two in which he played, Ted Williams bombed in his only Series appearance.

Some stars, like Joe DiMaggio and Stan Musial, played reasonably well but were overshadowed by less illustrious teammates. For some, the timing was wrong. Walter Johnson didn't get into a Series until the end of his career, and Bob Feller was past his prime by the time he got there.

And some great players—George Sisler, Nap Lajoie, Ernie Banks, Harry Heilmann, and Rube Waddell—never played in a Series. The first four played on teams that didn't make it; Waddell's one chance was eliminated when he hurt his shoulder before the 1905 Series and could not pitch in it.

So, though some of the game's biggest stars were also stars in the Series—Babe Ruth being the best example—there were also players whose October performances far outshone what they did during the regular season, Pepper Martin being perhaps the most obvious example.

Some players, like Hank Gowdy and Gene Tenace, had one spectacular Series and then subsided into ordinary performances. In general, I feel that sustained excellence is more important; one outstanding Series by itself is not enough to make the team.

That brings up the special problem engendered by the New York Yankees' long domination. Because Yankee teams were so often in the Series, their players have the most impressive cumulative records—most games, most at-bats, etc.

I don't feel it's fair to penalize non-Yankee players who had no chance to match these achievements simply because their teams did not play so frequently in the Series.

So, I have not let cumulative marks weigh heavily in my selections—unless they represented a consistent standard of excellence, as with Ruth and Lou Gehrig, for instance.

So, here's my team. Let the arguments begin.

CATCHER

For one Series, no catcher ever surpassed Gowdy's .545 mark in 1914—but he was only .226 in two other Series. Tenace hit four homers in 1972, but he was only .255 in three Series and actually caught only in the first one, being moved to his more natural position at first base after that.

Yogi Berra has the longevity records: most Series (14), most games (75), most at-bats (259), as well as most hits (71) and most doubles (10). He is second with 41 runs scored and 39 RBIs, third with 12 homers.

But, as I mentioned a few paragraphs earlier, Berra benefited because his team played so frequently in the Series. In four World Series, Johnny Bench batted slightly higher (.279 to .274) and had a higher slugging percentage (.523 to .452). Batting only a third as many times as Berra, he had five homers, four doubles, and 14 RBIs; prorated to as many at-bats as Berra, he would have had 15 homers, 12 doubles, 42 RBIs—all higher figures than Yogi's.

Berra started his career as a catcher who threw curves to second base and a part-time outfielder. He improved rapidly and became a solid defensive catcher. But nobody was ever as good a defensive catcher as Johnny Bench in his prime.

Bench is my World Series catcher.

FIRST BASE

There is no shortage of candidates. Jimmie Foxx hit .350, .333, and .348 in consecutive Series for the 1929–31 Philadelphia Athletics. Frank Chance hit .421 and stole five bases for the Chicago Cubs in 1908, and managed the team, too. Bill Terry hit .429 for the New York Giants in 1924.

But no first baseman ever dominated the way Gehrig did. In seven Series, he hit .361 with ten homers. Twice he hit over .500, with .545 in 1928 and .529 in 1932.

It was Gehrig's fate to be continually overshadowed by the flamboyant Ruth, and the World Series was no exception to that. When Gehrig hit .545 in 1928, Ruth hit .625. In 1932, Gehrig's bat was the key in all four Yankee wins, and he drove in nine runs and scored eight in those four games. But what do we remember about the 1932 Series: Babe Ruth "calling his shot" on a home run off Charlie Root.

SECOND BASE

Eddie Collins fielded brilliantly, hit .328, and stole a record 14 bases in six World Series. Charlie Gehringer hit .321 in three Series and nothing got by him in the field. Frankie Frisch hit .294 in eight Series and even managed the St. Louis Cardinals to a '34 Series win.

But Billy Martin was a great clutch performer for the Yankees in the '50s, with great statistics. Overall, he hit .333 for five Series. In 1952, he saved the Yankees with a great catch of Jackie Robinson's pop fly. In 1953, he hit .500.

It's close, but Martin is my choice.

SHORTSTOP

This is a difficult choice to make because shortstops traditionally are good-field, no-hit; it is one of two positions (catcher being the other) where managers will sacrifice offensive potential for defensive play.

Two shortstops, though, both hit well and fielded their positions well. Alvin Dark hit an overall .323 in three Series, including marks of .417 and .412 in 1951 and 1954. Dark was always a leader for the Giants, too.

But overall, the most impressive shortstop was probably Brooklyn's Pee Wee Reese, one of the most underrated players in the game throughout his career. Reese's overall average of .272 didn't match Dark's but he was a consistent threat for the Dodgers, not just with his hitting but with his alert base running. In the field, he participated in 25 double plays.

THIRD BASE

Stan Hack was an excellent lead-off man in three Series for the Chicago Cubs, batting .348 overall. No third baseman had a better offensive Series than Heinie Groh, who hit .474 for the New York Giants in 1922. In 1970, Brooks Robinson had a tremendous Series for the Baltimore Orioles, hitting .429 with two homers and making unbelievable plays in the field.

But overall, the best performance was that of Frank (Home Run) Baker, who hit .363 in six Series. Baker hit .429, .375, and .450 in consecutive Series in 1910, 1911, and 1913, and it was in 1911 that he earned his nickname by hitting home runs on consecutive days off the great Giant pitchers, Rube Marquard and Christy Mathewson.

LEFT FIELD

This is perhaps the toughest choice of all, between Lou Brock and Reggie Jackson.

Brock had back-to-back great Series in 1967 and 1968. The first year, he hit .414, got 12 hits, and stole seven bases. The next year, he was even better, hitting .464 with a record-tying 13 hits and stealing another seven bases, tying his own Series record of the year before.

But, as sensational as he was, Brock was not the dominant figure in either Series; that honor belonged to Bob Gibson in '67 and Mickey Lolich in '68.

Jackson, in contrast, was the Most Valuable Player twice, in 1974 with the Oakland A's and in 1977 with the New York Yankees. He hit .357 in five Series, has the all-time top slugging average in World Series play with .755 and is second only to Ruth in frequency of home runs. And his three home runs on consecutive swings in the final game of the '77 Series is probably the most impressive hitting performance in a single Series game.

CENTER FIELD

When the Yankees, Giants, and Dodgers all played in the metropolitan New York area, a debate raged constantly over the merits of center fielders Mickey Mantle, Willie Mays, and Duke Snider.

Mays, though he made one great catch in 1954, was not a standout performer in the Series, hitting just .239 in four Series. Mantle and Snider, though, were both outstanding.

Mantle holds Series records of 18 homers, 42 runs scored, and 40 RBIs, though he batted just .257. Snider hit .286 and, playing in only slightly more than half as many games as Mantle, had 11 home runs and 26 RBIs; in 1955, he hit four homers as the Dodgers won their first Series.

Prorated, Snider's statistics would be better than Mantle's, and he deserves the nod in a very close call.

RIGHT FIELD

No competition, though there have been several good players here. Roberto Clemente had a great Series in 1971, batting .414 with 12 hits and playing a tremendous defensive right field. Hank Bauer hit safely in 17 consecutive Series games, a record. Hank Aaron hit .364 in two Series, with three homers.

But Ruth stands alone. In ten Series, including three as a pitcher, Ruth hit .325, with 15 homers and 32 RBIs. He set a record with his .625 average in 1928, and he is the only player to twice hit three home runs in a game.

Ruth was a better outfielder than people remembered and a good base runner, despite his puzzling attempt at stealing second that ended the 1926 Series. He was also a great pitcher early in his career, and held the Series record for consecutive scoreless innings for more than four decades.

UTILITY

Pepper Martin defies categorization because he played center field in the 1931 Series and third base in 1934. But he has to be included on this team, and this is a natural spot. In 1931, Martin beat the Philadelphia A's almost singlehandedly, and his career (three Series) batting average of .418 is the highest ever.

RIGHT-HANDED PITCHER

Although there have been many outstanding ones, this boiled down to a two-man race between Christy Mathewson, the great Giant pitcher of the early 20th century, and fireballing Bob Gibson of the St. Louis Cardinals of the '60s.

Mathewson pitched three shutouts in the 1905 Series, a mark that will probably never be equalled. Although he was only 5–5 overall, that record is the result of simple bad luck. His talent is demonstrated by the awesome statistics he achieved: only 76 hits in 101⅔ innings in four Series, just ten walks and an earned run average of 1.15.

But Mathewson was pitching in the dead ball era. Gibson was pitching when the ball was very lively indeed, and his feats are even more impressive than Mathewson's. He lost his first Series decision and his last one, but in between won seven straight. He set a Series game record with 17 strikeouts in 1968 and struck out 92 in 81 Series innings. He gave up only 55 hits and had an ERA of 1.88.

Gibson has to be the choice.

LEFT-HANDED PITCHER

There have been some good ones. Johnny Podres won four of five decisions, including the game that won the first Series for the Dodgers in 1955. Ken Holtzman was also 4–1 for the Oakland A's, and Mickey Lolich won all three games he started in the '68 Series.

Lefty Gomez was a perfect 6–0 for the New York Yankees, Herb Pennock 5–0 for the same team. Ed Lopat was 4–1.

Sandy Koufax was just 4–3 for the Dodgers, who seldom got him any runs, but two of those wins were shutouts. He had 61 strikeouts in 57 innings (and, for a short time, the Series record with a 15-strikeout game in 1963) and an incredible 0.95 earned run average.

Whitey Ford had the most impressive record of all, 33⅔ consecutive scoreless innings. He holds the records for most Series (11), most starts (22), most openers (8), most innings (146), most strikeouts (94) and most wins (10).

But, except for the first record, all of Ford's marks are based on the fact that his team was in the Series so frequently. Overall, he was 10–8 with a 2.71 ERA, good but not great, and he completed only seven games in 22 starts.

Ford was usually pitching for a much stronger team than Koufax; in the '60s, the Dodgers won on pitching by Koufax and Don Drysdale and base running by Maury Wills.

Although Ford usually gets selected because of his Series records, Koufax was the better pitcher—in the World Series as well as in the regular season.

RELIEF PITCHER

Until the '40s, the relief pitcher was seldom a big factor in the Series, though Wilcy Moore pitched well for the Yankees in the 1927 and 1928 Series.

Since then, the relief pitcher has become a big factor. In recent Series, Kent Tekulve and Rich Gossage have been very impressive, and Bruce Sutter dominated the 1982 Series for the St. Louis Cardinals. Johnny Murphy pitched well in six Series for the Yankees in the '30s and '40s, and Joe Page was an important factor in the 1947 and 1949 Series for the Yankees.

But no reliever has quite equalled Rollie Fingers who, in three Series, won two games and saved a Series record six, with an ERA of 1.15.

MANAGER

The dominant manager of the early part of the 20th century, John McGraw, was only 3–5 in World Series play. The best in recent years, Earl Weaver, was just 1–3.

Connie Mack was 5–3 (his first pennant with the Philadelphia A's was in 1902, before Series play started).

As always, though, the choice has to come down to a Yankee manager. Joe

McCarthy, after losing one World Series as manager of the Chicago Cubs, was nearly perfect with the Yankees, winning seven of eight, 1936–43.

But Casey Stengel has to be the choice. Stengel won seven of ten, and in the three he lost, the Series was stretched to seven games. He won five straight, 1949–53, which no manager has ever done. And he did it with Yankee teams which were good but never the equal of the overwhelming teams McCarthy managed in his time.

The team:

> C—Johnny Bench, Cincinnati Reds.
> 1B—Lou Gehrig, New York Yankees.
> 2B—Billy Martin, New York Yankees.
> 3B—Frank "Home Run" Baker, Philadelphia A's and New York Yankees.
> SS—Pee Wee Reese, Brooklyn Dodgers.
> LF—Reggie Jackson, Oakland A's and New York Yankees.
> CF—Duke Snider, Brooklyn Dodgers.
> RF—Babe Ruth, New York Yankees.
> RHP—Bob Gibson, St. Louis Cardinals.
> LHP—Sandy Koufax, Los Angeles Dodgers.
> RP—Rollie Fingers, Oakland A's.
> UTILITY—Pepper Martin, St. Louis Cardinals.

28. The Best of the Best

(Who was the best of the best? My nomination for the best American League team of all time is the 1937 New York Yankees, better even than the more celebrated 1927 team. The best National League team was the 1976 Cincinnati Reds, though the Brooklyn Dodger teams of the 1950s were close. Had the Yankees and Reds met in a World Series, this is the way I think it would have gone.)

Vernon (Lefty) Gomez picked up the rosin bag behind the mound, less to dry his fingers than to give himself a chance to take a deep breath. He looked at the Cincinnati runners, Ken Griffey at second and Pete Rose at first, and past them, to his outfielders. "I'm not sure they're deep enough," Gomez thought wryly to himself.

Lefty had won the first game in the Series, a classic against the Reds' Don Gullett. Both left-handers had given up just four hits, but two of the hits off Gullett had been home runs. Bill Dickey had hit one in the second inning and then Joe DiMaggio had broken a 1–1 tie in the bottom of the ninth with a soaring drive into the left field stands.

In the second game the Yankees looked ready to take a 2–0 Series lead when they knocked Gary Nolan out of the box with a three-run second.

But the Reds' secret weapon was their bull pen, and manager Sparky Anderson used it all in this game, starting with left-hander Fred Norman. In the regular season, Norman had been primarily a starter, winning 12 games, but Anderson didn't figure on using Norman until late in the Series as a starter, and in the World Series, you hold nothing back.

Norman shut down the Yankees in the second and also the third, before giving way to Pedro Borbon. The Yankees got a run off Borbon in the fifth when George Selkirk tripled and Lou Gehrig brought him home with a sacrifice fly, but then, Will McEnaney put the Bronx Bombers down 1–2–3 for the next three innings.

Meanwhile, the Reds shocked the New Yorkers with a six-run explosion in the fifth that knocked out starter Red Ruffing.

Griffey led off with a double and Rose singled him home for the first run. Ruffing pitched too carefully to Morgan, the National League's Most Valuable Player for the second straight year, and walked him—and Johnny Bench homered on Ruffing's first pitch, a fastball over the plate.

Yankee manager Joe McCarthy left Ruffing in—the Yankee bull pen wasn't nearly so deep as the Reds—and Ruffing got Tony Perez to pop out for the first out of the inning.

But then George Foster, who had led the Reds with 29 homers during the season, got another Ruffing fastball that was out over the plate and drilled it down the left field line to tie the game at 5–5.

McCarthy had seen enough. He brought in Johnny Murphy, but the Reds weren't through. Cesar Geronimo, a .307 hitter who was only No. 7 in the powerful Cincinnati lineup, singled and stole second, and shortstop Dave Concepcion hit a high bouncer up the middle. Tony Lazzeri went behind second base to grab it, but he had no play on Concepcion and the fleet Geronimo came around third to score ahead of Lazzeri's frantic throw.

Finally, Murphy got pinch hitter Dan Driessen to ground out and Griffey, batting for the second time in the inning, to pop up.

Trailing by a run going into the ninth, the Yankees threatened when Selkirk singled with one out. The heart of the order—DiMaggio, Gehrig, and Dickey—followed, but Rawly Eastwick came in to get DiMaggio to fly out to deep center and Gehrig to pop out to end the game.

Nothing could stop the Yankee bats the next game, though, as they broke out against rookie Cincinnati starter Pat Zachry for a 10–3 win, Monte Pearson getting the win.

Gehrig got two home runs, good for five RBIs, in the blowout, and every Yankee starter except Myril Hoag got at least one hit. DiMaggio got three, including two triples.

That Yankee win led manager McCarthy to make a move that would be debated endlessly: Instead of coming back with Gomez, a 21-game winner during the regular season, he started rookie right-hander Spud Chandler.

McCarthy knew he was gambling, but he had been impressed with Chandler during the season. Although the rookie had won just seven games, he had had a 2.84 ERA, a good mark in the hitting-happy American League. He looked like a coming star.

If Chandler couldn't do it, the Yanks would still need only a win apiece from Gomez and Ruffing, and this move gave each of McCarthy's star pitchers an extra day of rest.

The move looked especially good for the Yankees when Gullett, after retiring the first nine batters to face him, fouled a ball off his instep while hitting in the third inning and had to come out of the game.

It was all too typical an occurrence for Gullett, whose frequent injuries had kept him from becoming the great pitcher everybody expected him to be.

But once again, the very deep Cincinnati bull pen came to the rescue, as Jack Billingham (another erstwhile starter used in long relief), McEnaney, and Borbon held the Yankees to single runs in the sixth and eighth innings.

Meanwhile, the Reds got two in the fourth when Morgan hit a two-run homer off Chandler, and another two in the eighth, off Murphy, when Driessen got a pinch-hit single, Griffey walked, and Rose doubled. Borbon got the win.

The well-rested Gomez came back with another masterpiece in the fifth game, as the Yankees once again took the lead in the Series with a 3–1 triumph.

All the New Yorkers' runs came in the fourth inning off Norman. DiMaggio, who had led the American League with 46 home runs in his second season, led off with a ball hit so deep into the left-center bleachers that left fielder Foster took only two steps in pursuit before watching it sail on by.

Gehrig and Dickey singled on successive pitches from Norman, while Anderson waved frantically to the Cincinnati bull pen. But before "Captain Hook" could run another pitcher in, Tony Lazzeri scored both Gehrig and Dickey with a double, once again showing why he had been nicknamed "Poosh 'em Up, Tony."

Going into the ninth, Gomez had allowed only two hits, a bunt single by Rose, his ninth hit of the Series, and a single in the sixth that was stretched into a double by Griffey. The Reds had had only three other base runners, two on walks and the third on an error by the usually reliable shortstop, Frankie Crosetti, and had never had more than one base runner in an inning.

Gomez weakened in the ninth, though, walking Morgan and then, after getting Bench to pop out, yielding a run-scoring double by Perez. Having lost the shutout, McCarthy didn't want to lose the game as well, so he brought in Murphy, who this time, struck out Foster and Geronimo to quickly end the game.

With a 3–2 lead, Ruffing ready to go in the sixth game, and the Series back in Yankee Stadium, where World Series seem to belong, the Yankees were in great shape to wrap it up.

But in every Series, there seems to be at least one star player who loses his effectiveness. In this one, it seemed to be Ruffing. A 20-game winner during the regular season, Ruffing had been no mystery to the Reds in the second game and he was even less of a mystery this time around. The Reds knocked him out with four runs in the first inning and feasted on a succession of Yankee pitchers for 14 hits. Oddly, none of the hits went out of the park, though Morgan had three straight doubles.

Given this cushion, Nolan breezed to an 8–2 win and that rarity: a complete game for a Cincinnati pitcher.

Writers descended on McCarthy in the Yankee dressing room after the game. "Who's pitching tomorrow?" asked the first reporter.

"Gomez, of course," said McCarthy.

"But he's had only two days of rest," said a writer, well aware that Gomez normally had at least three days between starts.

"He'll have all winter to rest up," said McCarthy, but privately, he was very worried. He doubted that Gomez could go very far the next day.

Ruffing came up to him after the writers had left. "I'll be in the bull pen tomorrow, Skip," he said. "Hell, I hardly broke a sweat today."

McCarthy smiled. He knew what a competitor Ruffing was, and he knew that the two pastings Ruffing had taken from the Reds would only make him more determined, not discourage him.

Meanwhile, Gomez was parrying questions from reporters. "Don't ask me how my arm feels, ask DiMaggio how his legs feel. Don't tell the Reds but I'm going to throw everything down the middle. Let them find out how deep center field is in this park. DiMag will run down anything that stays in the park."

Sitting on a stool nearby, DiMaggio showed no emotion, his face the dignified mask it always was. No reporter asked him about his legs.

The Reds were confident, even cocky, in their dressing room. Morgan had gotten only one hit off Gomez in the Yankee left-hander's two Series starts, but he assured reporters, "No pitcher gets Joe Morgan out forever. I saw some things."

Rose was bouncing around the room. "The Yankees don't scare me," he said. "Sure, they're good, but I don't know that they're any better than the Dodgers. DiMag? Great player—but I saw Willie Mays in his prime. I'd take Willie. Dickey's a great catcher, but he's not as good as Johnny here. Gomez? Hey, I batted against Koufax and Gibson!"

Manager Anderson wasn't so boastful, but he was confident, too. He had Gullett, completely recovered from his sore ankle, ready to go and well-rested; equally important, his bull pen hadn't thrown a ball in competition for two days, with the travel day between the fifth and sixth games and Nolan's complete game.

"I've got Gullett," he reminded reporters, "and Norman, Billingham, Borbon, McEnaney, and Eastwick. It don't make no difference to me if I use them all. There's no tomorrow after tomorrow."

As he warmed up, Gomez was as worried as his manager had been the day before. He could tell there was no zip in his arm; his fastball wasn't moving.

Griffey, the Reds' lead-off hitter, laid down a bunt down the first base line and beat it out. He took a long lead off first base, daring Gomez to throw over. Just coming into his own as a base stealer, Griffey had stolen 36 times that year, second only to Morgan's 60 on the Reds.

Gomez threw once, twice, three times over to first base. Griffey got back safely each time. Dickey called a pitch-out—but Griffey wasn't going. On the second pitch to Rose, Griffey took off, and Rose hit the ball through the right side of the infield, where

Lazzeri would have been if he hadn't broken to cover second on what looked like a steal. Griffey fled to third. The Reds had two men on, nobody out, and the batter was Joe Morgan.

Morgan was an offensive machine of almost unprecedented versatility. He had hit for average—.320—and power, with 27 homers and 30 doubles among his 151 hits. He had scored 113 runs, knocked in 111, and gotten 114 walks. He had stolen 60 bases and had been thrown out only ten times. And, as National League pitchers could have warned Gomez, he hit left-handers as well as he hit right-handers.

On his own, Ruffing got up in the Yankee bull pen and started throwing.

Gomez shook off a sign from his catcher, Dickey. Once, when Jimmie Foxx was batting, Gomez had shaken off sign after sign until the frustrated Dickey ran out to the mound. "What do you want to throw to this guy?" asked Dickey. "To tell you the truth, Bill, I don't want to throw him anything at all," said Gomez.

This time, though, he didn't feel like joking. He nodded his acceptance of the second signal, for a fastball on the outside corner, and he went into the stretch, looking over his shoulder at Griffey, then threw to the plate. Morgan cocked his bat, but let it slip by, just outside for a ball.

Contrary to what he had told reporters, Morgan hadn't noticed anything about Gomez's pitching: He had noticed something about himself. He hadn't been patient enough. Morgan had a very sharp eye, as evidenced by his many walks, but he had been biting on pitches outside the strike zone his first two games against Gomez. This time, he was determined to get his pitch.

The sellout crowd at Yankee Stadium was quiet, mesmerized by the classic duel between pitcher and hitter. Gomez tried a curve. Again, Morgan let it go by for a ball, and Gomez was now in a 2–0 hole.

The next pitch was a fastball on the inside corner of the plate, a pitch that usually handcuffed left-handed hitters. But Morgan was ready. He whipped his bat through the air and lined a vicious drive down the right field line, past Gehrig almost before Lou could react to it, and into the right field corner.

Griffey scored easily. Rose rounded third, waved on in because Selkirk was having trouble coming up with the ball in right field. As he did, Morgan came around second without slowing down. The throw came in to Lazzeri, who turned instantly and whipped it to third, but Morgan hit the dirt, belly-first, and just beat the throw.

It wouldn't get any easier for Gomez; the next hitter was Johnny Bench. Injuries had caused Bench to have a rare off-year, with only 16 homers and a .234 batting average, but he was healthy for the Series and very dangerous.

Gomez threw him a fastball, down and out, away from Bench's power. But Bench drove the ball through the night, deep to left-center. DiMaggio, already pulled toward left, was off with the crack of the bat, never looking back, just running, running,

running as the ball soared toward the fence. At the last moment, DiMag looked where he knew the ball would be, reached up, and caught it. But Morgan scored easily after the catch. The Reds were up, 3–0.

Gomez fiddled with the mound a little, then called Dickey out for a conference. "I'm just stalling, just giving Red more time to warm up," he told the startled catcher. "I can't stay in here."

Moments later, when the plate umpire came out to break up the conference, Gomez walked to the dugout and told McCarthy to take him out. "I don't have a thing, Joe," he said. "Take me out while we've still got a chance."

Ruffing was ready. He had started throwing hard when he saw Morgan's hit, and he was determined to prove something. He threw a fastball inside that spun Perez into the dirt, and then struck out Tony on three straight fastballs. Foster, too, went down, as he popped a fastball on the fists to Gehrig in foul territory.

For five more innings, it was more of the same as Ruffing, once again the pitcher who had won so many money games for the Yankees, set the Reds down easily. Rose walked in the third, Geronimo singled in the fourth. That was it.

But it didn't seem Ruffing's great pitching would be enough because Gullett was matching him pitch-for-pitch. The Yankees had gotten two hits off the Cincinnati left-hander, but both had been wasted. Hoag had gotten the first hit, leading off the third, but Crosetti, Ruffing, and Red Rolfe hadn't gotten the ball out of the infield. The next inning, Gehrig had singled with two outs but had been forced by Dickey.

Now, in the bottom of the sixth, Ruffing was the lead-off hitter for the Yankees. Red had started his career as an outfielder and, after being switched to the pitcher's mound, had been a dangerous hitter for a pitcher. He took a ball and a strike and then went to right field with a Gullett curve for the Yankees' third hit.

The Yankees seldom played for one run, but McCarthy did this time, reasoning that it was very important that his team get that first score. Rolfe sacrificed Ruffing to second, and then Selkirk laced a drive into right-center. Geronimo made a good play to cut it off and hold Selkirk to a single, but Ruffing scored the first Yankee run.

Now it was "window breaking" time for the Yankees. The term had been invented because of the homer-hitting 1927 team, but this one actually had more power, with 174 homers to 158 for the '27 Yankees. And the ones who had done most of the damage were coming up—DiMaggio (46), Gehrig (37), and Dickey (29).

Gullett, suddenly wild, walked DiMaggio. Anderson wasted no time; he brought in McEnaney to pitch to the left-handers coming up. But these were no ordinary left-handers. Gehrig took a strike and then doubled into right-center, with two runs scoring. The shaken McEnaney threw three straight balls to Dickey. McCarthy flashed the Yankee catcher the green light. This was the time to go for it. Dickey caught a waist-high fastball and rode it down the line, into the right field stands.

Just like that, the Yankees had a 5–3 lead, and Yankee Stadium erupted. This was the kind of big inning that had long been the Yankees' style, and they loved it in New York.

It didn't look good for the Reds, even when Geronimo led off the seventh with a single. Knowing he could pinch-hit for McEnaney, who had finally gotten out of the sixth by making Lazzeri pop out and Hoag strike out, Anderson called on Concepcion to bunt.

Concepcion bunted in front of the plate and Dickey pounced on it, throwing to second because he thought he could get Geronimo. But the Yankee catcher had underestimated Geronimo's speed; the throw was late and both runners were safe.

This time, Anderson used his famous pinch-bunter, Ed Armbrister, who advanced the runners with a perfect sacrifice.

Two runs up, the Yankees played back, conceding one run to avoid giving up two. Griffey grounded to the right side, and the Reds scored their run, but Ruffing then got Rose to fly out to end the inning. The Yankees were still up by one.

That one left in the eighth. Morgan led off with a single and took a long lead at first. Ruffing threw to first base, but Morgan was back. He threw again to first. Morgan got back again. The third time, he threw to the plate—but the umpire stepped out, calling a balk. Morgan advanced to second.

On the next pitch, Morgan took off for third, getting so big a jump on the flustered Ruffing that Dickey didn't even attempt a throw. Bench flied deep to center, and Morgan scored the tying run.

And then, the pitchers took over. The zeros kept going up on the scoreboard, through 12 innings. Ruffing had finally given way in the tenth to Murphy. Anderson, pulling every string, had used Borbon, Norman, and Billingham after McEnaney.

Rose led off the top of the 13th for the Reds. Running the count to 3–2, he fouled off three pitches from Murphy before finally coaxing a walk, running to first, as was his style.

The Yankees expected a bunt from Morgan, even though he was an extremely dangerous hitter. Joe shortened as if to bunt, made note of the defense as he took the first pitch for a ball.

On the next pitch, he took a half-swing and hit a soft liner down the third base line. Had Rolfe been in normal position, it would have been an easy out. Charging as he was, he had no chance for it. The ball landed just past the third base bag and rolled and rolled and rolled. Shortstop Crosetti finally ran it down in foul territory, but by that time, Rose had gone to third and Morgan to second with the shortest double of his career.

McCarthy ordered Bench walked intentionally to load the bases and set up a force at every base. The strategy worked as Perez hit a one-bouncer to Rolfe, who fired home to get Rose. Dickey's throw to first just got Perez for a double play.

It was all up to Foster now, and a fly ball wouldn't be enough to score the run.

Murphy went into his stretch and checked Morgan at third. Joe bluffed to go home but stayed as Murphy threw a strike to Foster. Again Morgan bluffed but stayed, and Murphy threw ball one.

On the third pitch, Morgan kept coming. "Ohmigawd, he's going to steal home," thought Murphy, and he hurried his motion to get the pitch there before Morgan. At that moment, Morgan stopped; he had only been bluffing, after all. But Murphy's hurried pitch went wide. Dickey made a desperate attempt to stop it, but it bounced off his glove, several feet away from the plate. Morgan, unexcelled at shifting into high gear quickly, raced to the plate. Dickey got to the ball but had no play; he could not beat Morgan to the plate and Murphy had not covered in time to take a throw. Morgan scored, and the Reds were ahead, 6–5.

In the confusion, Bench had gone to third, but he was left there when Foster struck out.

The Yankees were far from dead. They had, in fact, the heart of their order coming up in the 13th against Eastwick, the Cincinnati relief ace who was the sixth pitcher Anderson had thrown into the game, and their fans took heart when DiMaggio led off with a sharp single into left field.

Now McCarthy faced a dilemma: He hated to waste Gehrig's bat with a sacrifice, but the first baseman had slowed down near the end of his great career and was capable of hitting into a double play.

But McCarthy made his decision: He had won on the long ball, and he was not going to change his style now. He would let Gehrig hit away.

Lou took a ball and a strike and then hit a fastball far into right field. For a time, it seemed the ball was going out, or would at least be off the fence. DiMaggio went halfway to second base and waited. At the last moment, the ball dropped, and Griffey caught it against the fence. DiMag retreated to first.

Dickey was the next hitter. He knew Eastwick could be hit, despite that lively fastball; Gehrig's ball had taught him that. He was determined to take his cuts.

He lashed a vicious liner just to the right of second base, but Morgan reacted quickly to get to the ball on one bounce, and then fed it to Concepcion coming across the base. Double-play time.

But DiMaggio, though he was never used as a base stealer because McCarthy believed in the power game, was an excellent base runner. He came in high at second base and Concepcion threw off-balance to first base, his throw pulling Perez off the bag. The Yankees still had life.

It was all up to Lazzeri. At 34, Lazzeri was not the great hitter he had been—he had hit only .244 that season—but he was still dangerous, especially in a clutch situation.

Eastwick teased him with a fastball just outside, but Lazzeri let it go for a ball. Eastwick came back inside with a fastball, and Lazzeri fouled it into the screen.

There was no secret what was going on. Eastwick was throwing nothing but fastballs now, and Lazzeri knew it. The next one might have been just outside, but Lazzeri was up to swing, not take. He lashed out at the pitch and hit a liner down the right field line but foul by several feet.

"He can't get around on my fastball," thought Eastwick, remembering that the scouting report prepared for the Series had predicted that. He took a deep breath and then threw what he later called "the best fastball of my life." It started out chest high but by the time Lazzeri started his swing, it had risen up to his shoulders. He missed it cleanly.

The Reds erupted, mobbing Eastwick on the mound. The Yankees, gentlemanly in defeat as well as in victory, walked into the dressing room. The crowd sat in stunned silence, unable to believe that their awesome Yankees could be beaten.

Well, it could have happened that way.

Statistics

World Series Results and Receipts

Year	National League	American League	Games W-L	Attendance	Receipts	Winning Player's Share	Losing Player's Share
1903	Pittsburgh	*Boston	3-5	100,429	55,500.00	1,316.25	1,182.00
1905	*New York	Philadelphia	4-1	91,723	68,437.00	1,142.00	833.75
1906	Chicago	*Chicago	2-4	99,845	106,550.00	1,874.63	439.50
1907	*Chicago	Detroit	4-0a	78,068	101,728.50	2,142.85	1,945.96
1908	*Chicago	Detroit	4-1	62,232	94,975.50	1,317.58	870.00
1909	*Pittsburgh	Detroit	4-3	145,295	188,302.50	1,825.22	1,274.76
1910	Chicago	*Philadelphia	1-4	124,222	173,980.00	2,062.79	1,375.16
1911	New York	*Philadelphia	2-4	179,851	342,164.50	3,654.58	2,436.39
1912	New York	*Boston	3-4a	252,037	490,449.00	4,024.68	2,566.47
1913	New York	*Philadelphia	1-4	151,000	325,980.00	3,246.36	2,164.22
1914	*Boston	Philadelphia	4-0	111,009	225,739.00	2,812.28	2,031.65
1915	Philadelphia	*Boston	1-4	143,351	320,361.50	3,780.25	2,520.71
1916	Brooklyn	*Boston	1-4	162,859	385,590.50	3,910.28	2,834.82
1917	New York	*Chicago	2-4	186,654	425,878.00	3,669.32	2,442.61
1918	Chicago	*Boston	2-4	128,483	179,619.00	1,102.51	671.09
1919	*Cincinnati	Chicago	5-3	236,928	722,414.00	5,207.01	3,254.36
1920	Brooklyn	*Cleveland	2-5	178,737	564,800.00	4,168.00	2,419.60
1921	*New York	New York	5-3	269,976	900,233.00	5,265.00	3,510.00
1922	*New York	New York	4-0a	185,947	605,475.00	4,470.00	3,225.00
1923	New York	*New York	2-4	301,430	1,063,815.00	6,143.49	4,112.89
1924	New York	*Washington	3-4	283,665	1,093,104.00	5,969.64	3,820.29
1925	*Pittsburgh	Washington	4-3	282,848	1,182,854.00	5,332.72	3,734.60
1926	*St. Louis	New York	4-3	328,051	1,207,864.00	5,584.51	3,417.75
1927	Pittsburgh	*New York	0-4	201,705	783,217.00	5,592.17	3,728.10
1928	St. Louis	*New York	0-4	199,072	777,290.00	5,531.91	4,197.37
1929	Chicago	*Philadelphia	1-4	190,490	859,494.00	5,620.57	3,782.01
1930	St. Louis	*Philadelphia	2-4	212,619	953,772.00	5,785.00	3,875.00
1931	*St. Louis	Philadelphia	4-3	231,567	1,030,723.00	4,467.59	3,032.09
1932	Chicago	*New York	0-4	191,998	713,377.00	5,231.77	4,244.60
1933	*New York	Washington	4-1	163,076	679,365.00	4,256.72	3,019.86
1934	*St. Louis	Detroit	4-3	281,510	1,031,341.00	5,389.57	3,354.57
1935	Chicago	*Detroit	2-4	286,672	1,073,794.00	6,544.76	4,198.53
1936	New York	*New York	2-4	302,924	1,204,399.00	6,430.55	4,655.58
1937	New York	*New York	1-4	238,142	985,994.00	6,471.10	4,489.05
1938	Chicago	*New York	0-4	200,833	851,166.00	5,782.76	4,674.87

World Series Results and Receipts (Continued)

Year	National League	American League	Games W-L	Attendance	Receipts	Winning Player's Share	Losing Player's Share
1939	Cincinnati	*New York	0-4	183,849	745,329.00	5,614.26	4,282.58
1940	*Cincinnati	Detroit	4-3	281,927	1,222,328.21	5,803.62	3,351.81
1941	Brooklyn	*New York	1-4	235,773	1,007,762.00	5,943.31	4,829.40
1942	*St. Louis	New York	4-1	277,01	1,105,249.00	5,573.78	3,018.77
1943	St. Louis	*New York	1-4	277,312	1,105,784.00	6,139.46	4,321.96
1944	*St. Louis	St. Louis	4-2	206,708	906,122.00	4,626.01	2,743.79
1945	Chicago	*Detroit	3-4	333,457	1,492,454.00	6,443.34	3,930.22
1946	*St. Louis	Boston	4-3	250,071	1,052,900.00	3,742.34	2,140.89
1947	Brooklyn	*New York	3-4	389,763	1,781,348.92	5,830.03	4,081.19
1948	Boston	*Cleveland	2-4	358,362	1,633,685.56	6,772.05	4,651.51
1949	Brooklyn	*New York	1-4	236,710	1,129,627.88	5,665.54	4,272.73
1950	Philadelphia	*New York	0-4	196,009	953,669.03	5,737.95	4,081.34
1951	New York	*New York	2-4	341,977	1,633,457.47	6,446.09	4,951.03
1952	Brooklyn	*New York	3-4	340,906	1,622,753.01	5,982.65	4,200.64
1953	Brooklyn	*New York	2-4	307,350	1,779,269.44	8,280.68	6,178.42
1954	*New York	Cleveland	4-0	251,507	1,566,203.38	11,147.90	6,712.50
1955	*Brooklyn	New York	4-3	362,310	2,337,515.34	9,768.00	5,598.00
1956	Brooklyn	*New York	3-4	345,903	2,183,254.59	8,714.76	6,934.34
1957	*Milwaukee	New York	4-3	394,712	2,475,978.94	8,924.36	5,606.06
1958	Milwaukee	*New York	3-4	393,909	2,397,223.03	8,759.10	5,896.09
1959	*Los Angeles	Chicago	4-2	420,784	2,628,809.44	11,231.18	7,257.17
1960	*Pittsburgh	New York	4-3	349,813	2,230,627.88	8,417.94	5,214.64
1961	Cincinnati	*New York	1-4	223,247	1,480,059.95	7,389.13	5,356.37
1962	San Francisco	*New York	3-4	376,864	2,878,891.11	9,882.74	7,291.49
1963	*Los Angeles	New York	4-0	247,279	1,995,189.09	12,794.00	7,874.32
1964	*St. Louis	New York	4-3	321,807	2,243,187.96	8,622.19	5,309.29
1965	*Los Angeles	Minnesota	4-3	364,326	2,975,041.60	10,297.43	6,634.36
1966	Los Angeles	*Baltimore	0-4	220,791	2,047,142.46	11,683.04	8,189.36
1967	*St. Louis	Boston	4-3	304,085	2,350,607.10	8,314.81	5,115.23
1968	St. Louis	*Detroit	3-4	379,670	3,018,113.40	10,936.66	7,078.71
1969	*New York	Baltimore	4-1	272,378	2,857,782.78	18,338.18	14,904.21
1970	Cincinnati	*Baltimore	1-4	253,183	2,599,170.26	18,215.78	13,687.59
1971	*Pittsburgh	Baltimore	4-3	351,091	3,049,803.46	18,164.58	13,906.46
1972	Cincinnati	*Oakland	3-4	363,149	3,954,542.99	20,705.01	15,080.25
1973	New York	*Oakland	3-4	358,289	3,923,968.37	24,617.57	14,950.17
1974	Los Angeles	*Oakland	1-4	260,004	3,007,194.00	22,219.09	15,703.97
1975	*Cincinnati	Boston	4-3	308,272	3,380,579.61	19,060.46	13,325.87
1976	*Cincinnati	New York	4-0	223,009	2,498,416.53	26,366.68	19,935.48
1977	Los Angeles	*New York	2-4	337,708	3,978,825.33	27,758.04	20,899.05
1978	Los Angeles	*New York	2-4	337,304	4,650,164.57	31,236.99	25,483.21
1979	*Pittsburgh	Baltimore	4-3	367,597	4,390,766.14	28,236.87	22,113.94

1980	*Philadelphia	Kansas City	4-2	324,216	5,131,756.00	34,693.00	32,211.00
1981	*Los Angeles	New York	4-2	338,081	5,615,911.00	**	28,845.00
1982	*St. Louis	Milwaukee	4-3	348,570	6,421,055.00	43,279.00	31,934.00
1983	Philadelphia	*Baltimore	1-4	304,139	7,652,103.00	65,487.00	44,473.00

Note: Player's Shares for 1969 to date include League Championship Series

---

* indicates winning team   a indicates one game tied
** not announced

WORLD SERIES INDIVIDUAL BATTING RECORDS

8 Game Series records that tied or exceeded those shown are included under 7 Game Series.

	4 Games	5 Games	6 Games	7 Games
Highest Batting Average	.625 Ruth, AL: NY 1928	.500 McLean, NL: NY 1913 Gordon, AL: NY 1941	.500 Robertson, NL: NY 1917 Martin, AL: NY 1953	.500 Martin, NL: StL 1931 Garner, NL: Pitt 1979
Highest Slugging Average	1.727 Gehrig, AL: NY 1928	.929 Gordon, AL: NY 1941	1.250 Jackson, AL: NY 1977	.913 Tenace, AL: Oak 1972
Most At Bats	19 Koenig, AL: NY 1928	23 Janvrin, AL: Bos 1916 Moore, NL: NY 1937 Richardson, AL: NY 1961	28 Moore, NL: NY 1936	33 Harris, AL: Wash 1924 Rice, AL: Wash 1925 Moreno, NL: Pitt 1979 *36 Collins, AL: Bos 1903*
Most Runs	9 Ruth, AL: NY 1928 Gehrig, AL: NY 1932	6 Baker, AL: Phil 1910 Murphy, AL Phil 1910 Hooper, AL: Bos 1916 Simmons, AL: Phil 1929 May, NL: Cin 1970 Powell, AL: Balt 1970	10 Jackson, AL: NY 1977	8 Leach, NL: Pitt 1909 Martin, NL: StL 1934 Johnson, AL: NY 1947 Mantle, AL: NY 1960, 64 Richardson, AL: NY 1960 Brock, NL: StL 1967
Most Hits	10 Ruth, AL: NY 1928	9 Baker, AL: Phil 1910, 13 Collins, AL: Phil 1910 Groh, NL: NY 1922 Moore, NL: NY 1937 Richardson, AL: NY 1961 Blair, AL: Balt 1970 B. Robinson, AL: Balt 1970	12 Martin, AL: NY 1953	13 Richardson, AL: NY 1964 Brock, NL: StL 1968

WORLD SERIES INDIVIDUAL BATTING RECORDS (Continued)

	4 Games	5 Games	6 Games	7 Games
Most Long Hits	6 Ruth, AL: NY 1928	4 Murphy, AL: Phil 1910 Collins, AL: Phil 1910 Howard, AL: NY 1961 Clendenon, NL: NY 1969 May, NL: Cin 1970 B. Robinson, AL: 1970	6 Jackson, AL: NY 1977	7 Stargell, NL: Pitt 1979
Most Total Bases	22 Ruth, AL: NY 1928	17 B. Robinson, AL: Balt 1970	25 Jackson, AL: NY 1977	25 Stargell, NL: Pitt 1979
Most One Base Hits	9 Munson, AL: NY 1976	8 Chance, NL: Chi 1908 Baker, AL: Phil 1913 Groh, NL: NY 1922 Moore, NL: NY 1937 Richardson, AL: NY 1961 Blair, AL: Balt 1970 Garvey, NL: LA 1974	10 Rolfe, AL: NY 1936 Irvin, NL: NY 1951	12 Rice, AL: Wash 1925
Most Two Base Hits	3 Gowdy, NL: Bos 1914 Ruth, AL: NY 1928	4 Collins, AL: Phil 1910	5 Hafey, NL: StL 1930	6 Fox, AL: Det 1934
Most Three Base Hits	2 Gehrig, AL: NY 1927 Davis, NL: LA 1963	2 Collins, AL: Phil 1913 Brown, AL: NY 1949	2 Rohe, AL: Chi 1906 R. Meusel, AL: NY 1923 Martin, AL: NY 1953	4 *Leach, NL: Pitt 1903* 3 Johnson, AL: NY 1947
Most Home Runs	4 Gehrig, AL: NY 1928	3 Clendenon, NL: NY 1969	5 Jackson, AL: NY 1977	4 Ruth, AL: NY 1926 Snider, NL: Brk. 1952, 55 Bauer, AL: NY 1958 Tenace, AL: Oak 1972

WORLD SERIES INDIVIDUAL BATTING RECORDS (Continued)

	4 Games	5 Games	6 Games	7 Games
Most Runs Batted In				
	9 Gehrig, AL: NY 1928	8 Murphy, AL: Phil 1910 May, NL: Cin 1970	10 Kluszewski, AL: Chi 1959	12 Richardson, AL: NY 1960
Most Sacrifices				
	3 Westrum, NL: NY 1954	4 Lewis, AL: Bos 1916	3 Sheckard, NL: Chi 1906 Steinfeldt, NL: Chi 1906 Tinker, NL: Chi 1906 Barry, AL: Phil 1911 Lee, NL: Chi 1935	5 Clarke, NL: Pitt 1909 *Daubert, NL: Cin 1919*
Most Sacrifice Flies (Since 1954)				
	2 Westrum, NL: NY 1954	1 Daley, AL: NY 1961 B. Robinson, AL: Balt 1969 Weis, NL: NY 1969 Concepcion, NL: Cin. 1970	2 Washington, AL: KC 1980	2 Campanella, NL: Brk 1956 B. Robinson, AL: Balt 1971
Most Bases on Balls				
	7 Thompson, NL: NY 1954	7 Sheckard, NL: Chi 1910 Cochrane, AL: Phil 1929 Gordon, AL: NY 1941	9 Randolph, AL: NY 1981	11 Ruth, AL: NY 1926 Tenace, AL: Oak 1973
Most Strikeouts				
	8 R. Meusel, AL: NY 1927	8 Hornsby, NL: Chi 1929 Snider, NL: Brk 1949	12 Wilson, AL: KC 1980	11 Mathews, NL: Mil 1958 Garrett, NL: NY 1973
Most Stolen Bases				
	2 Deal, NL: Bos 1914 Maranville, NL: Bos 1914 Morgan, NL: Cin 1976 Geronimo, NL: Cin 1976	6 Slagle, NL: Chi 1907	4 Lopes, NL: LA 1981	7 Brock, NL: StL 1967, 68
Most Caught Stealing				
	2 Aparicio, AL: Balt 1966 Foster, NL: Cin 1976	5 Schulte, NL: Chi 1910	3 Devore, NL: NY 1911	4 *Neale, NL: Cin 1919* 3 Brock, NL: StL 1968

SERVICE

Most Series

14   L.P. Berra, AL: N.Y. 1947, 49-53, 55-58, 60-63

Most Series, Consecutive

5   By many. See rosters AL: N.Y. 1949-53; 60-64

CLUBS

Most Series, One Club

14   L.P. Berra, AL: N.Y. 1947, 49-53, 55-58, 60-63

Most Series, Winning Club

10   L.P. Berra, AL: N.Y. 1947, 49-53, 56, 58, 61-62

Most Series, Losing Club

6   H.H. Reese, NL: Brk. 1941, 47, 49, 52-53, 56
       E.G. Howard, AL: N.Y. 1955, 57, 60, 63-64; Bos. 67

Most Positions Played

4   G.H. Ruth, AL: Bos. 1915-16, 18 (p, 1f);
                N.Y. 21-23, 26-28, 32 (1f, rf, 1b)
       J.R. Robinson, NL: Brk. 1947, 49, 52-53, 55-56 (1b, 2b, 1f, 3b)
       A.C. Kubek, AL: N.Y. 1957-58, 60-63 (1f, 3b, cf, ss)
       E.G. Howard, AL: N.Y. 1955-58, 60-64 (1f, rf, 1b, c); Bos. 67 (c)

BATTING AVERAGE

Highest Batting Average

      Minimum: 20 games:

.391   L.C. Brock, NL: St.L. 1964, 67-68 (21gs)

Most Series, .300+

6   G.H. Ruth, AL: N.Y. 1921, 23, 26-28, 32

Most Series Leading Club

      Playing all games:

3   F.J. Baker, AL: Phil. 1911, 13-14
       H.H. Reese, NL: Brk. 1947, 49, 52
       E.D. Snider, NL: Brk. 1952, 55-56
       G.R. Hodges, NL: Brk. 1953, 56; L.A. 59
       S.P. Garvey, NL: L.A. 1974, 77, 81

SLUGGING AVERAGE

Highest Slugging Average
     Minimum: 20 games:
.755   R.M. Jackson, AL: Oak, 1973-74; N.Y. 77-78, 81 (27 gs)

GAMES

Most Games
  75   L.P. Berra, AL: N.Y. 1947, 49-53, 55-58, 60-63

Most Games, One Club
  75   L.P. Berra, AL: N.Y. 1947, 49-53, 55-58, 60-63

Most Games, Consecutive
  30   R.E. Maris, AL: N.Y. 1960-64
       R.C. Richardson, AL: N.Y. 1960-64

AT BATS

Most At-Bats
  259   L.P. Berra, AL: N.Y. 1947, 49-53, 55-58, 60-63

Most At-Bats, Game
  6   P.H. Dougherty, AL: Bos. Oct. 7, 1903
      J.J. Collins, AL: Bos. Oct. 7, 1903
      J.T. Sheckard, NL: Chi. Oct. 10, 1908
      H.K. Groh, NL: Cin. Oct. 9, 1919
      G.J. Burns, NL: N.Y. Oct. 7, 1921
      M.A. Koenig, AL: N.Y. Oct. 6, 1926
      F.P. Crosetti, AL: N.Y. Oct. 2, 1932
      W.M. Dickey, AL: N.Y. Oct. 2, 1932
      J.W. Sewell, AL: N.Y. Oct. 2, 1932
      R.A. Rolfe, AL: N.Y. Oct. 6, 1936
      J.P. DiMaggio, AL: N.Y. Oct. 6, 1936
      J.R. Brown, NL: St.L. Oct. 4, 1942
      A.F. Schoendienst, NL: St.L. Oct. 10, 1946
      E.B. Slaughter, NL: St.L. Oct. 10, 1946
      H.H. Reese, NL: Brk. Oct. 5, 1956
      A.C. Kubek, AL: N.Y. Oct. 6, 1960
      W.J. Skowron, AL: N.Y. Oct. 6, 1960
      C.L. Boyer, AL: N.Y. Oct. 12, 1960

R.C. Richardson, AL: N.Y. Oct. 9, 1961
A.C. Kubek, AL: N.Y. Oct. 9, 1961
P.L. Molitor, AL: Mil. Oct. 12, 1982
R.R. Yount, AL: Mil. Oct. 12, 1982
Extra inning game:
7   D.A. Hahn, NL: N.Y. Oct. 14, 1973 (12)

Most Appearances, No At-Bats, Game
5   F.C. Clarke, NL: Pitt. Oct. 16, 1909

Most At-Bats, Inning
2   By many

RUNS

Most Runs
42   M.C. Mantle, AL: N.Y. 1951-53, 55-58, 60-64

Most Runs, Game
4   G.H. Ruth, AL: N.Y. Oct. 6, 1926
E.B. Combs, AL: N.Y. Oct. 2, 1932
F.P. Crosetti, AL: N.Y. Oct. 2, 1936
E.B. Slaughter, NL: St.L. Oct. 10, 1946
R.M. Jackson, AL: N.Y. Oct. 18, 1977

Most Runs, Inning
2   F.F. Frisch, NL: N.Y. Oct. 7, 1921 (7th)
A.H. Simmons, AL: Phil. Oct. 12, 1929 (7th)
J.E. Foxx, AL: Phil. Oct. 12, 1929 (7th)
R.J. McAuliffe, AL: Det. Oct. 9, 1968 (3rd)
M.J. Stanley, AL: Det. Oct. 9, 1968 (3rd)
A.W. Kaline, AL: Det. Oct. 9, 1968 (3rd)

Most Games, Consecutive, Runs
9   G.H. Ruth, AL: N.Y. 1927-28, 32

HITS

Most Hits
71   L.P. Berra, AL: N.Y. 1947, 49-53, 55-58, 60-63

Most Hits, Game
5   P.L. Molitor, AL: Mil. Oct. 12, 1982

Most Games, 4+ Hits, Lifetime

2   R.R. Yount, AL: Mil. Oct. 12 & 17, 1982

Most Games, 4+ Hits, One Series

2   R.R. Yount, AL: Mil. Oct. 12 & 17, 1982

Most Hits, 2 Consecutive Games

7   P.L. Molitor, AL: Mil. Oct. 12-13, 1982

Most Hits, Inning

2   R.M. Youngs, NL: N.Y. Oct. 7, 1921 (7th)

      A.H. Simmons, AL: Phil. Oct. 12, 1929 (7th)

      J.E. Foxx, AL: Phil. Oct. 12, 1929 (7th)

      J.J. Dykes, AL: Phil. Oct. 12, 1929 (7th)

      J.G. Moore, NL: N.Y. Oct. 4, 1933 (6th)

      J.H. Dean, NL: St.L. Oct. 9, 1934 (3rd)

      J.P. DiMaggio, AL: N.Y. Oct. 6, 1936 (9th)

      H.E. Leiber, NL: N.Y. Oct. 9, 1937 (2nd)

      S.F. Musial, NL: St.L. Oct. 4, 1942 (4th)

      E.G. Howard, AL: N.Y. Oct. 6, 1960 (6th)

      R.C. Richardson, AL: N.Y. Oct. 6, 1960 (6th)

      R.H. Cerv, AL: N.Y. Oct. 8, 1960 (1st)

      F.R. Quilici, AL: Minn. Oct. 6, 1965 (3rd)

      A.W. Kaline, AL: Det. Oct. 9, 1968 (3rd)

      N.D. Cash, AL: Det. Oct. 9, 1968 (3rd)

      M.W. Rettenmund, AL: Balt. Oct. 11, 1971 (5th)

Most Hits, Consecutive

7   T.L. Munson, AL: N.Y. 1976-77

Most Games, Consecutive, Hits

17   H.A. Bauer, AL: N.Y. 1956-58

Fewest Hits

    Most at bats, lifetime

0   G.L. Earnshaw, AL: Phil. 1929-31 (22)

    Most at bats, consecutive:

0   M.J. Owen, AL: Det. 1934-35 (31)

    Series, most at bat:

0   C.D. Maxvill, NL: St.L. 1968 (22)

    Game, most at bats:

0   T.C. Jackson, NL: N.Y. Oct. 10, 1924 (6-ab, 12 inn)

H.M. Critz, NL: N.Y. Oct. 6, 1933 (6ab, 11 inn)
F.B. Millan, NL: N.Y. Oct. 14, 1973 (6ab, 12 inn)

LONG HITS

Most Long Hits
26   M.C. Mantle, AL: N.Y. 1951-53, 55-58, 60-64

Most Long Hits, Game
4   W.F. Isbell, AL: Chi. Oct. 13, 1906 (4-2b)

Most Long Hits, Inning
2   R.M. Youngs, NL: N.Y. Oct. 7, 1921 (7th; 2b, 3b)

TOTAL BASES

Most Total Bases
123   M.C. Mantle, AL: N.Y. 1951-53, 55-58, 60-64

Most Total Bases, Game
12   G.H. Ruth, AL: N.Y. Oct. 6, 1926; Oct. 9, 1928
      R.M. Jackson, AL: N.Y. Oct. 18, 1977

Most Total Bases, Inning
5   R.M. Youngs, NL: N.Y. Oct. 7, 1921
     A.H. Simmons, AL: Phil. Oct. 12, 1929

ONE BASE HITS

Most One Base Hits
49   L.P. Berra, AL: N.Y. 1947, 49-53, 55-58, 60-63

Most One Base Hits, Game
5   P.L. Molitor, AL: Mil. Oct. 12, 1982

Most One Base Hits, Inning
2   J.E. Foxx, AL: Phil. Oct. 12, 1929 (7th)
     J.G. Moore, NL: N.Y. Oct. 4, 1933 (6th)
     J.P. DiMaggio, AL: N.Y. Oct. 6, 1936 (9th)
     H.E. Leiber, NL: N.Y. Oct. 9, 1937 (2nd)
     R.H. Cerv, AL: N.Y. Oct. 8, 1960 (1st)
     A.W. Kaline, AL: Det. Oct. 9, 1968 (3rd)

N.D. Cash, AL: Det. Oct. 9, 1968 (3rd)
M.W. Rettenmund, AL: Balt. Oct. 11, 1971 (5th)

TWO BASE HITS

Most Two Base Hits
10   F.F. Frisch, NL: N.Y. 1921-24; St.L. 28, 30-31, 34
      L.P. Berra, AL: N.Y. 1947, 49-53, 55-58, 60-63

Most Two Base Hits, Game
4   W.F. Isbell, AL: Chi. Oct. 13, 1906

Most Two Base Hits, Inning
1   By many

THREE BASE HITS

Most Three Base Hits
4   T.W. Leach, NL: Pitt. 1903, 09
      T.E. Speaker, AL: Bos. 1912, 15; Clev. 20
      W.R. Johnson, AL: N.Y. 1943, 49-50

Most Three Base Hits, Game
2   T.W. Leach, NL: Pitt. Oct. 1, 1903
      P.H. Dougherty, AL: Bos. Oct. 7, 1903
      W.H. Ruether, NL: Cin. Oct. 1, 1919
      R.C. Richardson, AL: N.Y. Oct. 12, 1960
      H.T. Davis, NL: L.A. Oct. 3, 1963

Most Three Base Hits, Inning
1   By many

HOME RUNS

Most Home Runs
18   M.C. Mantle, AL: N.Y. 1951-53, 55-58, 60-64

Most Home Runs, Game
3   G.H. Ruth, AL: N.Y. Oct. 6, 1926; Oct. 9, 1928
      R.M. Jackson, AL: N.Y. Oct. 18, 1977

Most Home Runs, Game, Rookie
2   C.E. Keller, AL: N.Y. Oct. 7, 1939
      A.C. Kubek, AL: N.Y. Oct. 5, 1957

W.D. McGee, NL: St.L. Oct. 15, 1982

Most Games, Consecutive, Home Runs
4   H.L. Gehrig, AL: N.Y. Oct. 5, 7(2), 9, 1928; Sept. 28, 1932
     R.M. Jackson, AL: N.Y. Oct. 15, 16, 18(3), 1977; Oct. 10, 1978

Most Home Runs, First Game
2   T.B. Kluszewski, AL: Chi. Oct. 1, 1959
     F.G. Tenace, AL: Oak. Oct. 14, 1972
     W.M. Aikens, AL: K.C. Oct. 14, 1980

Most Games, 2+ Home Runs
4   G.H. Ruth, AL: N.Y. Oct. 11, 1923; Oct. 9, 1928;
                 Oct. 6, 1926; Oct. 1, 1932

Most Games, One Series, 2+ Home Runs
2   W.M. Aikens, AL: K.C. Oct. 14, 18, 1980

Most Home Runs, Consecutive At Bats
4   R.M. Jackson, AL: N.Y. Oct. 16-18, 1977

Most Home Runs, Inning
1   By many

Most Home Runs, Consecutive Innings
2   G.H. Ruth, AL: N.Y. Oct. 11, 1923 (4-5)
     G.H. Ruth, AL: N.Y. Oct. 9, 1928 (7-8)
     T.B. Kluszewski, AL: Chi. Oct. 1, 1959 (3-4)
     R.M. Jackson, AL: N.Y. Oct. 18, 1977 (4-5)
     W.M. Aikens, AL: K.C. Oct. 18, 1980 (1-2)

Home Run, First Series At Bat

J. Harris, AL: Wash. Oct. 7, 1925	B.C. Robinson, AL: Balt. Oct. 5, 1966
G.A. Watkins, NL: St.L. Oct. 2, 1930	J.R. Santiago, AL: Bos. Oct. 4, 1967
M.T. Ott, NL: N.Y. Oct. 3, 1933	M.S. Lolich, AL: Det. Oct. 3, 1968
G.A. Selkirk, AL: N.Y. Sept. 30, 1936	D.A. Buford, AL: Balt. Oct. 11, 1969
J.L. Rhodes, NL: N.Y. Sept. 29, 1954	F.G. Tenace, AL: Oak. Oct. 14, 1972
E.G. Howard, AL: N.Y. Sept. 28, 1955	J.P. Mason, AL: N.Y. Oct. 19, 1976
R.E. Maris, AL: N.Y. Oct. 5, 1960	D.V. DeCinces, AL: Balt. Oct. 10, 1979
D.R. Mincher, AL: Minn. Oct. 6, 1965	A.J. Otis, AL: K.C. Oct. 14, 1980
	R.J. Watson, AL: N.Y. Oct. 20, 1981

Most Home Runs, First Two Series At Bats
2 F.G. Tenace, AL: Oak. Oct. 14, 1972

Most Home Runs, Leading Off, Game
1 P.H. Dougherty, AL: Bos. Oct. 2, 1903 W.H. Bruton, NL: Mil. Oct. 2, 1958

D.J. Jones, AL: Det. Oct. 13, 1909
P.F. Rizzuto, AL: N.Y. Oct. 5, 1942
L.D. Mitchell, AL: Clev. Oct. 10, 1948
E.R. Woodling, AL: N.Y. Oct. 4, 1953
A.E. Smith, AL: Clev. Sept. 30, 1954

L.C. Brock, NL: St.L. Oct. 6, 1968
D.A. Buford, AL: Balt. Oct. 11, 1969
T.L. Agee, NL: N.Y. Oct. 14, 1969
P.E. Rose, NL: Cin. Oct. 20, 1972
R.W. Garrett, NL: N.Y. Oct. 16, 1973
D.E. Lopes, NL: L.A. Oct. 17, 1978

Most Home Runs, Bases Full, Inning

1 E.J. Smith (RF) AL: Clev. (Brk.)
  Oct. 10, 1920 (1st: Grimes)
  A.M. Lazzeri (2B) AL: N.Y. (N.Y.)
  Oct. 2, 1936 (3rd: Coffman)
  G.J. McDougald (2B) AL: N.Y. (N.Y.)
  Oct. 9, 1951 (3rd: Jansen)
  M.C. Mantle (CF) AL: N.Y. (Brk.)
  Oct. 4, 1953 (3rd: Meyer)
  L.P. Berra (C) AL: N.Y. (Brk.)
  Oct. 5, 1956 (2nd: Newcombe)
  W.J. Skowron (1B) AL: N.Y. (Brk.)
  Oct. 10, 1956 (7th: Craig)

  R.C. Richardson (2B) AL: N.Y. (Pitt.)
  Oct. 8, 1960 (1st: Labine)
  C.J. Hiller (2B) NL: S.F. (N.Y.)
  Oct. 8, 1962 (7th: Bridges)
  K.L. Boyer (3B) NL: St.L. (N.Y.)
  Oct. 11, 1964 (6th: Downing)
  J.A. Pepitone (1B) AL: N.Y. (St.L.)
  Oct. 14, 1964 (8th: Richardson)
  J.T. Northrup (CF) AL: Det. (St.L.)
  Oct. 9, 1968 (3rd: Jaster)
  D.A. McNally (P) AL: Balt. (Cin.)
  Oct. 13, 1970 (6th: Granger)

RUNS BATTED IN

Most Runs Batted In
40   M.C. Mantle, AL: N.Y. 1951-53, 55-58, 60-64

Most Runs Batted In, Game
6   R.C. Richardson, AL: N.Y. Oct. 8, 1960

Most Runs Batted In, Inning
4   By many

SACRIFICE HITS

Most Sacrifice Hits
8   E.T. Collins, AL: Phil. 1910-11, 13-14; Chi. 17, 19

Most Sacrifice Hits, Game
3   J.B. Tinker, NL: Chi. Oct. 12, 1906

Most Sacrifice Hits, Inning
1   By many

SACRIFICE FLIES
(Since 1954)

Most Sacrifice Flies
   3   B.C. Robinson, AL: Balt. 1966, 69-71)

Most Sacrifice Flies, Game
   2   W.N. Westrum, NL: N.Y. Oct. 2, 1954

Most Sacrifice Flies, Inning
   1   By many

Most Runs Batted In, Sacrifice Fly
   2   T.M. Herr, NL: St.L. Oct. 16, 1982 (2nd inn)

BASES ON BALLS

Most Bases on Balls
   43   M.C. Mantle, AL: N.Y. 1951-53, 55-58, 60-64

Most Bases on Balls, Consecutive
   5   H.L. Gehrig, AL: N.Y. Oct. 7-9, 1928

Most Bases on Balls, Game
   4   F.C. Clarke, NL: Pitt. Oct. 16, 1909
         G.H. Ruth, AL: N.Y. Oct. 10, 1926
         D.V. DeCinces, AL: Balt. Oct. 13, 1979
         Extra inning game:
         R.C. Hoblitzel, AL: Bos. Oct. 9, 1916 (14)
         R.M. Youngs, NL: N.Y. Oct. 10, 1924 (12)
         J.R. Robinson, NL: Brk. Oct. 5, 1952 (11)

Most Bases on Balls, Inning
   2   V.L. Gomez, AL: N.Y. Oct. 6, 1937 (6th)
         R.J. McAuliffe, AL: Det. Oct. 9, 1968 (3rd)

HIT BY PITCH

Most Hit By Pitch
   3   J.P. Wagner, NL: Pitt. 1903, 09
         F.L. Chance, NL: Chi. 1906-07
         F.C. Snodgrass, NL: N.Y. 1911-12

M.G. Carey, NL: Pitt. 1925
L.P. Berra, AL: N.Y. 1953, 55
E.G. Howard, AL: N.Y. 1960, 62, 64
F. Robinson, NL: Cin. 1961; AL: Balt. 71
D.B. Campaneris, AL: Oak. 1973-74
R.M. Jackson, AL: N.Y. 1977-78

Most Hit By Pitch, Game
2   M.C. Carey, NL: Pitt. Oct. 7, 1925
L.P. Berra, AL: N.Y. Oct. 2, 1953
F. Robinson, NL: Cin. Oct. 8, 1961

Most Hit By Pitch, Inning
1   By many

STRIKEOUTS

Most Strikeouts
54   M.C. Mantle, AL: N.Y. 1951-53, 55-58, 60-64

Most Strikeouts, Consecutive
5   J. Devore, NL: N.Y. Oct. 16-17, 1911
G. Mogridge, AL: Wash. Oct. 7-10, 1924
G.W. Pipgras, AL: N.Y. Oct. 1, 1932
M.C. Mantle, AL: N.Y. Oct. 2-3, 1953
T.M. Shannon, NL: St.L. Oct. 12-14, 1964

Most Strikeouts, Game
5   G.W. Pipgras, AL: N.Y. Oct. 1, 1932

Most Strikeouts, Inning
1   By many

GROUNDED INTO DOUBLE PLAYS

Most Grounded Into DP
7   J.P. DiMaggio, AL: N.Y. 1936-39, 41-42, 49-51

Most Grounded Into DP, Game
3   W.H. Mays, NL: N.Y. Oct. 8, 1951

STOLEN BASES

Most Stolen Bases

14   E.T. Collins, AL: Phil. 1910-11, 13-14; Chi. 17, 19
     L.C. Brock, NL: St.L. 1964, 67-68

Most Stolen Bases, Game

3   J.P. Wagner, NL: Pitt. Oct. 11, 1909
    W.H. Davis, NL: L.A. Oct. 11, 1965
    L.C. Brock, NL: St.L. Oct. 12, 1967; Oct. 5, 1968

Most Stolen Bases, Inning

2   J.F. Slagle, NL: Chi. Oct. 8, 1907 (10th)
    G.E. Browne, NL: N.Y. Oct. 12, 1905 (9th)
    T.R. Cobb, AL: Det. Oct. 12, 1908 (9th)
    E.T. Collins, AL: Chi. Oct. 7, 1917 (6th)
    G.H. Ruth, AL: N.Y. Oct. 6, 1921 (5th)
    L.C. Brock, NL: St.L. Oct. 12, 1967 (5th)
    D.E. Lopes, NL: L.A. Oct. 15, 1974 (1st)

Most Stolen Home

2   R.W. Meusel, AL: N.Y. 1921, 28

Most Stolen Home, Game

1   See following item

Most Stolen Home, Inning

1   W.F. Dahlen, NL: N.Y. Oct. 12, 1905 (5th)
    G.S. Davis, AL: Chi. Oct. 13, 1906 (3rd)
    J.F. Slagle, NL: Chi. Oct. 11, 1907 (7th)
    T.R. Cobb, AL: Det. Oct. 9, 1909 (3rd)
    C.L. Herzog, NL: N.Y. Oct. 13, 1912 (1st)
    C.J. Schmidt, NL: Bos. Oct. 9, 1914 (8th)
    M.J. McNally, AL: N.Y. Oct. 5, 1921 (5th)
    R.W. Meusel, AL: N.Y. Oct. 6, 1921 (8th); Oct. 7, 1928 (6th)
    M.M. Irvin, NL: N.Y. Oct. 4, 1951 (1st)
    J.R. Robinson, NL: Brk. Sept. 28, 1955 (8th)
    T.J. McCarver, NL: St.L. Oct. 15, 1964 (4th)

CAUGHT STEALING

Most Caught Stealing, Game
2   F.W. Luderus, NL: Phil. Oct. 8, 1915
       T.O. Livingston, NL: Chi. Oct. 3, 1945
       A.M. Martin, AL: N.Y. Sept. 28, 1955

Most Caught Stealing, Inning
1   By many

PINCH-HITTING

Most Games
10   J.E. Blanchard, AL: N.Y. 1960-62, 64

Games, One Series
5   H.E. McCormick, NL: N.Y. 1912
       B.E. Paschal, AL: N.Y. 1926
       F.E. Secory, NL: Chi. 1945
       H.A. Lavagetto, NL: Brk. 1947
       C.W. Warwick, NL: St.L. 1964
       T.M. Shopay, AL: Balt. 1971
       G. Marquez, AL: Oak, 1972
       A.L. Mangual, AL: Oak, 1973
       T.M. Crowley, AL: Balt. 1979
       H.P. Kelly, AL: Balt. 1979

Most At-Bats
10   J.E. Blanchard, AL: N.Y. 1960-62, 64

Most Hits
3   J.K. O'Dea, NL: Chi. 1935; St.L. 42, 44
       R.W. Brown, AL: N.Y. 1947
       J.R. Mize, AL: N.Y. 1949, 52
       J.L. Rhodes, NL: N.Y. 1954
       C.A. Furillo, NL: Brk. 1947; L.A. 59
       R.H. Cerv, AL: N.Y. 1955-56, 60
       J.E. Blanchard, AL: N.Y. 1960-61, 64
       C.W. Warwick, NL: St.L. 1964
       G. Marquez, AL: Oak, 1972
       K.G. Boswell, NL: N.Y. 1973

Hits, One Series

3   R.W. Brown, AL: N.Y. 1947
      J.L. Rhodes, NL: N.Y. 1954
      C.W. Warwick, NL: St.L. 1964
      G. Marquez, AL: Oak, 1972
      K.G. Boswell, NL: N.Y. 1973

Total Bases, One Series

8   C.A. Essegian, NL: L.A. 1959
      B. Carbo, AL: Bos. 1975

Home Runs

2   C.A. Essegian, NL: L.A. Oct. 2 (7th), 8 (9th), 1959
      B. Carbo, AL: Box. Oct. 14 (7th), 21 (8th), 1975
1   L.P. Berra, AL: N.Y. Oct. 2, 1947 (7th)
      J.R. Mize, AL: N.Y. Oct. 3, 1952 (9th)
      G.T. Shuba, NL: Brk. Sept. 30, 1953 (6th)
      J.L. Rhodes, NL: N.Y. Sept. 29, 1954 (10th)
      H. Majeski, AL: Clev. Oct. 2, 1954 (5th)
      R.H. Cerv, AL: N.Y. Oct. 2, 1955 (7th)
      E.G. Howard, AL: N.Y. Oct. 5, 1960 (9th)
      J.E. Blanchard, AL: N.Y. Oct. 7, 1961 (8th)
      J.W. Johnstone, NL: L.A. Oct. 24, 1981 (6th)

Runs Batted In, One Series

6   J.L. Rhodes, NL: N.Y. 1954

Runs Batted In, Game

3   J.L. Rhodes, NL: N.Y. Sept. 29, 1954
      H. Majeski, AL: Clev. Oct. 2, 1954

Bases on Balls, One Series

3   H.B. Tate, AL: Wash. 1924

Strikeouts, One Series

3   C.L. Harnett, NL: Chi. 1929
      R.B. Hemsley, NL: Chi. 1932

WORLD SERIES INDIVIDUAL PITCHING RECORDS

8 Game Series records that tied or exceeded those shown are included under 7 Game Series.

	4 Games	5 Games	6 Games	7 Games
Earned Run Average (Most innings, 10+)	0.00 James, NL: Bos 1914 (11)	0.00 Mathewson, NL: NY 1905 (27)	0.00 Benton, NL: NY 1917 (15⅔)	0.00 Hoyt, AL: NY 1921 (27); Ford, AL: NY 1960 (18)
Games	3 By four pitchers	5 Marshall, NL: LA 1974	6 Quisenberry, AL: KC 1980	7 Knowles, AL: Oak 1973
Games Started	2 By many. Last: McNally, AL: Balt 1966	3 Mathewson, NL: NY 1905; Coombs, AL: Phil 1910	3 By many. Last: Wynn, AL: Chi 1959	5 Phillippe, NL: Pitt 1903; 3 By many. Last: Tiant, AL: Bos 1975; Gullett, NL: Cin 1975
Complete Games	2 Rudolph, NL: Bos 1914; Hoyt, AL: NY 1928; Ruffing, AL: NY 1938; Koufax, NL: LA 1963	3 Mathewson, NL: NY 1905; Coombs, AL: Phil 1910	3 Bender, AL: Phil 1911; Vaughn, NL: Chi 1918	5 Phillippe, NL: Pitt 1903; 3 Adams, NL: Pitt 1909; Mullin, AL: Det 1909; Coveleski, AL: Clev 1920; Johnson, AL: Wash 1925; Newsom, AL: Det 1940; Burdette, NL: Mil 1957; Gibson, NL: StL 1967-68; Lolich, AL: Det 1968
Games Finished	3 Reniff, AL: NY 1963	5 Marshall, NL: LA 1974	6 Quisenberry, AL: KC 1980	6 Casey, NL: Brk 1947
Saves (Since 1969)	2 McEnaney, NL: Cin 1976	2 Fingers, AL: Oak 1974	2 McGraw, NL: Phil 1980; Gossage, AL: NY 1981	3 Tekulve, NL: Pitt 1979
Shutouts	1 By nine pitchers	3 Mathewson, NL: NY 1905	1 By twelve pitchers	2 Burdette, NL: Mil 1957; Ford, AL: NY 1960; Koufax, NL: LA 1965
Most Games, Relief Pitcher	3 French, NL: Chi 1938; Mossi, AL: Clev 1954; Reniff, AL: NY 1963	5 Marshall, NL: LA 1974	6 Quisenberry, AL: KC 1980	7 Knowles, AL: Oak 1973

Won				
	2 — Rudolph, NL: Bos 1914; James, NL: Bos 1914; Hoyt, AL: NY 1928; Ruffing, AL: NY 1938; Koufax, NL: LA 1963	3 — Mathewson, NL: NY 1905; Coombs, AL: Phil 1910	3 — Faber, AL: Chi 1917	*3 — Phillippe, NL: Pitt 1903; Dineen, AL: Bos 1903; Adams, NL: Pitt 1909; Wood, AL: Bos 1912;* Coveleski, AL: Clev 1920; Brecheen, NL: StL 1946; Burdette, NL: Mil 1957; Gibson, NL: StL 1967; Lolich, AL: Det 1968
Lost				
	2 — Sherdel, NL: StL 1928; Lee, NL: Chi 1938; Walters, NL: Cin 1939; Lemon, AL: Clev 1954; Ford, AL: NY 1963; Drysdale, NL: LA 1966	2 — By many. Last: Messersmith, NL: LA 1974	3 — Frazier, AL: NY 1981	*3 — Williams, AL: Chi 1919*; 2 — By many. Last: McClure, AL: Mil 1982
Innings				
	18 — Rudolph, NL: Bos 1914; Hoyt, AL: NY 1928; Ruffing, AL: NY 1938; Koufax, NL: LA 1963	27 — Mathewson, NL: NY 1905; Coombs, AL: Phil 1910	27 — Mathewson, NL: NY 1911; Faber, AL: Chi 1917; Vaughn, NL: Chi 1918	*44 — Phillippe, NL: Pitt 1903*; 32 — Mullin, AL: Det 1909
Runs				
	11 — Alexander, NL: StL 1928; Lemon, AL: Clev 1954	16 — Brown, NL: Chi 1910	10 — By 4, Last: Sutton, NL: LA 1978	*19 — Phillippe, NL: Pitt 1903*; 17 — Burdette, NL: Mil 1958
Hits				
	17 — Ruffing, AL: NY 1938	23 — Coombs, AL: Phil 1910; Brown, NL: Chi 1910	25 — Mathewson, NL: NY 1911	*38 — Phillippe, NL: Pitt 1903*; 30 — Johnson, AL: Wash 1924
Home Runs				
	4 — Sherdel, NL: StL 1928; Root, NL: Chi 1932; Thompson, NL: Cin 1939	4 — Nolan, NL: Cin 1970	4 — Reynolds, AL: NY 1953	5 — Burdette, NL: Mil 1958; Hughes, NL: StL 1967
Bases on Balls				
	8 — Lemon, AL: Clev 1954	14 — Coombs, AL: Phil 1910	11 — Tyler, NL: Chi 1918; Gomez, AL: NY 1936; Reynolds, AL: NY 1951	11 — Johnson, AL: Wash 1924; Bevans, AL: NY 1947
Strikeouts				
	23 — Koufax, NL: LA 1963	18 — Mathewson, NL: NY 1905	20 — Bender, AL: Phil 1911	35 — Gibson, NL: StL 1968

SERVICE

Most Series
   22   E.C. Ford, AL: N.Y. 1950, 53, 55-58, 60-64

Most Series, Relief Pitcher
   6   J.J. Murphy, AL: N.Y. 1936-39, 41, 43

GAMES

Most Games
   22   E.C. Ford, AL: N.Y. 1950, 53, 55-58, 60-64

Most Games, Relief Pitcher
   16   R.G. Fingers, AL: Oak. 1972-74

Games, Consecutive
   7   D.D. Knowles, AL: Oak. 1973

STARTED

Most Started
   22   E.C. Ford, AL: N.Y. 1950, 53, 55-58, 60-64

Started, Consecutive
   22   E.C. Ford, AL: N.Y. 1950, 53, 55-58, 60-64

Opening Games Started
   8   E.C. Ford, AL: N.Y. 1955-58, 61-64

COMPLETE

Most Complete
   10   C. Mathewson, NL: N.Y. 1905, 11-13

Complete, Consecutive
   8   R. Gibson, NL: St.L. 1964, 67-68

FINISHED

Most Finished
   10   R.G. Fingers, AL: Oak, 1972-74

Finished, Consecutive

7   C.W. Labine, NL: Brk. 1953, 55-56
       D.J. McMahon, NL: Mil. 1957-58; AL: Det. 68

SAVES

Most Saves

6   R.G. Fingers, AL: Oak. 1972-74

SHUTOUTS

Most Shutouts

4   C. Mathewson, NL: N.Y. 1905, 13

Shutouts, Consecutive

3   C. Mathewson, NL: N.Y. 1905
       E.C. Ford, AL: N.Y. 1960-61

Scoreless Innings

       Complete game:
10   C. Mathewson, NL: N.Y. Oct. 8, 1913
       C.W. Labine, NL: Brk. Oct. 9, 1956
       Game, consecutive:
13   G.H. Ruth, AL: Bos. Oct. 9, 1916
       Consecutive:
33   E.C. Ford, AL: N.Y. 1960-62

WON

Most Won

10   E.C. Ford, AL: N.Y. 1950, 53, 55-58, 60-64

Won, Consecutive

7   Robert Gibson, NL: St.L. 1964, 67-68

LOST

Most Lost

8   E.C. Ford, AL: N.Y. 1950, 53, 55-58, 60-64

Lost Consecutive

5   L.A. Bush, AL: Phil. 1914; Bos. 18; N.Y. 22-23

INNINGS

Most Innings
146   E.C. Ford, AL: N.Y. 1950, 53, 55-58, 60-64

Innings, Game
14   G.H. Ruth, AL: Bos. Oct. 9, 1916

RUNS

Most Runs
51   E.C. Ford, AL: N.Y. 1950, 53, 55-58, 60-64

Runs, Game
9   A.J. Coakley, AL: Phil. Oct. 12, 1905
M.P. Brown, NL: Chi. Oct. 18, 1910
W.P. Johnson, AL: Wash. Oct. 15, 1925

Runs, Inning
7   G.L. Wiltse, NL: N.Y. Oct. 26, 1911 (7th)
C.O. Hubbell, NL: N.Y. Oct. 6, 1937 (6th)

EARNED RUNS

Most Earned Runs
44   E.C. Ford, AL: N.Y. 1950, 53, 55-58, 60-64

Earned Runs, Game
7   M.P. Brown, NL: Chi. Oct. 18, 1910

Earned Runs, Inning
6   G.L. Wiltse, NL: N.Y. Oct. 26, 1911 (7th)

HITS

Most Hits
132   E.C. Ford, AL: N.Y. 1950, 53, 55-58, 60-64

Hits, Game
15   W.P. Johnson, AL: Wash. Oct. 15, 1925

Hits, Inning
7   J. Wood, AL: Bos. Oct. 15, 1912 (1st)

Hits, Consecutive, Inning
6   O.E. Summers, AL: Det. Oct. 10, 1908 (9th)

Hitless Innings, Consecutive
11⅓   D.J. Larsen, AL: N.Y. 1956-57

HOME RUNS

Most Home Runs
9   J.A. Hunter, AL: Oak, 1972-74; N.Y. 76-78

Home Runs, Game
4   C.H. Root, NL: Chi. Oct. 1, 1932
      E.E. Thompson, NL: Cin. Oct. 7, 1939
      R.H. Hughes, NL: St.L. Oct. 11, 1967

Home Runs, Inning
3   R.H. Hughes, NL: St.L. Oct. 11, 1967 (4th)

Home Runs, Consecutive, Inning
2   By 9 pitchers. Last:
      R.A. Guidry, AL: N.Y. Oct. 25, 1981 (7th)

Home Runs, Bases Full
1   By 12 pitchers

BASES ON BALLS

Most Bases on Balls
34   E.C. Ford, AL: N.Y. 1950, 53, 55-58, 60-64

Bases on Balls, Game
10   F.C. Bevans, AL: N.Y. Oct. 3, 1947

Bases on Balls, Inning
4   W.E. Donovan, AL: Det. Oct. 16, 1909 (2nd)
      A.C. Reinhart, NL: St.L. Oct. 6, 1926 (5th)
      G.T. Bush, NL: Chi. Sept. 28, 1932 (6th)
      D.E. Gullett, NL: Cin. Oct. 22, 1975 (3rd)
      R.E. Castillo, NL: L.A. Oct. 20, 1981 (4th)
      Consecutive:
3   J.R. Shawkey, AL: N.Y. Oct. 7, 1921 (4th)
      A.C. Reinhart, NL: St.L. Oct. 6, 1926 (5th)

G.T. Bush, NL: Chi. Sept. 28, 1932 (6th)
K. Heintzelman, NL: Phil. Oct. 6, 1950 (8th)
J.W. Hoerner, NL: St.L. Oct. 3, 1968 (9th)
R.E. Castillo, NL: L.A. Oct. 20, 1981 (4th)

HIT BATSMEN

Most Hit Batsmen
4   W.E. Donovan, AL: Det. 1907, 09
E.S. Plank, AL: Phil. 1905, 11, 13-14

Hit Batsmen, Game
3   B.E. Kison, NL: Pitt. Oct. 13, 1971

Hit Batsmen, Inning
2   R.E. Willett, AL: Det. Oct. 11, 1909
W.A. Granger, NL: St.L. Oct. 9, 1968

STRIKEOUTS

Most Strikeouts
94   E.C. Ford, AL: N.Y. 1950, 53, 55-58, 60-64

Strikeouts, Game
17   R. Gibson, NL: St.L. Oct. 2, 1968
Relief pitcher:
11   M.W. Drabowsky, AL: Balt. Oct. 5, 1966

Strikeouts, Inning
4   O. Overall, NL: Chi. Oct. 14, 1908 (1st)

Strikeouts, Consecutive
6   H.O. Eller, NL: Cin. Oct. 6, 1919
M.W. Drabowsky, AL: Balt. Oct. 5, 1966
Start of game:
5   M.C. Cooper, NL: St.L. Oct. 11, 1943
S. Koufax, NL: L.A. Oct. 2, 1963

WILD PITCHES

Most Wild Pitches
5   H.H. Schumacher, NL: N.Y. 1933, 36-37

Wild Pitches, Game

2 C.M. Tesreau, NL: N.Y. Oct. 15, 1912   J.O. Carleton, NL: Chi. Oct. 9, 1938
   E.J. Pfeffer, NL: Brk. Oct. 12, 1916   J.A. Bouton, AL: N.Y. Oct. 5, 1963
   R.J. Shawkey, AL: N.Y. Oct. 5, 1922   J.A. Stuper, NL: St.L. Oct. 13, 1982
   V.E. Aldrich, NL: Pitt. Oct. 15, 1925   G.F. Medich, AL: Mil. Oct. 19, 1982
   J.K. Miljus, NL: Pitt. Oct. 8, 1927

Wild Pitches, Inning

2 R.J. Shawkey, AL: N.Y. Oct. 5, 1922 (5th)
   V.E. Aldrich, NL: Pitt. Oct. 15, 1925 (1st)
   J.K. Miljus, NL: Pitt. Oct. 8, 1927 (9th)
   J.O. Carleton, NL: Chi. Oct. 9, 1932 (8th)
   G.F. Medich, AL: Mil. Oct. 19, 1982 (6th)

STADIUM DIMENSIONS

National League

Active Stadiums

| Team | Stadium | Home Run Distances (in ft.) | | | Seating |
		LF	CF	RF	Capacity
Atlanta Braves	Atlanta Stadium	330	402	330	52,870
Chicago Cubs	Wrigley Field	355	400	353	37,741
Cincinnati Reds	Riverfront Stadium	330	404	330	51,726
Houston Astros	Astrodome	330	400	330	44,500
Los Angeles Dodgers	Dodger Stadium	330	395	330	56,000
Montreal Expos	Olympic Stadium	325	404	325	59,511
New York Mets	Shea Stadium	341	410	341	55,300
Philadelphia Phillies	Veterans Stadium	330	408	330	56,581
Pittsburgh Pirates	Three Rivers Stadium	340	410	340	50,235
St. Louis Cardinals	Busch Memorial Stadium	330	404	330	50,100
San Diego Padres	San Diego Stadium	330	410	330	47,634
San Francisco Giants	Candlestick Park	335	410	335	58,000

Former Stadiums

| Team | Stadium | Home Run Distances (in ft.) | | | Seating |
		LF	CF	RF	Capacity
Houston Colts 45	Colt Stadium	360	420	360	32,601
Brooklyn Dodgers	Ebbets Field	365	389	352	31,902
Pittsburgh Pirates	Forbes Field	365	457	300	35,000
New York Giants	Polo Grounds	279	483	257	55,000
St. Louis Cardinals	Busch Stadium	315	426	310	30,490
Cincinnati Reds	Crosley Field	328	390	366	29,488
San Francisco Giants	Seals Stadium	375	415	350	22,900
Milwaukee Braves	County Stadium	320	420	315	43,799
Montreal Expos	Jarry Park	340	417	340	30,000
Philadelphia Phillies	Connie Mack Stadium	334	410	329	43,608
Los Angeles Dodgers	Coliseum	251	420	333	94,600

American League

Active Stadiums

Team	Stadium	Home Run Distances (in ft.)			Seating
		LF	CF	RF	Capacity
Baltimore Orioles	Memorial Stadium	309	405	309	52,860
Boston Red Sox	Fenway Park	315	390	302	33,538
California Angels	Anaheim Stadium	333	404	333	43,250
Chicago White Sox	Comiskey Park	352	445	352	44,492
Cleveland Indians	Cleveland Stadium	320	400	320	76,713
Detroit Tigers	Tiger Stadium	340	440	325	53,676
Kansas City Royals	Royals Stadium	330	410	330	40,760
Milwaukee Brewers	County Stadium	320	402	315	53,192
Minnesota Twins	Metropolitan Stadium	343	406	330	45,919
New York Yankees	Yankee Stadium	312	417	310	57,545
Oakland Athletics	Oakland Coliseum	330	400	330	50,000
Seattle Mariners	The Kingdome	316	410	316	59,438
Texas Rangers	Arlington Stadium	330	400	330	41,907
Toronto Blue Jays	Exhibition Stadium	330	400	330	43,737

Former Stadiums

Team	Stadium	Home Run Distances (in ft.)			Seating
		LF	CF	RF	Capacity
Philadelphia Athletics	Connie Mack Stadium	334	440	331	33,233
St. Louis Browns	Sportsman's Park	351	422	310	30,000
Washington Senators	Griffith Stadium	408	426	328	29,731
Kansas City A's	Municipal Stadium	353	421	353	32,561
California Angels	Chavez Ravine Stadium	330	410	330	56,000
California Angels	Wrigley Field	340	412	339	20,543
Seattle Pilots	Sicks Stadium	305	405	320	28,500

Bibliography

Allen, Lee. *The World Series.* New York: G. P. Putnam's, 1969.

Allen, Maury. *Damn Yankee.* New York: Times Books, 1980.

———. *Mr. October.* New York: Times Books, 1981.

———. *You Could Look It Up.* New York: Times Books, 1979.

Anderson, Dave; Chass, Murray; Creamer, Robert; Rosenthal, Harold. *The Yankees.* New York: Random House, 1981.

Angell, Roger. *Five Seasons.* New York: Simon and Schuster, 1977.

———. *Late Innings.* New York: Simon and Schuster, 1982.

Asinoff, Eliot. *Eight Men Out.* New York: Holt, Rinehart and Winston, 1963.

Bergman, Ron. *The Mustache Gang.* New York: Dell Publishing, 1973.

Berry, Henry. *The Boston Red Sox.* New York: Rutledge Books, 1975.

Broeg, Bob. *The Pilot Light and the Gashouse Gang.* St. Louis: Bethany Press, 1980.

———. *The Redbirds.* St. Louis: River City Publishers, 1981.

Cohen, Richard M.; Neft, David S.; Johnson, Roland T.; Deutsch, Jordan A. *The World Series.* New York: Dial Press, 1976.

Dickey, Glenn. *The Great No-Hitters.* Radnor, Pa.: Chilton Book Co., 1976.

———. *The History of National League Baseball.* New York: Stein and Day, 1979.

———. *The History of American League Baseball.* New York: Stein and Day, 1980.

Enright, Jim. *The Chicago Cubs.* New York: Rutledge Books, 1975.

Falls, Joe. *The Detroit Tigers.* New York: Rutledge Books, 1975.

Hertzel, Bob. *The Big Red Machine.* Englewood Cliffs, N.J., 1976.

Holmes, Tommy. *The Brooklyn Dodgers.* New York: Rutledge Books, 1975.

Honig, Donald. *The October Heroes.* New York: Simon and Schuster, 1979.

———. *The Brooklyn Dodgers.* New York: St. Martin's, 1979.

———. *Baseball Between the Lines.* New York: Coward, McCann and Geoghegan, 1976.

———. *Baseball When the Grass Was Green.* New York: Coward, McCann and Geoghegan, 1975.

———. *Baseballs' 10 Greatest Teams.* New York: Macmillan, 1982.

———. *The Men in the Dugout.* Chicago: Follett, 1977.

Lieb, Fred. *Baseball As I Have Known It.* New York: Coward, McCann and Geoghegan, 1977.

Reichler, Joe, ed. *The World Series.* New York: Simon and Schuster, 1978.
Ritter, Lawrence S. *The Glory of Their Times.* New York: Macmillan, 1966.
Schaap, Dick. *Steinbrenner!* New York: G. P. Putnam's Sons, 1982.
Shecter, Leonard. *Once Upon the Polo Grounds.* New York: Dial Press, 1970.
Thorn, John. *The Relief Pitcher.* New York: E. P. Dutton, 1979.

Index